CONTENTS

CHILD DEVELOPMENT

A TEXT FOR THE CARING PROFESSIONS

ROBERT B. BURNS

CROOM HELM
London & Sydney

NICHOLS PUBLISHING COMPANY
New York

© 1986 Robert B. Burns
Croom Helm Ltd, Provident House, Burrell Row,
Beckenham, Kent, BR3 1AT

Croom Helm Australia, 44-50 Waterloo Road,
North Ryde, 2113, New South Wales
Reprinted 1987

British Library Cataloguing in Publication Data

Burns, Robert B.
    Child development: a text for the caring
    professions.
    1. Child development
    I. Title
    155.4 BF721

    ISBN 0-7099-3232-4
    ISBN 0-7099-3233-2 Pbk

First published in the United States of America 1986 by
Nichols Publishing Company, Post Office Box 96,
New York, NY 10024

Library of Congress Cataloging in Publication Data

Burns, R.B.
Child development.

Includes index.
1. Child development. I. Title.
HQ767.9.B87 1986   305.2'3   85-21583

ISBN 0-89397-236-3

Phototypeset by Words & Pictures Ltd, Thornton Health, Surrey
Printed and bound in Great Britain
by Billing & Sons Limited, Worcester.

INTRODUCTION

The aim of this book is to introduce students in the helping services, particularly health, social work and teaching, to some of the important aspects of child development from a psychological perspective. The book is aimed less at students specialising in psychology than those such as teachers or nurses who will work with children.

Psychology is the scientific study of behaviour. The aspects of psychology to be dealt with in this book are concerned with the development of behaviour in human beings from the onset of life at conception to the age at which their most important functions have become mature viz., the end of adolescence. The text makes no claims to be comprehensive. It introduces particular areas of child development that would seem most appropriate for an introductory text relevant to the above professional groups.

The early years illustrate the major features of human development. Each child has his own rate of development, some maturing more rapidly than others; e.g., some infants walk at eleven months, others not until 15 months. Development also follows a fairly orderly sequence which in general is the same for all children, e.g. crawling is followed by standing which is then followed by walking. Thus while the pattern of development is to some extent predictable, considerable individual differences in rates exist. This makes us aware of the uniqueness of each child, a uniqueness that stems from the continuous interaction of biological or inherited elements of the organism with environmental elements that impinge on the organism and that are interpreted in idiosyncratic ways by the organism.

I am indebted to numerous typists throughout the world, but particularly in Australia, Britain and South Africa, who have typed various chapters while I was an itinerant academic. I wish also to give my thanks to my wife who continually encouraged me in this undertaking.

R.B. Burns
Cape Town

1 THE BACKCLOTH

Why Study Child Development?

A study of the psychology of childhood provides a rich background of information about children's behaviour and psychological growth under a variety of environmental conditions. It provides information about psychological methods for appraising a child's developmental status: indicates what behaviour and development is usual at particular times; gives understanding of basic psychological processes like learning, motivation, maturation, and socialisation; provides knowledge of the general principles of development with which to evaluate critically new trends and 'fads' in child care and training; and promotes practical suggestions for guiding the psychological growth of children who experience difficulties in adjusting to adults, other children and other aspects of their environment.

Furthermore, extended study in this scientific area promotes a better understanding of adult behaviour. Familiar aphorisms such as 'The child is the father of the man,' and 'As the twig is bent so grows the tree' document man's belief in the major contributions of childhood experiences to the personality and behaviour of the mature individual. The principles of psychoanalysis, criminology and psychosomatic medicine all emphasise the importance of childhood experiences. It therefore seems important to understand the child because every stage of childhood is itself important, and also because an understanding of the child gives a better understanding of all the effective characteristics of the adult, as well as the foibles and idiosyncrasies of later years.

Adults have no doubt speculated on how an apparently helpless dependent novice newborn or neonate who could not survive without the ministrations of adults, can develop into a relatively independent person, capable of coping with, and in, a complex environment within two decades. Our major questions concern how this development occurs, can it be influenced, what sequence of changes occurs and at what ages, why is each person's development unique in terms of timing and characteristics manifest? Some answers can be given but the study of human development is nowhere near complete or comprehensive and on a considerable number of issues our knowledge is still partial and even speculative. Our knowledge in this area continues to advance year by year. In popular wisdom there are different, contradictory viewpoints about the nature of childhood. Sometimes a youngster is regarded as a bundle of animal instincts in need of control, sometimes as a being whose fate has been preordained. On the other hand, a newborn child may be seen as an organism with few, if any, predispositions — a blank slate on which environmental experience will write. Such contradictory beliefs lead to questions about how children should be raised. Should they be guided and carefully taught or allowed to develop with little pressure and control? These points of view have changed again and again over the centuries, and have been reflected in child-rearing practices, and in the research and theories of child psychologists.

Human Complexity

Human psychological development is a problematic area to study. Firstly, human development is like a complex puzzle, the pieces of which gradually fit together to create an individual whose wholeness is greater than the sum of the parts. This makes it hard to pull out separate pieces of human development to look at them separately. Their abstraction from the integrated functioning organism loses the human qualities only experienced within the ambit of the totality.

As one step toward dealing sensibly with this difficult task it seems helpful to think about the 'whole person' in terms of three broad categories of behaviour and personal characteristics. One category, *physical-motor*, includes body build and configuration, size, strength, rate of physical maturation, motor skill coordination, physical health, and the like. Temperament, interpersonal relationship skills, emotional adjustment and morality are included in a second category, *personal-social*. Within the third category, *cognitive-intellectual*, are included perception, memory, language, problem-solving and thinking abilities, academic achievement and so on.

But even with this perspective the considerable interaction between these three areas blurs the distinction. For example, children's mobility and self-help skills (eating, dressing, toileting) are all based heavily on physical-motor development, but children's accomplishments may both reflect and affect personal-social developments, such as a growing sense of autonomy or independence. Physical-motor accomplishments also make it possible to seek and enjoy social relationships with other children, as in play, which provide further opportunities for the acquisition and practice of problem-solving skills. Opportunities for, and patterns of, success (or failure) in games and social relationships may affect later development in a variety of ways. The chapters in this book will focus on specific aspects of development but make references where relevant to other interlocking aspects.

Another problem that arises is that human development is not a one-way street. It is a network of two-way flows and junctions, for just as children's development may be influenced by parents and other social forces (such as peers or the mass media), children influence their parents and the environment in which development occurs (Bijou, 1976; Schaffer 1971). Whatever pattern of influence is attempted by parents, children respond in turn, usually to influence the tempo and style with which their parents seek to 'train' or 'control' their young. Similarly, children's efforts to master their broader physical and social environment will produce effects on other people and the environment, the responses from which further influence development. We can thus think about the process of human development as a series of feedback loops whereby conditions of the individual and the environment operate continuously to produce change. The extent to which this interaction series is positive and constructive, or negative and destructive, depends largely upon a child's genetic make-up and the environment in which he operates.

Individuals are very active and potent forces in their own development. Even the very culture they live in can be influenced by children and the young. Political activities and consumer power are but two examples of how the young affect their elders and thus the broader culture of which everyone is a part.

Development

If human beings simply grew, we would all be six feet bouncing babies! However, we also develop. Development involves both growth and maturation, and eventually stagnation and decline. Development means change through the process of living through time. Throughout this text the term is used to include all change associated with time in both the structure and the functioning of the living organism. This development is also termed maturation. As the body grows it is also maturing. This maturing aspect of change is not directly measurable in quantitative terms. New and qualitatively different features become incorporated in the inner structural organisation of a body part — features that are discrete and discontinuous. This aspect of developmental change is called maturation.

For example, changes in the structure of the brain during childhood are largely maturational in nature. These changes apparently do not consist of cell proliferation; they are characterised, not by the addition of dimensional increments, but rather by a subtle rearrangement and organisation of interconnections between neurons already present, thus preparing for functioning at progressively higher levels.

But growth and development are intimately related since changes in size and strength can facilitate new patterns of behaviour which are learned. Learning is a more or less permanent change in behaviour as a result of experience. So development involves learning, too, as well as growth and maturation. This text is concerned with the various forms of development that occur such as physical, emotional, social and intellectual, and how such developments are influenced by maturation and learning, the latter being the more important and itself determined by an individual's environmental experiences.

The Concept of Stages

Development appears as a change in kind, that is, the change consists of a series of qualitatively different events, features or stages. It is not then amenable to measurement by any standard scale of units. Other means must be devised for the appraisal of this sort of development. In this connection the concept of stages becomes useful. Changes in kind usually follow one after another in a fixed sequence. Most aspects of development seem to be subject to definite sequences, each new skill developed out of or dependent on a previous one. A child crawls before it can walk; it babbles before it can talk; it uses the whole hand as a gripping tool before it can press the thumb against the fingers (the opposable thumb). When such an invariable sequence of events or stages is observed, that sequence can be made the basis for the assessment of an individual's status with reference to that particular line of development.

The term 'stage', however, has little, if any, scientific or explanatory value. We often hear people say of an awkward child,

'He's just passing through a negative stage'. In this type of context the term has no meaning. Stage theory to the developmental psychologist is not as simple. We speak of stages in development when some striking change in behaviour has occurred, or some task has been achieved which rapidly and significantly alters the total functional effectiveness of the organism.

A number of developmental psychologists have proposed 'stage theories'. We will be referring later to, particularly, the stage theories of Piaget (on cognitive and moral development), Erikson (socio-emotional development), Freud (psycho-sexual development) and Kohlberg (moral development).

What then is implied by the concept of stage? Three criteria stand out. Firstly, there must be qualitative changes in development and not just quantitative ones. Many changes are simply quantitative in that the child gets better at doing something. It would, for example, be pointless to speak of a child moving from a stage in which he can recall four items to a stage where he can recall eight items as he grows older. All that has occurred is a quantitative increment in a specific ability. For a stage theory we need qualitative changes such as those Piaget indicates as characterising the child's manner of thinking at different periods of development. A second criterion is that the stages emerge in an invariant sequence, i.e. the order always remains the same, with each stage built upon the preceding one. The third criterion is that each stage can be identified by specific characteristics that distinguish it clearly from previous and future stages.

The notion of stage does not imply that stages must emerge at fixed chronological ages. Age *per se* is not relevant to the stage concept. It does not imply, either, that development is solely due to biological maturation without any contribution from environment. Finally, the notion of stage does not imply that these are abrupt jumps in development, with the child moving overnight from one stage to the next. Transitions are, in fact, gradual with much overlap. A stage theory is a model, an idealised abstraction; real development is never so tidy. But, despite the structure above, stage has become strongly linked with age.

An Age Concept of Development

The most commonplace framework for describing development derives from the study of children and youth according to their chronological ages. Thus, a generalised picture of children's developmental status is ordered by age typicalness and cross-age differences. A popularised example of this approach has resulted in labelling children successively as 'terrible twos', 'trusting threes', 'fascinating fours', 'frustrating fives', and so on (Gessell and Ilg, 1943). Such a way to order behaviour development is sensible if for no other reason than that children do appear different and behave differently at successive ages for, as they grow older, they learn new and more complex tasks.

Table 1.1 contains generalised age-based descriptions of behaviour, usually called norms. Such norms refer to the average, or typical, case and do not explain developmental changes in behaviour. Nevertheless, norms are useful to gain a general picture of normal development and as reference points for considering deviation from the average. Plans for children and adolescents, such as schooling, can be made with only partial accuracy by the person's age, because emotional and intellectual maturity (to name only two factors) are responsible for wide variations in behaviour among children of the same age. Age alone provides only a general but convenient shorthand index for cataloguing development change over time. There are very wide variations around these averages. Some 14 year olds, for example, are 5ft tall; others are 6ft 1in tall. Some 14 year olds are fully mature sexually; others have not yet even entered puberty. In other words, for an accurate picture of development one must move beyond the average (or mean) and consider the range in developmental variation at different ages. As seen in Table 1.1, organising data around the average, and the range of children and youth around this average, results in behavioural norms.

But a person's age does not specify the exact biological and cultural factors that contribute to development. The intellectual, problem-solving superiority of an adolescent over a pre-school child is not explained at all by saying, 'The adolescent is older'. Specifying the precise characteristics of intellectual behaviour at these two periods of development and charting the forces that produce these characteristics are much more helpful than a simple statement of age.

Limitations aside, the universality of an age-dependent concept of development cannot be denied. In fact, judging by the way in which society is organised, educationally, economically and legally, it is tempting to suggest that developmental changes and expectancies for children's behaviour are 'programmed in' by virtue of pre-established chronological age-based standards. For example, such important life

Table 1.1: Some Descriptive Norms

Behaviour	No. of cases	Median age in weeks	Range in weeks
Toes to mouth	13	26	22 – 36
Grasp person's face	13	27	21 – 44
Sit alone	22	28	16 – 41
Pat, beat or strike	14	28	14 – 46
Roll several feet	13	31	23 – 41
Rise to sitting	10	35	17 – 48
Pull to kneeling	10	38	23 – 61
Stand, holding furniture	11	38	28 – 44
Creep	24	40	16 – 58
Walk holding furniture	19	47	34 – 59
Pull to standing	25	47	29 – 62
Walk when led	14	49	34 – 60
Stand alone	10	53	43 – 67
Few steps alone	25	61	45 – 69

Source: Gesell and Ilg, 1943; Gesell and Amatrada, 1941.

events as school entrance, marriage without parental permission and voting are usually determined solely by chronological age-based standards. Why age should be the criterion for such wide-ranging privileges is not easily explained. Within most societies, however, chronological age seems to represent the best single indicator of successive levels of maturity.

An orientation to development based on chronological age has led many authors to organise their writings about children and youth by age level. That is, it is common for a textbook in developmental psychology to consist of generalised descriptions by basic age categories: e.g. infancy (the first two years of life), the preschool years, and the like. This book selects an alternative framework in an effort to better preserve the stream of development in critical areas such as language, cognitive development, moral development and the like. Moreover, because individual children differ in their rates of development, the range of individual differences in behaviour increases markedly with time. This makes it increasingly difficult to construct meaningful portraits of behaviours based only on an age-related concept of development.

Normality

This book deals with normal development, though, where

relevant, factors related to the development of 'abnormality' will be discussed. This division between what is normal and what is not is certainly not clear cut in psychological development, and definitions of normality/abnormality are contentious and of doubtful value even if thought feasible.

Many references are made in mass media papers and magazines to juvenile delinquents, problem children and neurotics with comment about their abnormal behaviour. In this sense, then, abnormal implies extremely undesirable and unhealthy behaviour and by implication normal is healthy and desirable. The association of psychology with the sort of clients mentioned above creates the illusion in the eyes of the general public that psychology is solely concerned with the abnormal. This is erroneous; psychology is the study of all behaviour whether it is abnormal, in the sense of unusual, or within a range of common behaviour patterns. In this latter sense, we are really looking at 'normal' as being synonymous with average. The word 'norm' means a standard or average.

For measurable variables like height or weight or performance on a standardised test, the standard of normality is not difficult to ascertain, since the average can be calculated and the distribution round the average evaluated so that the range of variation is known. Here, therefore, we are interpreting 'normal' as a statistical concept. 'Abnormal' would be some performance or behaviour which was in a statistical sense at the extreme ends of the normal range and thus synonymous with 'unusual' or 'uncommon'.

So far our brief discussion has suggested that there are two senses of normal, one implying the dichotomy healthy/unhealthy or desirable/undesirable, the other implying common/infrequent. The former is a subjective, value-laden and cultural conception of normality. The latter is an objective quantitative measure. Both senses are found very commonly in writing on developmental psychology without this distinction being made apparent.

What is regarded as normal in both senses defined above may differ from one age group to another. For example, bed wetting (enuresis) and thumb sucking are normal (i.e. both common and healthy) in the infant but certainly abnormal (i.e. both infrequent and unhealthy) in the adolescent. It is also true that most people possess some undesirable and abnormal traits. For example, 60 per cent of children show some sign of neurotic symptoms such as irrational fears, obsessions or psychosomatic illnesses. On this basis it is more normal (statistically speaking) to be slightly neurotic than not, although such symptoms are not disposed towards desirable ways of coping with life. In fact there seem to be many highly specific abnormalities (or eccentricities) that children who on the whole appear normal can display. There are also so many variables, traits and characteristics that compose the individual, that it is impossible to suggest that anyone is normal, i.e. around the average in all the multitude of personal characteristics.

Valentine (1957) quotes research suggesting that in a sample of 500 problem children, 40 per cent had mothers who manifested neurotic symptoms. Among adults, about 25 per cent in a general population display at least one neurotic symptom. Hence a sizeable number of families will have at least one parent who is slightly neurotic.

Abnormal tends to be associated with derogatory connotations. This can be seen in the different views held of the gifted child and of the educationally sub-normal child. Both in a statistical sense are well away from the normal range of intellectual performance but only the latter child is regarded as abnormal. Giftedness, on the other hand, is eminently desirable even if so very different and uncommon. In view of these difficulties in understanding what is really implied by the term 'normal' and the pejorative value-laden use of the term abnormal it would be better if we looked at each individual child's behaviour, development and characteristics in terms of their effectiveness as coping strategies to deal with the environment as the child perceives it. Where the child is not coping, instead of labelling him we encourage him to adopt new strategies more suitable to successful and happy living.

The Present View

Some of the views of childhood promulgated through the centuries reveal a startling difference of opinions from era to era, and from one theorist to another. The pendulum has swung from belief in the innate badness of children to the rejection of such a belief, from biological determinism to environmental determinism, from a model of the child as a miniature adult to a model of a child qualitatively different from an adult. The present emphasis appears to be of a conception of childhood development based on an interaction between heredity and environment, with newborn infants predisposed genetically to learn certain things, and able to perceive more than was once thought. The neonate is not a *tabula rasa* and indeed initiates social contact with his mother in mutual interaction. The infant is not simply a passive recipient of environmental experience but works hard to obtain stimulation and to modify his environment. So a more balanced view of development currently exists with the child not developing at the whim of the environment or of deliberate reinforcement ploys, but exposing more of his potentials given a favourable context. Extreme environmentalism, extreme behaviourism and extreme biological determinism have all given way to a view of the human organism as the interplay between heredity and environment.

Summary

Child development seeks to understand the processes underlying human behaviour in the first two decades of life, and covers three broad areas, physical-motor, personal-social and cognitive-intellectual. Child development involves reciprocal interaction between child and significant adults in its life. It is important to study child development because childhood experiences affect later adult behaviour and because it provides practical knowledge in rearing children. It is difficult to differentiate between normal and abnormal behaviour since statistical and value questions are involved. A useful way of conceptualising development has been to adopt an age or stage concept of development, but such norms only describe; they do not explain. Currently the child is seen as an interaction of environment and genetic forces, able to act on his environment from a very early age.

Questions

1. Why do you regard the study of child development as important?
2. What do you understand by the terms 'normal' and 'abnormal' as used in this chapter?
3. What is a 'norm'? Of what use is a 'norm' in child development?
4. Compare the 'age' and 'stage' concepts of development.
5. What is the value of discovering developmental norms for various aspects of growth? What is the danger in applying such norms to individuals?

Further Reading

Baldwin, A.L. *Theories of Child Development*, New York: Wiley, 1967

Dennis, W. (ed.) *Historical Readings in Developmental Psychology*, New York: Appleton-Century-Crofts, 1972. Selection of thirty-seven leading authors, including Darwin, Galton, Preyer, Hall, Thorndyke, Binet, Freud, Terman, Watson, Gesell, Piaget, and Hebb. Each article is preceded by editor's introductory comments about the significance of the paper and often of the author himself.

Goulet, L.R. and Baltes, P.B. (eds.) *Life-span Developmental Psychology: Research and Theory*, New York: Academic Press, 1970. A volume of twenty contributors on history, theories, methods, and several aspects of development, emphasising cognition and learning.

Jones, M.C., Bayley, N., Macfarlane, J.W., and Honzik, M.P. (eds.) *The Course of Human Development*, Waltham, Mass.: Xerox College Publishing, 1971. A selection of 64 articles organised in twelve chapters, three of which were newly written for this text. Most of the authors present original data and summarise their previous work. This volume reflects reasonably well what developmental psychology has to offer in longitudinal research.

Langer, J. *Theories of Development*, New York: Holt, Rinehart and Winston, 1969

Lerner, R.M. *Concepts and Theories of Human Development*, Reading, Mass.: Addison-Wesley, 1976

Sears, R.R. 'Your ancients revisited: A history of child development' in E.M. Hetherington (ed.) *Review of Child Development Research*, Vol. 5, Chicago: University of Chicago Press, 1975

References

Bijou, S. (1976) *Child Development*, Englewood Cliffs, New Jersey: Prentice Hall

Gesell, A. and Amatrada, C. (1941) *Developmental Diagnosis*, New York: Heuber

Gesell, A. and Ilg, F. (1943) *Infant & Child in the Culture of Today*, New York: Harper

Schaffer, H.R. (1971) *The Growth of Sociability*, London: Penguin

Valentine, C. (1957) *Development of the Normal Child*, Harmondsworth: Penguin

2 HEREDITY AND ENVIRONMENT

Introduction

A controversial issue throughout the history of psychology has been the debate about, and investigation of, the relative roles of heredity and environment in the development of individual differences, a debate that has been greatly confused by difficulties over what is meant by the concepts of heredity and environment.

Despite beliefs that men ought to be born equal, they are not. Each person is a unique amalgam of inherited genetic material endowing them with variations in aptitude, development and capacities which, in turn, are acted on by their interpretation of unique environmental experiences some of which influence the organism even before birth.

The answer to the question of what are the relative roles of heredity and environment is important because it affects decisions about social policy and action. If genes are the sole arbiters of development and behaviour, then, of course, social intervention, say by preschool play group and nursery experience for disadvantaged children, will have no effect. But if environmental influences have even a minimal effect, we need to know which environmental influences affect which human characteristics and how their positive effects can be maximised while their negative ones are minimised.

As to the relative importance of these two variables, few psychologists today hold extreme genetic or environmental determinist stances. Most contemporary psychologists take an interactionist approach, i.e. differences between individuals are the outcome of the interactions between heredity and environment. Heredity sets the upper limit of what an individual can attain while environment affects the degree to which the potentialities can be realised. But even those who believe in the interaction of both variables still tend to favour one factor or the other as the more important, such as Jensen's claim that genetic factors account for 80 per cent of a person's intelligence and the environment for 20 per cent (Jensen 1969).

However, to try to say which is the more important for human development is like asking which is more important to water, H_2 or O, or asking if length or width is more important in calculating the area of a rectangle. More recently, scientists have moved to thinking about how heredity and environment combine and interact in behaviour and development. Since there is little or nothing we can do about selective breeding (the only clear way to influence heredity), we are now mainly preoccupied with discovering what environments permit optimum growth for individuals of all types of heredity.

Heredity

To the layman, genetics explains why people are alike, why children resemble their parents and why certain traits run in families. But equally important is the fact that genetics explains why individuals are different. The major biological advantage of sexual reproduction is that it ensures that no two individuals are alike in the total complement of genes (identical twins excepted). Man has at least 25,000 genes (and probably more) and with random matings the odds against two individuals obtaining the same set are astronomical. For all practical purposes, such an event can be regarded as an impossibility.

The particular set of genes received is really all that can be meant by 'heredity'. The role of genetic factors by themselves as determinants of human attributes, behaviour and performance is limited and apart from sex determination is restricted essentially to minor physical characteristics (e.g. eye colour) and medical problems (e.g. associated with chromosomal irregularities). For example an extra chromosome causes mongolism or Down's syndrome which accounts for about 25 per cent of admissions to hospitals for the mentally severely impaired. Females with a missing 'X' chromosome (Turner's syndrome) tend to suffer from difficulty in spatial perception.

Males with an extra 'Y' chromosome are found to excess in institutions for the hard-to-manage, persistent criminal. In a special hospital in Scotland for such cases, one patient in 35 was found to have an extra 'Y' chromosome, compared with about one in 700 among newly-born males in Scotland. Similar incidences have been noted in America (Telfer *et al.*, 1968) and in an Australian study (Wiener *et al.*, 1968).

Examples of single genes with a major and specific effect on behaviour are those which cause Huntington's chorea, phenylketonuria and colour blindness. The first two conditions are rare. Huntington's chorea is a disease which leads to mental deterioration in middle life.

Phenylketonuria is one of the recessively inherited inborn errors of metabolism. With appropriate dietary treatment early on, the gross effects on intelligence are preventable. Red-green colour blindness, a sex-linked recessive trait in which carrier mothers pass the trait to half their sons, affects about 8 per cent of males.

The effects of chromosomal abnormalities and single mutant genes account for only a small proportion of the total variation in psychological behaviour. One does not think of single causes, genetic or environmental, but rather of multicausal origins in which both genetic and environmental variations play a part.

Questions about possible genetic programming in human behaviour have been raised recently by a growing interest in the science of ethology (Eibl-Eibesfeldt, 1975). Ethology is a biologically oriented discipline concerned with the comparative study of behaviour across all animal species, including the human. Ethologists seek to identify inborn skills, drive mechanisms, dispositions to learn and adaptation patterns common to various species that are relatively uninfluenced by individual experience e.g. animals' warning and distress calls, curiosity behaviour, play, imprinting and territoriality.

The relevance of ethology to human behaviour is perhaps most specifically marked by still more recent developments in the emerging and closely related discipline called sociobiology (Barash, 1979). Sociobiology confines its study to the biological basis of all forms of social behaviour across species. Its purpose is to establish general principles of the evolution and biology of uniquely social behaviour, again with an eye toward discovering patterns of potentials for such behaviour that are 'built in' to the heredity of a whole species. For example, humans everywhere — regardless of cultural membership — seem to use the same facial configurations to express basic emotions of joy, fear, perplexity and disgust. Likewise, humans everywhere show a strong tendency for social organisation and have developed elaborate kinship rules for this purpose. Sociobiology may ultimately clarify the exact construction of humankind's inherent social nature and distinguish distinctively evolutionary social traits from those that are determined more strongly by idiosyncratic learning experiences.

Environment

While we may feel fairly certain what constitutes heredity in that it is the genetic material transmitted at conception from father and mother, the definition of environment is difficult. In one sense it is the sum of all the non-genetic influences. The environment is not something one can quantify easily since it consists of a plethora of elements which are individually interpreted and made meaningful by each person in the light of past experience, expectations, attitudes, values etc. Each individual makes sense of his environment in his own way; it becomes a personal construct.

Hence, an environment cannot be defined by an outside observer but only subjectively by the experiencing person. The sociologists may be able to define environments in crude terms by unemployment rates, income levels, number of children per family, percentage of owner occupiers, etc., but this tells us nothing about how those who live there perceive their environment. In any case, there are far more subtle environmental elements than these crude variables that influence behaviour and development in psychological terms. The socio-emotional environment and its interpretation is a vital though subjective and unquantifiable element. This poses problems for investigations of environmental influences. For example, studying identical twins reared in different homes assumes that the twins actually interpret these homes differently. We suspect that they may but in what ways and to what extent is impossible to say. Many workers studying the relative roles of heredity and environment do tend to take a simplistic view of environment.

Genotype and Phenotype

The term genotype is used to refer to the genetic characteristics of individuals, transferred in the genes of the parents at fertilisation. Hair and eye colour, potential for height and body dimensions, are all examples of features carried through from previous generations. But many of these inherited components cannot be observed directly because external influences are at work from the moment of conception. The term phenotype refers to the results of the interaction of genetic potential and environmental effects. The child as we see him is a phenotype.

Prenatal Environmental Influences

Prenatal growth constitutes a major critical period in the total cycle of human development. It determines the soundness of the foundation for postnatal development. Despite the long history of myths and superstitions about the effect of environmental influences and maternal experiences on the unborn child, the scientific evidence demonstrating adverse effects of environmental factors on developing organisms dates back only half a century. A voluminous body of evidence testifies that the prenatal organism is at risk and that the maternal organism cannot protect it against all of the many environmental factors that are potentially hazardous to the developing organism. We can define the environment as everything outside the prenatal organism, including the amniotic fluid, uterus, the maternal body and the environment external to the mother. The scientific study of the deleterious effects of the environment on developing organisms is called teratology, and the noxious influences themselves are termed teratogens:

X-Rays and Drugs

The possibility that external factors can adversely affect foetal development has been taken increasingly seriously since the discovery in the 1820s that X-radiation in pregnancy could cause foetal death or malformation. Subsequently, it was discovered in Australia in 1940, that contraction of rubella (German measles) during the first three months of pregnancy increased the incidence of congenital blindness, deafness and heart disease. The Thalidomide disaster in 1960-2 increased concern about the effects of drugs on the foetus.

Administration of opiates (e.g. morphine, heroin) repeatedly during pregnancy because of drug addiction leads to a state of drug dependence in the newborn, with a withdrawal syndrome occurring up to six weeks after birth, usually giving rise to irritability and often convulsions. All drugs that act on the central nervous system (anaesthetics, analgesics, etc.) can cross the placenta and, frequently, give rise to respiratory depression in the newborn.

The most critical prenatal period is the first trimester of pregnancy, which includes the embryonic stage and the early phase of foetal development. Any diseased or toxic condition of the mother significantly affecting her metabolic rate and blood composition is detrimental to the growth of the child, because most toxins penetrate the placenta and invade the foetus.

Smoking and Drinking

The relationship between maternal smoking and prenatal development has attracted much attention. Cigarette smoke contains a
number of toxic substances that are absorbed by the maternal body
and possibly transferred to the foetus. Simpson (1957) reports higher
rates of premature births among smoking mothers compared to those
not smoking. Since then, an array of studies have confirmed this
general finding, e.g. Yerushalmy (1973).

Although a statistical relationship exists between maternal
cigarette smoking during pregnancy on the one hand, and such
variables as birth size, birth weight and prematurity on the other, no
direct, causal relationship can be convincingly established by
correlational techniques. It may be the general characteristics of the
smoker that produce differences in prenatal development and not
smoking itself.

The literature dealing with the prenatal effects of alcohol is also
equivocal. Although alcohol quickly crosses the placental barrier,
very little is known about its teratogenicity. Green (1974) suggests
that chronic and excessive drinking of alcohol can have deleterious
prenatal effects, such as higher mortality rates, reduced birth size and
weight, and malformations.

Maternal Malnutrition

Maternal malnutrition during pregnancy is associated with deficit in
body weight in offspring at birth and deficit in brain development.
(Birch and Gussow, 1970). Through malnutrition, the maternal
bloodstream may become deficient in protein, minerals and vitamins.
Since the foetus is dependent on the maternal bloodstream for its
nutrition, it follows that maternal malnutrition is foetal malnutrition
also in many instances; the effects of such malnutrition may never be
completely overcome. This is particularly likely with respect to brain
development. The numbers and size of brain cells increase in linear
fashion between conception and birth. After birth, the rate of increase
slows down considerably, consequently the deficiency in number of
brain cells associated with malnutrition *in utero* is likely to be
permanent and irreversible. Clear evidence relating malnutrition to
impaired brain development and subsequent intellectual development
is lacking. However, Stein, Susser, Saenger and Morolla (1972)
found no relationship between mental performance at age 19 of
125,000 males and exposure to severe prenatal malnutrition. These

investigators studied the effect of the maternal starvation during pregnancy that occurred in the Dutch famine of 1944-45 in Nazi-occupied Holland. Despite the severe nutritional and caloric deprivation imposed on women in various stages of pregnancy (450 calories per day) no differences could be found in adult mental performance of their children as a function of prenatal malnutrition compared to matched controls.

It is extremely difficult to isolate maternal dietary factors and deficiencies from the many other complicating conditions associated with, and arising from, the many other complicating conditions associated with, and arising from, malnutrition. Disease states, hormonal and metabolic disruption and physical trauma may all accompany malnutrition.

Blood Incompatibility

Blood incompatibility is another serious condition afflicting some foetuses whose blood type is Rh+ while the mother's is Rh−. During her first such pregnancy Rh+ in the foetal blood, inherited from an Rh+ father, sensitises the mother, and she produces antibodies, usually several weeks after delivery. These antibodies become activated about 30 weeks after the next conception of an Rh+ foetus. Many of them penetrate the placenta and cause a breakdown of the foetal blood cells. In the past, massive blood transfusions after birth saved about half of the afflicted infants. In 1968 a vaccine was introduced which, when administered once after every Rh+ childbirth, prevents complications due to this blood incompatibility.

Emotional Adjustment

Pregnancy brings new bodily sensations and new feelings, often toward the foetus. Joyful and welcome as pregnancy may be, there are some discomforts, such as nausea, heartburn and fatigue to be borne. The expectant mother may have doubts about her potential as a mother and wife. She is aware of children being born with a variety of defective conditions and may fear that this will happen to her child. In one of the early empirical studies at the Fels Research Institute, Sontag (1941) demonstrated that strong emotional reactions are irritating to the foetus. The movements of foetuses increased several hundred per cent while their mothers were under emotional stress. Even when the disturbance was brief, heightened behavioural irritability of the foetus lasted as long as several hours. An unusually large amount of activity seems to correlate with a 'hyperactive, irritable, squirming, crying infant after birth' – a 'neurotic' baby (Sontag, 1941).

Laboratory research with animals also suggests that maternal stress may produce increased emotional reactivity in offspring (Joffe, 1969) and disruptions in maternal-infant relations (Smith, Hesletine and Corson, 1971). But such effects appear to be species specific and are not always consistent in their direction. While it is plausible that chronic, high-level emotional states in humans may contribute to pregnancy and perinatal complications, the evidence remains unconvincing (Carlson and LaBarba, 1979). Numerous reports have related maternal emotional disturbances to increased incidence of prematurity, spontaneous abortion, stillbirths, delivery problems and a variety of behavioural disturbances during infancy and early childhood (Gorsuch and Key, 1974; Harper and Williams, 1974) but correlations can never imply cause and effect. During emotional arousal the body's autonomic nervous system causes certain chemical substances, adrenalin in particular, to be released into the bloodstream. These also find their way through the placental barrier and the resulting changes in the circulatory system of the foetus may have an effect upon cell metabolism. So where the mother is in a constant state of tension or stress, associated, for example, with prolonged grief or with marital disharmony, there may be enduring adverse consequences for the child.

About two-thirds of pregnant women experience heightened irritability, the 'blues', and crying spells for no apparent reason other than pregnancy. Moods swing more powerfully during this phase of life than at other times. The expectant mother needs support and frequent approval and reassurance, especially from her husband; additionally she needs lines of communication with other significant persons in her life. If they express approval and understanding of her condition, this helps to raise her sense of worth and dignity as a woman, fulfilling her unique function in the family and society. Opportunities to talk about pregnancy or impending birth when she wishes to are deeply gratifying and reassuring. It reduces the emotional tension resulting from the pregnancy, from the anticipation of the delivery and from the changes likely in her future way of life.

High levels of maternal emotional disturbances are often accompanied by alcohol and drug abuse, nutritional neglect and other forms of potentially harmful behaviour that present hazards to the foetus and mother. It is also possible that abnormal intrauterine conditions and their effects on the maternal body may precipitate emotional states in the mother in which case foetal damage would be independent of her emotional condition.

Empirical Investigations of the Heredity/Environment Issue

The major approach to the investigation of the relative contributions of heredity and environment is the study of family resemblances.

If genes have some effect, there should be some degree of family resemblance. If this can be shown to be non-existent or illusory, the genetic hypothesis is refuted. If, however, there is a family resemblance in respect of a particular measure, one can see how far it parallels the proportion of genes shared by relatives of different kinds. On average, parent and child, brother and sister, and fraternal or dizygotic (genetically dissimilar) twins, all have half their genes in common. Uncle and nephew, grandparent and grandchild, share a quarter of their genes. Identical twins (monozygotic) have identical genes while adopted children have no genetic material in common with their adopted families.

A classic experimental design to investigate the effects of several independent variables on a dependent variable is to manipulate one variable at a time, holding the others constant. So, in this area of concern we need to vary heredity and environment in turn while holding the other constant. Nature provides us with a way of holding heredity constant while varying environment. This situation occurs with identical twins who derive from a single fertilised ovum and, therefore, possess identical genes. We can then compare identical twins (monozygotic or MZ) reared in the same home, with identical twins that have been separated soon after birth and brought up in different homes. Any differences are presumably due to environmental effects. We can also compare MZ with DZ (dizygotic or fraternal) twins. If resemblance is due to the social, cultural or physical environment and the genes make no difference, then a DZ pair of twins of like sex should be about as similar as an MZ pair of twins who are identical in all their genes. If on the other hand MZ pairs are significantly more alike than DZ pairs, the hypothesis that the genes make a difference receives support.

It is, of course, impossible to devise the alternative experiment involving the holding of environment constant and varying the genetic material raised in it. The closest we can come is using adopted and foster children, usually comparing the adopted child/adopted mother correlation with the adopted child/real mother correlation on particular characteristics.

At this point, we would do well to recall the problem raised earlier, of specifying the environment. When investigators talk glibly about placing separated twins in different environments, we have no real way of knowing how different such environments were as perceived and evaluated by the twins placed in them. What constitutes the perceived environment for any individual is not fully open to the inspection of others. Additionally, many features of the environment defy quantification owing to their qualitative nature. Most of the research has looked at the question of genetic influence on intelligence possibly due to the existence of a plethora of tests which are assumed to measure the trait.

Family Resemblance Studies

Twin Studies. Data on intelligence in families have been reported in many publications scattered over several decades. Some of this information was assembled and reviewed by Erlenmeyer-Kimling and Jarvik (1963) in a well-known article. The review was based on 52 independent investigations from eight countries and four continents, involving over 30,000 correlational pairings. The findings are described in the form of ranges and median values for relatives of each type. The median values of genetic predictions are shown in Table 2.1.

Table 2.1: Median Correlation Coefficients in Studies of IQ Test Scores Assembled by Erlenmeyer-Kimling and Jarvik (1963).

Degree of relationship	Reared apart	Genetic prediction	Reared together	Genetic prediction
Unrelated Foster parent-child	0.01	0.00	0.23	0.00
Parent-child	0.40	0.50	0.50	0.50
Sibs			0.49	0.50
DZ twins	0.49	0.50	0.53	0.50
MZ twins	0.75	1.00	0.87	1.00

Source: Adapted from Shields (1973, p. 561).

The IQs of unrelated persons are uncorrelated, as expected. There are small but statistically significant correlations between the IQs of unrelated persons reared together and between foster parents and children. The medians for siblings and for DZ twins are not far from 0.50 even when siblings are reared apart. The very much larger correlations between MZ twins over DZ ones, even when the MZ are reared apart is taken as support for the genetic hypothesis. The 'MZ together' median of 0.87 is nearly as high as the correlation obtained when testing the same person twice with the same test, as might be done in assessing test-retest reliability. Two things are remarkable about the Erlenmeyer-Kimling and Jarvik data. Firstly, they were assembled from such scattered sources, from numerous investigators working independently employing a variety of tests. The second impressive feature is that the pattern of correlations resembles so closely that expected if genetic factors contributed substantially more to the variation in intelligence between individuals than do environmental ones. It must be noted that these are median correlations for each category which do hide a considerable range within each category.

This range is likely to be due to the wide range of tests, to the age range of the subjects and to substantial differences in experimental design. However, this amalgam of studies constitutes a formidable case for the major role of hereditary factors in 'intelligence'. Few would dispute such an interpretation, though there remains doubt about the mechanisms and processes involved. Nevertheless, the median values approximate remarkably closely to the theoretical values that would be expected on a genetic hypothesis, with correlations increasing regularly with increasing degrees of kinship. Using certain statistical manipulations Jensen (1969) claims that twin study data indicate an environmental contribution to variations in intelligence between individuals only of the order of 20 per cent.

Interaction. Only a few studies of kinship have considered the interaction between heredity and environment. Most studies have taken a simple view of heredity and environment as being additive effects. The interaction (statistically known as covariance) refers to the likelihood that parents with 'superior' genes to transmit to their offspring will also provide above-average environments while parents who transmit to their children genes of lower potential are more likely to provide less stimulating environmental conditions.

Three studies of kinship data by Morton (1972), Loehlin (1975) and Jensen (1973) have separated off this component and there is a fairly close agreement between the three studies, viz. a genetic percentage of around 65 per cent, environmental 23 per cent, and covariance 12 per cent. Note, too, that the genetic percentage is well below the 80 per cent which Jensen originally advocated in 1969.

The precise figures do not matter for they will vary with population groups tested and with the attribute being measured; what is important is that it is recognised (1) that both environment and heredity have substantial influences on most human capabilities and attributes, and (2) that generally the component of heredity tends to be the larger effect. Equally important to remember is that: (1) these figures have been obtained from intelligence tests that purport to measure intelligence, an assumption that is queried in many quarters because measured intelligence is affected by learning, motivation and personality among other things (Chapter 7); (2) these figures therefore do not reflect the proportionate effects for any attribute other than measured intelligence, in fact commonsense would tell us this with individual eye colour, for instance, being 100 per cent genetically controlled, and reading ability being controlled largely in 'normal' children by home and school (environmental) variables; and (3) these figures relate to group data and no meaningful statement can be made for any individual; for each person there is his unique blend of heredity and environment for each specific attribute.

Family Resemblance in Personality. Applying personality questionnaires in twin studies (Eysenck and Prell 1951; Eysenck 1956) reveals that MZ twins are more similar than DZ twins for neuroticism and extraversion (Table 2.2).

Table 2.2: Twin Study Correlations for Personality

	Extraversion	Introversion
MZ	0.50	0.85
DZ	−0.33	0.22

Source: Data derived from Eysenck, 1956.

In a study of nearly 150 pairs of twin school children, Gottesman (1966) found that the MZ pairs resemblances were significantly greater than those of DZ pairs on several scales of a personality inventory including those for dominance and sociability.

Psychotic illnesses, such as schizophrenia, appear to have a strong genetic basis, too. Schizophrenia may manifest itself, frequently after puberty, in many forms, though the most prominent features are usually bizarre thinking and a divorce between thought, feeling and reality such that horrifying ideas, delusion and hallucinations rack the thinking and behaviour of the sufferer. However, apart from 'hardcore' cases where doctors agree on the diagnosis, borderline cases present situations where less agreement exists. Since genetic studies must rely on counts of the number of affected relatives of individuals known to be schizophrenic, the presence of 'schizoid' persons as well as clearly schizophrenic patients in some families leads to uncertainties about the count.

Heston (1966) traced 47 adults who had been born to schizophrenic mothers in Oregon, separated from their mothers within the first month of life, and placed in adoptive homes. These were compared with a 'normal' group of adopted children. The first group had a significantly higher frequency of institutionalisation in prison or mental hospital, discharge from the armed forces on psychiatric or behavioural grounds and a higher incidence of mental deficiency. Nine of this group were schizophrenic but no schizophrenics occurred among the controls.

Slater and Cowie (1971) found that when both parents are affected, about one-half of the children are also diagnosed as having the same disorder. Kallman (1953) provides a wealth of data on the concordance rates for schizophrenia for varying degrees of blood relationships. A selection of his percentages is listed in Table 2.3.

Table 2.3: Concordance Rates for Schizophrenia

Identical twins 91.5%	Grandchildren 4.3%
Fraternal twins 14.5%	Nephews & Nieces 3.9%
Full siblings 14.2%	First cousins 1.8%
General population 0.9%	

Source: Data derived from Kallman (1953).

Studies of Adopted/Foster Children. In view of the many difficulties associated with twin or other kinship data, the chief alternative approach is through foster children. There is a fair consensus that adoption at an early age into a good home tends to raise the IQs of adoptees, though probably not more than 10 points on average. The correlations between child's IQ and measures of foster parent ability, or education or the home rating, are mostly quite small. From a range of studies, Vernon (1979) found a median figure of 0.23 and this is almost certainly boosted by the tendency for selective placement, that is the attempt by the adoption agency to match the child with the foster home level. In some studies it was possible to get estimates of the ability of the true or biological parents though the data are seldom complete. Here a median figure of 0.30 was calculated by Vernon (1979).

There is no avoiding a conclusion that the consistently higher correlations with true parents with whom the children had had next to no contact testify to the greater influence of genetic factors over environmental ones. This line of evidence adds weight to the conclusions from the twin study data. Although adopted children do resemble their natural parents more than their adopted parents, their IQs are higher than would be predicted by their natural parents' IQs (Scarr-Salapatek and Weinberg, 1974). This suggests some environmental effect.

Criticism of Twin and Adopted Children Studies

Those who feel that the case for the primacy of genetic factors has been overstated produce four counter arguments.

Alternative Explanations. Some of the above similarities can be explained by selective placement by which is meant that the separated monozygotic twins are reared in similar environments either due to being reared by relations or by being deliberately placed in similar types of family by the adoption agencies concerned.

It can be argued that identical twins in fact share a more uniform environment than do fraternal twins. Identical twins are more likely to be dressed alike, to have the same friends (each has a similar companion in the other) and are more frequently mistaken for one another than are fraternal twins. Thus, environmental influences may well make a significant contribution to the greater association in intelligence which obtains for identical twins.

Marked differences in IQ scores do arise in identical twins, particularly in the case of twins reared apart. Moreover, these differences are associated with environmental factors. For example, Anastasi (1958) showed a relationship between the size of the discrepancy in IQ scores and the educational opportunities available to separated identical twins.

Invalid Data. The second argument is to attack the figures. The most outspoken critic would seem to be Kamin (1974) on this and other matters. He points out that the Erlenmeyer-Kimling and Jarvik summary misses out some research but his amended figures, while increasing the correlation of DZ raised together to r = 0.63, are themselves also based on an arbitrary selection.

There is concern as to whether one can generalise results to the whole population from twins who are not a random sample of the population. Many twins were volunteers obtained through advertising in the media.

Methodological Objections. The chief doubt raised about the genetic hypothesis is the suggestion that the pattern of correlations is an artefact of a great many biases in the sampling of cases, analysis of data, the selection of studies cited as typical in the field and even the scientific integrity of some workers. Such a massive and systematic distortion of the evidence seems improbable, although the integrity of one proponent of the genetic case, Burt, has been shown to be completely lacking (Gillie, 1976). None of Burt's material relevant to the heredity issue can be relied upon.

Simple Views of What Constitutes Environment and Intelligence. Stinchcombe (1969) argues that the proponents of the heredity argument have tended to interpret 'environment' in an insufficiently complex way. Stinchcombe prefers to talk in terms of the 'cumulative environment', a personally sensed context rather than the objective sum of income, length of parental education, family size etc. Cronbach (1969, p. 342) hits many of the relevant nails on the head.

> The phrase 'improve the environment', born of the enthusiasm of the social Darwinists, has misled environmentalists for two generations. Environments cannot be arrayed from good to bad, from rich to poor. The highly stimulating environment that most of us think of as 'rich' promotes optimal growth for some persons and may not be suitable for others. Environments can be varied along many dimensions . . . .

Much of the debate has focused on the area of intelligence, since intelligence has been one of the major areas of psychological interest up to the present decade, and a vast armoury of tests existed which purported to measure it. However, intelligence itself is subject to controversy since there is no adequate definition of the concept, and one has to employ some median of the environment with which to measure it, i.e. subjects must know letters, numbers, words and arithmetic to answer intelligence tests. So learning, experience and culture can never be removed from the measure obtained (see Chapter 7).

If intelligent behaviour depends on so many factors, there is obviously great scope for variability in addition to any variability attributable to the genes. Since intelligence depends primarily on the capacity to use information acquired from the environment, the quality of the environment must itself be a factor in the growth of intelligence.

Studies Supporting Environmental Influences

A number of pieces of work testify to the importance of the environment in creating individual differences.

The Milwaukee Project (Heber and Garber, 1977)

This project was designed to intervene in the environment of disadvantaged children. Forty infants of mothers with low IQs living in a slum area were divided into an experimental and control group, each of 20 children. All subjects were selected at birth. The experimental group was given an 'enriched life curriculum', being taken from their homes to the project site where they spent seven hours a day five days per week with a specially-trained teacher. At home the mothers received help, training and advice on child-care. The control group were brought up at home. Up to the age of 14 months the two groups remained closely parallel on the Gesell scale, but the control group fell behind at 18 months. On preschool scales given between two and four and one-half years, Heber found mean IQs of 122.6 and 95.2, a superiority of 27.4 points for the experimental group. Up to the age of six the Experimental means stayed between 110 and 120, whereas the Controls dropped to around 85. The special programme ceased when the children entered school. By ages eight to nine, the Experimentals had dropped to an average of 104, while the Controls now averaged 80. The Milwaukee Project provides a dramatic demonstration of the efficacy of appropriate environmental modifications in accelerating the cognitive development of children with poverty backgrounds.

Skeels' Study

Perhaps equally impressive for showing the effect of environment and experience is the work done by Skeels and Dye (1939) and Skeels (1966). Their study showed the effects of differential stimulation on mentally retarded children.

Two girls aged 13 months and 16 months, with IQs of 46 — both of them from a state orphanage — were placed in an institution for the feeble-minded in a ward for moron girls. When retested after six months it was found that the younger scored 95; at 43 months the older scored 93. Examination of the ward environment showed that the two girls were constantly played with by the girls in the ward, taken out by the attendants, given toys. On this evidence a group of 13 with a mean IQ of 64.3 ranging between 36 and 89 points, aged from

7–30 months, was also transferred to such wards for periods ranging from 6 to 30 months. All 13 showed gains, the minimum gain being 7 points and the maximum gain 58 points. A group of 11 children with a mean IQ of 87 points was left in the orphanage as a control group. On retesting, the group showed a decrease of between 18 and 45 points. Some 25 years later Skeels (1966) traced all these cases and found the transferred ones to be normal, self-supporting adults, holding quite a range of skilled jobs, or else they were married women. The non-transferred ones were still either institutionalised or in very low-grade jobs. It seems reasonable to conclude that, as adults, the transferred cases averaged at least 30 IQ points higher than the others. Both the Milwaukee and Skeel's studies can be faulted on matters of design e.g. non-randomness of samples, inadequate matching of groups in not reporting all details, and in placing too much credence on unreliable early childhood IQ tests. Nevertheless the studies do call into question the concept of fixed intelligence and they do suggest that environmental factors play some part in the development of measured intelligence.

Role of Dietary and Environmental Deprivation

Malnutrition at critical stages during ontogeny of experimental animals may lead to permanent impairment of the brain, including diminution of brain size. Shapiro and Vukovich (1970), for example, showed that nerve cells in the brains of stimulated animals develop complex branchings (dendrite spines) earlier than those in the brains of environmentally deprived animals. This is also apparent in humans (Eayrs and Horn, 1955). Eichenwald and Fry (1969) and Baraitser and Evans (1969) have all noted functional impairments of the human brain following early malnutrition.

Belated after-effects of starvation and other forms of maltreatment of Second World War prisoners held in concentration camps have been investigated in Norway (Strom, 1968). Nearly 20 years later, a number of survivors showed a reduction in the size of the brain, accompanied by signs of intellectual deterioration. Stock (1967) followed up S. African coloured children severely malnourished in the first two years of life for over five years, comparing them with a group of adequately nourished children of similar socioeconomic level. The experimental group scored 15.7 IQ points lower than the control group.

Thus evidence strongly points to some environmental factors as reducing neurological development in the brain which in turn must influence performance in various spheres.

The 'Self determined' Environment

The child with high genetic potentiality may create a better environment for himself. Parents and teachers who note his quick mind react by providing more stimulation than they would to an average child. If they fail to do so he is likely to seek out experiences on his own, through reading, hobbies, etc. Conversely, the lower the genetic potential, the more he is likely to prefer routine, unstimulating experiences, and adults will meet this need. Social psychologists are currently coming to reject the notion that socialisation of the child results simply from 'shaping' by his social environment, and see the child himself as determining the kind of experiences he receives (Schaffer, 1974).

General Points

It is far more difficult to assess the effects of environment than appears at first sight. Environmental effects are hard to demonstrate unequivocally. We often assume such effects because we feel intuitively that they ought to happen, without bothering to search for evidence.

While the cumulative impact of the environmental manipulation is really only shown up in extreme cases of deprivation, when some total immersion in a project will produce considerable change (e.g. Heber's work), short term educational interventions produce small and often superficial change that soon disappears.

We are now only beginning to understand how complex and subtle the mechanisms are for transmitting abilities, skills, attitudes and beliefs from one generation to another. For example, Firkowska, Otrowska, Sokolwska, Stein, Susser, and Wald (1978) reported that the post-Second World War reconstruction of Warsaw along strongly egalitarian lines has failed to eliminate or even to reduce to any great extent the traditional association between cognitive performance, social class, and occupation of parents. Environmental intervention may turn out to be complex, time-consuming and a costly process.

Summary

Each person is an amalgam of genetic and environmental forces. Controversy exists over the relative influence of each of these variables in the determination of human characteristics and performances. Only in a few rare medical cases and in such traits as eye and hair colour do genetic factors have the sole influence. While environment does have varying degrees of influence depending on the trait in question, it is difficult to define what specific environmental elements are the important ones. Moreover, environment cannot fully be defined in terms of objective variables; a phenomenological perspective is also required.

The environment can affect a child before birth since drugs, maternal illness, hormones and dietary deficiencies are not barred by the placenta from influencing the prenatal organism.

The investigations of the relative influences of heredity and environment have been generally conducted through twin, kinship and adopted child studies. Intelligence has been the main attribute considered since tests abound and are easy to administer. The results of such studies generally reveal that heredity is more important than environment though investigators disagree on the precise ratios, which in any case can only refer to the particular sample studied. Personality variables also reveal a stronger hand for genetics. Family resemblance studies have been criticised mainly on account of sampling bias, sample size, problems of generalisation of results, selective placement by adoption agencies and problems of measuring intelligence and defining concepts such as environment and intelligence.

Questions

1. What do you understand by the concepts (i) 'heredity' and (ii) 'environment'?
2. Why are twin studies used in investigations of this controversy? What criticisms would you make of the twin study method?
3. Discuss the view that the question as to which is the more important, heredity or environment, is one for which there can never be a general answer.
4. What is teratogen? How might some teratogens influence human development?
5. Suppose you are a professional in the health education or social work field and have been invited to talk to a local PTA on the environmental influences on children's development. Indicate what you would include in your talk.
6. Suppose you were in a debating team supporting the notion that

genetic influences are more important than environmental ones in human development. Outline your argument.

Further Reading

Anastasi, A. (1958) 'Heredity, environment, and the question, how?' *Psychological Review*, *65*, 197–208

Ausubel, D.P. (1964) 'How reversible are the cognitive and motivational effects of cultural deprivation?' *Urban Education*, *Summer*, 16–37

Halsey, A.H. (ed.) (1977) *Heredity and Environment*, London: Methuen

Eysenck, H.J. and Kamin, L. (1981) *Intelligence: The Battle for the Mind*, London: Pan

Jensen, A.R. (1969) 'How much can we boost IQ and scholastic achievement?' *Harvard Educ. Review*, *39*, 1–123

Jensen, A.R. (1973) *Educability and Group Differences*, New York: Harper Row

Kamin, L. (1974) *The Science and Politics of IQ*, Potomac: Erlbaum

Mittler, P. (1971) *The Study of Twins*, Harmondsworth: Penguin

Scarr-Salapatek, S. (1971) 'Unknowns in the IQ equation', *Science*, *174*, 1223–8

Scarr-Salapatek, S. (1975) 'Genetics and the development of intelligence' in F.D. Horowitz (ed.), *Review of Child Development Research*, 4, Chicago: University of Chicago Press, pp. 1–57

Vernon, P.E. (1979) *Intelligence: Heredity and Environment*, New York: Freeman

References

Anastasi, A. (1958) *Differential Psychology*, London: Macmillan

Baraitser, M. and Evans, D. (1969) 'The effect of undernutrition on brain rhythm development', *S. African Medical Journal*, *43*, 56–58

Barash, D. (1979) *Sociobiology: The Whisperings Within*, New York: Harper Row

Birch, R. and Gussow, J. (1970) *Disadvantaged Children*, New York: Grune and Stratton

Carlson, D. and LaBarba, R. (1979) 'Maternal emotionality and reproductive outcomes', *Int. J. Beh. Develop.*, *2*, 343–76

Cronbach, L.J. (1969) 'Heredity, environment and educational policy', *Harvard Educ. Review*, *39*, 338–47

Eayrs, J. and Horn, G. (1955) 'The development of cerebral cortex in hypothyroid and starved rats', *Anat. Record.*, *121*, 53–61

Eibl-Eibesfeldt, I. (1975) *Ethology*, New York: Holt

Eichenwald, H.F. and Fry, P.C. (1969) 'Nutrition and learning', *Science*, *163*, 664–8

Erlenmeyer-Kimling, L. and Jarvik, L.F. (1963) 'Genetics and intelligence: a review', *Science*, *142*, 1477–8

Eysenck, H.J. (1956) 'The inheritance of extraversion-introversion', *Acta. Psychology*, *12*, 95–110

Eysenck, H.J. and Prell, D. (1951) 'The inheritance of neuroticism', *J. Mental Sc.*, *97*, 441–65

Firkowska, A., Ostrowska, J., Soloska, V., Stein, Z., Susser, P. and Wald, M. (1978) 'Cognitive development and social policy', *Science*, *200*, 1357–62

Gillie, O. (1976) *Who Do You Think You Are?* London: Hart Davis

Gorsuch, R. and Key, M. (1974) 'Abnormalities of pregnancy as a function of anxiety and life stresses', *Psychosomatic Med.*, *36*, 352–62

Gottesman, I. (1966) 'Genetic variance in adaptive personality traits', *J. Child Psychol. and Psychiat.*, 7, 199–208

Green, H.G. (1974) 'Infants of alcoholic mothers', *American J. Obs. and Gynaec.*, 118, 713–16

Harper, J. and Williams, S. (1974) 'Early environmental stress and infantile autism', *Med. J. Aust.*, 1, 341–6

Heber, F.R. and Garber, H. (1977) The Milwaukee Project in P. Mittler (ed.) *Research to Practice in Mental Retardation*, Baltimore: University Park Press

Heston, L.L. (1966) 'Psychiatric disorders in foster home reared children of schizophrenic mothers', *Br. J. Psychiat.*, 112, 819–25

Jensen, A.R. (1969) 'How much can we boost IQ and scholastic achievement?' *Harvard Educ. Review*, 39, 1–123

Jensen, A.R. (1973) *Educability and Group Differences*, New York: Harper Row

Joffe, J.M. (1969) *Prenatal Determinants of Behaviour*, London: Oxford University Press

Kallman, F.J. (1953) 'The genetic theory of schizophrenia', *American J. Psychiat.*, 13, 309

Kamin, L.J. (1974) *The Science and Politics of IQ*, Potomac: Erlbaum

Loehlin, J.C. (1975) *Race Differences in Intelligence*, San Francisco: Freeman

Morton (1972) 'Human behavioural genetics' in L. Ehrman (ed.) *Genetics Environment and Behaviour*, New York: Academic Press

Scarr-Salapatek, S. and Weinberg, R.A. (1974) 'IQ test performance of black children adopted by white families', *American Psychol.*, 31, 726–39

Schaffer, H.R. (1974) *The Growth of Sociability*, Baltimore: Penguin

Shapiro, S. and Vukovich, K. (1970) 'Early experience effects on cortical dendrites', *Science*, 167, 992–4

Shields, J. (1973) 'Heredity and psychological abnormality' in H.J. Eysenck (ed.) *Handbook of Abnormal Development*, London: Pitman

Simpson, W.J. (1957) 'Preliminary report on cigarette smoking and the incidence of prematurity', *American J. Obs. and Gynaec.*, 73, 808–15

Skeels, H.M. and Dye, H. (1939) 'A study of the effects of differential stimulation on mentally retarded children', *Proc. Amer. Assoc. for Mental Deficiency*, 44, 114–36

Skeels, H.M. (1966) 'Adult status of children with contrasting early life experience', *Monogr. Soc. Res. in Child Dev.*, 31, No. 105

Slater, E. and Cowie, V. (1971) *The Genetics of Mental Disorder*, London: Oxford University Press

Smith, D., Hesletine, G. and Corson, J. (1971) 'Prepregnancy and prenatal stress', *Life Science*, 10, 233–42

Sontag, L.W. (1941) 'The significance of fetal environment differences', *American J. Obst. and Gynaec.*, 42, 996–1003

Stein, Z., Susser, P., Saenger, A. and Morolla, P. (1972) 'Nutrition and performance', *Science*, 178, 708–13

Stinchcombe, A.L. (1969) 'Environment: the cumulation of effects is yet to be understood', *Harvard Educ. Review*, 39, 511–22

Stock, M.B. (1967) 'The effects of undernutrition during infancy on brain growth and intellectual development', *S. African Med. J.*, 41, 1027–31

Strom, A. (1968) *Norwegian Concentration Camp Survivors*, Oslo: Universitetsforlaget

Telfer, M.A. *et al.* (1968) 'Incidence of gross chromosomal errors among tall criminal American males', *Science*, 159, 1249–60

Vernon, P.E. (1979) *Intelligence: Heredity and Environment*, San Francisco: Freeman

Wiener, S.G. (1968) 'XYY males in a Melbourne prison', *Lancet*, 1, 150

Yerushalmy, J. (1973) 'Smoking in pregnancy', *Devel. Med. Child Neurol.*, 15, 691–2

3 PHYSICAL, SOCIAL AND PERCEPTUAL DEVELOPMENT IN EARLY CHILDHOOD

The Heredity & Environment Issue Again

The birth of a child is marked by two fundamental changes in functioning. Infants are now subjected to states of deprivation or discomfort, i.e. hunger, pain, and they encounter a variety of events and experiences which shape their perception of the environment and their reactions to it. Another person usually comes to tend the crying child and with this action the child's development comes under the partial control of the social environment. From the moment a person begins to care for the infant, certain behaviours become selectively strengthened and others weakened. The infant also begins to develop attachments to human beings and is initiated into a system in which human beings are viewed as the basic objects to whom one turns for help and from whom one learns values, motives and complex behaviours.

A superficial view of the neonate suggests that it possesses very little to begin the long and complex development towards adulthood beyond a set of rudimentary and not very useful reflexes. The baby mostly sleeps, and wakens irregularly. Periods of alert activity are few and far between. Motor movements that occur seem to be fairly uncoordinated and purposeless most of the time. Strong noise or pain produces gross reactions of the whole body and crying may be frequent.

To some the infant presents itself as a primitive and naive organism, highly dependent on environmental influences to produce learning and organisation. Many of the earlier behaviourists believed this to be the case and assumed a strong empiricist view. This means they believed that the child was an empty receptacle to be filled with experience and knowledge and that the primitive behaviour of the infant reflected this lack of abilities and skills, which had to be learned. However, evidence exists to the contrary.

For example, if tadpoles are anaesthetised during the period in which swimming ability normally develops and then allowed to recover from the effects of the anaesthetic, it is found that they are soon just as able to swim as a control group which has not been anaesthetised. The same is true of human development, e.g. some cultures like the Eskimos and the Hopi Indians severely restrict the body movements of their infants by 'swaddling' or tying them to boards during the time when, in our culture, they normally learn to crawl, pull themselves up on objects, walk holding on to things and then walk unaided. The restricted infants show no obvious signs of the physical deprivation they have undergone; their walking does not appear to be retarded in any long-term way. This exemplifies the other extreme, the nativist position which asserted that all knowledge and skills were innate and would express themselves as the person matured. This is the *tabula rasa* (clean slate), or extreme empiricist view. An example supporting it is given by Gardner (1972). The phenomenon of deprivation dwarfism was studied in the context of hospitals and orphanages with different régimes. It was noticed that differences in the psychological, rather than nutritional, conditions of the environments affected the rate of children's physical growth. The investigators were thus able to make a tentative statement that a necessary and important condition for physical growth is the presence of a positive personal relationship with a caregiver. The investigators looked more closely at the physiological processes involved, and found suggestive evidence that one feature of deprivation dwarfism is a decrease in the secretion of growth-producing hormones.

Obviously, even on the basis of these two sets of evidence, a simple answer to the nature-nurture question is impossible. For some behaviours we may expect 'nature' to predominate, for others, 'nurture'. In general, however, we find that there is an inter-action between the two, so that both genes and environment contribute to development.

Physical & Physiological Growth

It is important to know something about physical growth and development because the child's level of physical development sets limits on the interaction it can have with the environment, and feelings about its own body can affect it strongly.

Height, Weight and Body Proportions

Physiological growth is a highly uneven process. The prenatal stage, the first and second years of life, and the years of early childhood are periods of tremendous though decelerating physiological growth.

Development tapers off during childhood until it reaches its low ebb at about nine or ten years of age. After about another two years there is a renewed acceleration of growth, which becomes turbulent during the major pubertal changes. A year later, a final deceleration phase begins, and physiological growth nearly ceases by the age of sixteen or eighteen. Each child has his or her own rate and pattern of physical growth, yet in most aspects these are comparable to those of other children. Among the most striking visible properties of physical growth are height, weight and the changing proportions of various parts of the body. By the second birthday, children attain about one-half their adult height. At one year of age most babies are somewhat fat, but at two or three they come into their own — increased physical activity reduces the amount of surplus fat.

In the analysis of physiological growth there are two fundamental questions: How does the individual grow? Why does one grow the way one does? The first question is in part answered by comparing the measurements with the general norms for that age. Height and weight are standard examples. Additional measurements include assessment of head circumference and X-rays revealing the level of bone ossification. The ossification stage of certain bones (hand and wrist, for example) indicates the level of physical maturity of the child X-rayed for that purpose. Bone X-ray analysis serves well as an index to estimate present status as well as future growth, including timing of major pubertal changes (Greulich, 1950). A basic answer to the second question lies in the individualised genetic code which, periodically, releases genetic material into the organising cells. These genetic agents initiate growth changes, provided there are nutritional materials available, to effect the structural changes according to the blueprint of the genetic code.

The most obvious development in early childhood is increase in height. It is possible to categorise growth in height into periods, as follows:

— rapid decline in rate (birth to 2–3 years)
— constant rate (2–3 years to 11–12 years)
— adolescent spurt (11–12 years to 15–16 years)
— final decline (15–16 years to 18–19 years)
— adult (18–19 years onwards)

It is interesting to note that at least the first two periods correspond to some extent with Piaget's categories of sensory-motor and pre-operational periods (see Chapter 5).

Weight, although following the same pattern as the development of height, is more prone to variation because of illnesses and nutritional factors, and as a result will usually show more individual differences. In cases of severe illness, e.g. the childhood infectious diseases (measles, mumps etc.), weight may temporarily be reduced, although this is not, of course, true of height. However, after such events, the rate of weight development will tend to increase to compensate for the temporary setback. Both weight and height are affected in deprivation dwarfism, a disorder caused by severe maternal deprivation.

Most measurements of the body show a pattern of growth similar to that already described in height. However, there are two important differences, in that the brain and the skull develop much earlier, and the reproductive organs and lymphoid tissues (tonsils, adenoids and parts of the intestines) develop later, undergoing their major period of growth during adolescence. The growth of the brain will be considered in further detail later but at this point it is worth noting that it has virtually reached its full adult size when the child is five years old.

The shape of the new-born child is very different from that of the adult. For one thing, the head is extremely large in relation to the rest of the body, and the arms and legs are also proportionately smaller. The head is almost 25 per cent of the length of the body at five months but in adults is only 10 per cent. During childhood the lower parts of the body, particularly legs and trunk, grow proportionately more.

From birth to the age of one year, the trunk is the fastest growing portion, accounting for about 60 per cent of the total increase in body length during this time. From the age of one year to the onset of adolescence, the legs grow the fastest. They account for about 66 per cent of the total increase in height during this period. During adolescence, the trunk again becomes the fastest growing portion, accounting for about 60 per cent of the adolescent height increase.

Development of the Nervous System and Brain

Patterns of response in most animals other than man appear to be predominantly determined by genetic factors. Man, however, depends primarily on learning to acquire these patterns. This is reflected, as we shall see, in the state of development of the brain at birth.

Although the new-born has many abilities which have only recently been clearly identified, and our view of the neonate now includes a more complex set of potential behaviours, the brain at this stage is very much 'uncommitted'. The 'wiring-up' of the complex electrical computer of the brain depends heavily on learning experiences. Because of this, there are many things that the young child is simply unable to learn.

The relationship between brain development and the abilities of the individual is not one-way, but interactive. Experience facilitates neural development, and neural development facilitates higher levels of learning and behaviour.

Although the major effects of brain development are seen in the period from birth to three years old, there are indications that the completion of this development covers much of the statutory schooling period. The general implication for teaching is that what can be expected of a child's intellectual performance depends on the levels of development of his thinking apparatus, and that this development is itself facilitated or hindered by the stimulation it receives.

In the physically mature person, nerves are insulated by a sheath of surrounding fatty tissue, known as myelin. This appears to act in a similar way to rubber insulation around electric wires, though it is not exactly the same because the speed of neural conductance is partly affected by the amount of myelin. This is because the nervous impulse is electrochemical, not just electrical. In fact, the speed of signals is much slower than that of electricity; in adults, it is about 60 to 80 metres per second.

Although virtually all the nerve cells in the spinal cord are already formed at birth, in the brain and the muscular and sensory pathways their myelination is incomplete, and this is reflected in the speed of neural conductance which at birth is no more than half the adult value. It takes some three years for the rate to reach the adult value. However, myelination is probably still not complete by the age of three, and there are some indications that neural development is not wholly completed before adolescence. For example, speed of reaction, which depends also on synapses and brain mechanisms, becomes faster between the ages of 14 and 17 in boys (Atwell and Albel, 1948).

Since rapid myelination occurs between birth and age two, poor nutrition during this time can impair the synthesis of the fatty compounds that form myelin, retard this process, and thereby impair intellectual functioning.

One of the consequences of a lack of full myelination is that impulses tend to 'spread' from the original nerve to those nearby, and this may be a partial explanation for the 'grossness' of infants' body movements and reflexes. The progressive development of fine muscular control is probably a consequence of neural maturation as well as learning.

The Brain

Most motor behaviour and all intellectual activity are controlled in the brain. The brain can be considered, for developmental purposes, as being in three main parts — the brain stem, the cerebellum and the cerebral cortex. The brain stem is an extension of the spinal column into the brain. The cerebellum is a tightly ridged set of lobes lying behind the brain stem and beneath the cerebral cortex. The cortex itself, which is the largest part of the brain, encloses the brain stem and is in two halves, right and left. These are the two cerebral 'hemispheres'.

The cortex is covered with numerous folds, and each hemisphere is bisected by a major fissure running from the area by the ear up to the top of the head, and down into the gap that separates the two hemispheres. Some parts of the brain appear to have quite specific functions, whereas other parts fulfil a whole range of functions. The brain stem serves to control the level of excitation of the brain itself, and acts as a filter on impulses entering and leaving the brain from the spinal column. The brain is the main regulating organ for all bodily processes; it is probably part of this structure that 'shuts down' the connections between the brain and the rest of the body in sleep. The cerebellum's primary role is in controlling posture and balance; it keeps opposing muscles in equilibrium and maintains muscle tone, i.e. the slight degree of tension in which muscles are kept when a person is awake. It is also involved in the coordination of body movements.

The reception of sensory information from all parts of the body (except the eyes and ears) is dealt with by the fold of cortex which lies to the rear of the central fissure running across each hemisphere, and motor movements originate from the fold in front of the fissure. Information from the eyes goes first to the parts of each hemisphere at the extreme rear corners, while auditory information is received in the temporal lobes, one of which is on each hemisphere lying underneath the ear region.

The sources of this information are twofold:

(1) from anatomical evidence of damage to different areas found in post-mortem examination or during surgery, related to symptoms such as aphasia (inability to speak)
(2) electrical stimulation of specific areas.

Most of the rest of the cortex, apart from those specific areas described above along with the speech area, which lies on the main cortex just above the auditory area on the temporal lobe, has a more general function, and it is in these areas that intellectual abilities develop. In man, these areas are much more highly developed than in other animals. There is a progression in other animals by which the development of the 'general' areas of the cortex is closely related to intelligence, or the ability to learn and solve problems, the higher primates such as chimpanzees being closest to man in their brain-structure.

The head is the most developed part of an infant's body, at least in terms of size, and in general it remains advanced relative to the rest of the body. At birth, the brain is about one-quarter of its adult weight; at six months after birth it is nearly half of its adult weight; at one year, 60 per cent, at two-and-a-half, 75 per cent, and 90 per cent at the age of five. By contrast, the rest of the body only reaches half of its adult weight at the age of about ten.

However, the different parts of the brain do not all develop at the same rate. Some are more developed at birth, and continue to develop faster. The development of the body occurs from the head downwards. In the brain, this direction is reversed, in that it develops from the lower part upwards, although the cerebellum lags behind. As can be seen from Figure 3.1, the mid brain, pons and medulla (brain stem) have finished their major period of growth and are thus the most developed parts at birth and in the first year-and-a-half, and the cerebrum (the cortical hemispheres) develops in advance of the cerebellum.

These patterns of growth relate to brain volume — for information on the detail of structural development of the cortex we have to rely on the work of Conel (1939–1959), who carried out a series of post-mortem micro-anatomical studies of human brains from birth to two years. Information beyond this point is virtually non-existent.

The sequence of development in the first two years of life follows this progression:

— the primary motor area, which lies just forward of the central fissure

Figure 3.1: Growth of Major Parts of the Brain

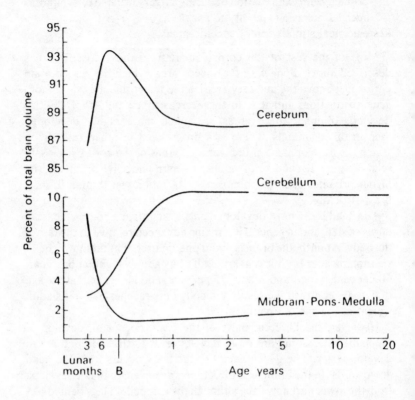

— the primary sensory area, which lies just behind the central fissure
— the visual area
— the auditory area

Most of the development is in the connections between neurons, and between the cortex and other parts of the brain, since at birth the brain has virtually its full complement of neurons. The 'general' areas of associations and intellectual abilities develop after the 'primary' motor and sensory areas listed above — and in general those areas closest to the primary areas develop faster than those further away.

In the motor area, those parts which control the upper parts of the body develop before those which control the lower trunk and legs. An exception to this is that the development of the control of the head is slower for the first month after birth, but after this period it is in advance of the rest of the body. Myelination follows the pattern described above and is probably only fully laid down just before adolescence.

This pattern of development makes Piaget's description of the sensory-motor period seem reasonable, since the sensory and motor areas are the most advanced in the cortex during the first two years of life. It is interesting to note that the motor area tends to develop in advance of the sensory area, which also gives some support to Piaget's view that the child is inwardly motivated; motor activity may occur partly because this area is more developed, and thus more able to stimulate activity (see Chapter 5).

That the brain continues to mature in its function to some extent after the age of two can be assumed from the development of electroencephalogram (EEG) records. The brain, like nerves in other parts of the body, produces electrical impulses, and with sensitive amplifying equipment these impulses can be picked up from electrodes attached to the scalp. The form of this electrical activity is a complex pattern of waves of different frequencies ranging from five cycles per second to bursts of much higher frequencies.

The EEG gradually shows more and more evidence of high frequency activity though the full adult pattern, which has an average frequency of about nine-and-a-half cycles per second, is not reached until between eleven and thirteen years of age. At birth, the EEG consists mainly of 'delta' waves, i.e. irregular, large amplitude, low frequency (less than seven cycles per second) activity. By the age of five, the 'alpha' rhythm predominates (about eight cycles per second), and from then on, higher frequencies gradually develop until the adult value is reached at about eleven years of age.

The proportion of time spent in sleep decreases as the child grows older. Neonates on average spend 80 per cent of their time asleep, while one-year-olds on average spend about 50 per cent of their time asleep. The rhythms and depth of sleep also change rapidly during the first year. For the first three or four weeks, the average infant takes seven or eight short naps a day, but thé number is reduced to between two and four longer periods of sleep by six weeks of age. By 28 weeks, most children will sleep through the night, and from then until they are about one year old, will require only two or three daytime naps. Night sleep also becomes less broken as the child matures — to the considerable relief of weary mothers and fathers.

There are at least two physiologically different kinds of sleep. In one, the person displays short, rapid movements of the eyes, and brain wave patterns characteristic of wakefulness. In the other, the brain wave patterns are different, and the eye movements are typically absent. In adults, dreams are most likely to occur during the rapid eye movement phase (called REM sleep), but it is not known whether young infants are dreaming when they display these eye movements. REM sleep is most frequent during the first 3–5 months (40 per cent of sleep time), and decreases with age.

The increase in quiet (non-REM) sleep is correlated with greater control of physiological mechanisms such as respiration and heart beat by the cerebral cortex. It also appears that by five months of age maturational changes in the brain may influence aspects of psychological functioning such as attentiveness and motor coordination.

Endocrine Glands

Glandular functioning is in part the answer to why the child grows in a normal or deviant way. Malfunctioning of a single endocrine gland — the pituitary or thyroid in particular — produces accelerating, retarding and other undesirable effects on the total organism. Genetic factors influence endocrine gland growth and activity, but the mechanisms involved are not yet fully understood. A thalamic centre acts to stimulate the pituitary gland, but its own stimulation probably comes from a centre in the brain. The sympathetic function of the autonomic nervous system affects the output of most endocrine glands. Height and bodily proportion are highly dependent on the pituitary gland, located at the base of the brain. The anterior lobe of the pituitary gland produces growth-stimulating hormone (STH).

The pituitary's influence extends to the sexual aspects of child and adolescent growth. Its anterior lobe generates gonadotrophic hormone (GTH), stimulating the growth of testes or ovaries. There are cases of insufficient growth of genital organs, as well as cases of precocious sexual maturation occurring at seven or nine years of age. *Pubertas praecox* is the term used to designate an unusually early structural and functional maturation of the sexual glands. Early sexual maturation produces adjustment problems for many girls. They feel 'out of place' with the preadolescents but also have difficulty being accepted by older girls. Physical growth also has much to do with the functional capability of the thyroid gland, as protein synthesis and many functions of the metabolic process are controlled by its hormone, thyroxin. As compared with that of the adult, the metabolic rate is highly accelerated throughout infancy and childhood.

Maturation

Maturation refers to the sequence of biological changes that occurs in almost all infants. These changes permit a psychological function to appear, given the proper environmental conditions. Maturation is a major developmental process involving physical growth, which brings about changes in the size and complexity of the physiology of the individual. Thus, an individual will not only increase his height and weight as he develops, but internal organic changes will also occur. One of the most important aspects of internal change is that associated with the maturation of the nervous system, for the level of development of the nervous system sets limits to learning; in general the more mature and complex the nervous system, the greater potential there will be for learning.

The emergence of speech between one and three years in almost all children in all societies is one of the best examples of the influence of maturation on a psychological function. The three-month-old, whose brain is mature enough, will not speak unless exposed to the language of other people. Maturation does not cause a psychological function to occur; it only sets the limits on the earliest time of its appearance. Puberty is also a maturational event, dependent upon the release of certain hormones from the pituitary gland located at the base of the brain. But environmental events, such as disease and poor nutrition, can retard the emergence of puberty by several months or even years.

We do not possess a detailed understanding of the biological changes that permit new capabilities to emerge, but we can describe some of the psychological milestones in the first year — the emergence of new abilities that are likely to be correlated with changes in the central nervous system.

The child's sitting, crawling and standing also exemplify the role of maturation in development. They occur during the first two years of life as a consequence of the opportunity to use the body plus the maturation of certain neural tissues, expansion and increased complexity of the central nervous system, and growth of bones and muscles. In many instances, these seemingly unlearned behaviour patterns improve and become better coordinated, more precise and more accurate after practice. Although these abilities will develop without any special teaching by adults, extreme degrees of environmental restriction of opportunity for motor development can retard the first appearance of walking and specific practice or teaching can facilitate an earlier appearance of these abilities.

Despite maturational developments being rooted in physiological growth the environment is important in that it is the medium through which potentialities are expressed, e.g. a child cannot crawl if he has no floor to crawl on. A child will not bother speaking if he finds his parents don't bother to answer him, i.e. no reward value. Speech needs encouragement.

The most suitable environment for the practice and display of the maturing feature must be provided, for although maturation will occur there must be opportunity then to allow practice which will make all the difference between a skilled and clumsy performance. As Shakespeare put it, 'There is a tide in the affairs of men, which, taken at the flood leads on to fortune' but 'omitted all the voyage of their lives is bound in shallows and miseries'. Whether deliberate training and extra practice can speed up the achievement of some maturational developments still remains a controversial issue.

Special training can lead the child to master certain skills that normally would not be learned until later in the developmental sequence. The question is whether or not such early training is practical and advisable. Although each case has to be evaluated on its own merits, the following generalisations seem to have theoretical, as well as empirical, support:

(a) Early training tends to be uneconomical and wasteful because it requires special instruction and many repetitions to learn what later would come readily. The extent to which special training leads to performance beyond what would occur naturally varies with the nature of the task. In skills where muscular strength, speed and precision of movement are crucial factors, maturation is essentially a sufficient determinant of proficiency and special practice is correspondingly futile. In tasks of greater complexity such as those of the classroom, on the other hand, opportunity and training play a more crucial role in determining efficiency.

(b) Such training may be definitely harmful. Forcing the child to the limit of his ability may well result in frustration and discouragement and, eventually, negative attitudes and personal maladjustment, all of which will interfere with subsequent learning.

(c) Early training may also be of great benefit. It may result in outstanding performances which could never be equalled by a child denied this early training. It can also result in positive attitudes, e.g. confidence, which can carry over into all aspects of life. It may forestall the development of the bad habits that can arise when a child learns something by himself, and it may provide the child with a start in learning certain skills which would then be the basis for the early learning of other skills further along the sequence.

Even more significant, however, are the many indications that early stimulation is essential to later learning. Not only must certain learnings take place by a certain time, if they are not to act as roadblocks to the learning of other material higher on the spiral, but also certain learnings are best mastered at an early age: in addition early learnings exert a beneficial effect on future learning capacity, including the promotion of the necessary physiological maturity. It also seems clear that we have grossly underestimated the ability of both human and animal subjects to learn under proper conditions.

(d) The crucial point seems to be the manner in which training is given. Too often parents and teachers get anxious and try to push the child. Unfortunately, far from building up the background he needs, such efforts are more likely to make him unready by building emotional blocks and a negative self-concept. Recent evidence suggests the importance of early training in the development of the child, but one must not overlook the possibility of harm. In all cases, the approach must be one of positive encouragement; patience and understanding are paramount.

Critical Periods

One concept intimately related to maturation is that of the critical period. The concept of the critical period was first used in animal studies, which demonstrated the critical nature of some early phases of life in setting a pattern for later life. Konrad Lorenz's concept (1955) of *imprinting*, whereby young birds attach themselves to a moving object, living or nonliving, is pertinent here. Imprinting is thought to occur during a critical time in the physiological and social development of the bird. The duration of this critical period is about one and a half days but varies somewhat for different species. Depending on resources at the critical time, goslings and ducklings have learned to follow people, hens, and a variety of decoy objects. No attachment will occur if there are no objects to follow during this period of heightened sensitivity.

Whether critical periods exist in human behavioural development in the same way as for other animals is still a subject of much dispute. Disputes are mainly in the area of attachment to, and need for, the mother. The issue is treated later (Chapter 9).

It is clear that critical periods do exist in humans in the sense that some learning is dependent on the adequate development of neural pathways. For example, toilet training is unsuccessful until the necessary paths from the bladder and bladder sphincter nerves to the spinal cord are developed. The area of maternal attachment and deprivation is one of the major areas of debate concerning critical periods in humans, as mentioned above.

After surveying imprinting on animals and humans, Gray (1958) placed the critical period for social imprinting in human beings from the age of about six weeks to about six months (from the onset of conditionability to the fear reaction to strangers). At this time deprivation of perceptual and social stimuli can be seriously damaging. He provides some evidence suggesting that 'wild children' and delinquent teenagers may have lacked imprinting, in addition to having stressful experiences, during the period of infantile helplessness. The main principle of the 'critical periods' hypothesis is that certain dispositions and sensitivities appear in clusters rather than individually and grow when stimulated by proper influences. If relevant stimuli are absent or are present only at an earlier period or a later period, contingent development fails to occur. When a fundamental growth does not take place, any advanced development of the same power or trait is impossible. If affection is not shown to the baby, he or she will fail to return it, and the capacity for genuine love in later life is thus diminished (Chapter 9).

The stress of children being separated from mother declines in intensity with age and they are able to tolerate being a greater distance from her. In a number of studies, the mother has been asked to leave the child alone or with a stranger for a few minutes (Maccoby and Feldman, 1972); in others, naturally occurring separations have been observed (Clarke-Stewart and Hevey, 1981). During the period from one to four years of age, children show less and less distress at brief separations from mother, and from two to four years they also seek less and less proximity and physical contact with her. Rheingold and Eckerman (1971) found an impressive mathematical regularity in the distance children would venture from mother: for each additional month of age, children went one-third of a metre farther during fifteen minutes of free play outside.

If a stranger is present, or the situation is otherwise stressful, children three years of age may still be upset at separation from mother. Murphy (1962) found that one-third of the three-year-olds she studied still had trouble separating from their mothers to leave home or to go upstairs with an examiner. Even at this age, it seems, children want physical comfort and reassurance from mother in times of mild stress. Not until the child is four years old is distress at a brief separation really rare (Marvin, 1977).

The fact that older children need not be as near mother does not mean that they care less for her than at the 'peak' of manifesting attachment to her. Although *physical* contact diminishes, the *relationship* remains strong and is evident in other patterns of behaviour.

Perception

A question which has puzzled many parents, psychologists and, indeed, philosophers is what a newly born baby sees.

If our perceptual abilities for space perception are innate, they should be present in the very young. If perception is a learned skill on the other hand then the world of the infant should be in, as William James has put it, '. . . a blooming, buzzing confusion'. In other words, the baby 'sees' very little; the visual world is chaotic, confusing and overwhelming and it takes a long time for the infant to 'learn to see', since eyes have only been used to the dim diffuse light that penetrates the womb. Unfortunately, human infants cannot tell us what the world looks like to them and so many of our questions about infant perception remain unanswered. Thus experimenters have had to stretch their ingenuity to try to measure visual abilities, often in animals, and then generalise perhaps invalidly to man. Research on attentional processes suggests, however, that the infant's world may actually be quieter than our own, because infants may not be able to shift attention rapidly from one event to another. When baby is watching mother, it may not hear other sounds in the room.

Sperry (1952), showed that in the visual systems of various species there appeared to be a strong genetic element which predetermined visual perception. He found that if the eyeballs of certain animals were severed from the optic nerves, turned through 180 degrees, replaced and allowed to reconnect, these animals showed every sign of seeing the world upside down. This suggested that the development of perception did not depend wholly on learning or, otherwise, these animals would have learned to see the world the correct way up.

At the same time, work of even greater significance was proceeding on a detailed study of the messages that travel along the optic nerve to the brain. Until this point, the eye had been regarded as a rather passive organ, merely collecting images and passing them on to the brain.

Hubel (1963) discovered by examining the eye-grain system of cats that a great deal of active processing of the retinal image occurs at the retinal level. It was found that spots, bars, slits and edges are all 'recognised' by particular arrangements of light-receiving cells and other associated cells and that the information passed on to the brain is already in a highly coded form.

However, it is a long way, both phylogenetically and conceptually from cats to humans. It could well be that perceptual and behavioural processes of simpler organisms are more predetermined by their genetic endowment than those of higher, more complex ones; after all, the behaviour of ants and many other insects seems to be almost entirely genetically pre-programmed. The pioneer in extending this work to human infants was Fantz (1961). He found that two-week-old infants had strong visual preferences for complex, rather than simple, patterns, and that the infant's visual ability is quite well developed soon after birth. Carpenter (1974) has shown that by the third week of life an infant can discriminate its mother's face from that of a stranger. Fantz also found preferences for human faces rather than other objects. But we do not really know whether it is the face itself or the complexity of the face pattern that attracts the infant. So, it seems that visual ability may be innate. Gibson and Walk (1960) investigated depth perception in infants, a vital ability as mobility develops, since it enables individuals to avoid potentially injurious falls. Human infants are normally protected from falls by things like gates on stairs, cot-sides and rails. This is based on a belief that crawling babies tend to fall over brinks. But why do they do this? Is it that they do not perceive the differences in depth or is it that they can perceive them but are likely to fall because of clumsy motor coordination?

The experiments by Gibson and Walk give an indication that this second hypothesis is more likely. They constructed a 'visual cliff' consisting of a central walkway with a shallow drop (an inch or so) on one side and a deep drop (about three feet) on the other. Each side was covered, at a level slightly lower than the walkway, with a sheet of strong glass to avoid injury to the subjects. The basic procedure (for human infants) was to place them on the walkway and then to encourage them to crawl to their mother over the two drops.

In one experiment, children between 6.5 and 14 months were placed on the board, and the mothers called to the children from the deep and shallow sides alternately. Nine of the children did not leave the board, possibly because they could not crawl adequately but 24 of the 27 who did crawl did so on to the shallow side but not the deep. The remaining three crawled on to both sides. So it seems that most children, by the time they can crawl, can perceive and avoid a dangerous drop. By implication, then, it would seem that many cases of babies falling off high objects are failures of motor-coordination rather than of perception. Experiments with other animals show that even one-day-old chickens, kids and lambs did not go off the deep end so it does seem that this ability is independent of specific learning. This tendency is clearly very strongly inbuilt; even after neo-decortication, a cat avoids the deep side. Experiments with much younger babies, some only a few days old, have shown that visual events like the sight of an object looming up on a hit path are interpreted by the baby just as they would be by an adult (Bower, 1977). The baby moves its head back and raises its arms as if to defend itself against impending contact.

These experiments cannot show whether depth perception is an innate abilty because they can only be carried out when the subject is old enough to move around. Nevertheless, they do show that the ability to discriminate depth is present by the time that it is needed, i.e. as soon as a child starts to crawl. Thus the dangerous falls to which very young children seem prone are much more likely to result from immature coordination of movement than from a lack of ability to perceive depth. This selection of research reveals that the infant is not an empty organism but one that is well prepared in a variety of ways for its development into an adult.

A large number of studies carried out on the development of perception in infants seems to make no decision about the objects to which the infants will pay attention. For instance, infants will observe one object for a very long time — up to 35 minutes by the ninth or tenth day. Since they are fixating objects it is clear that they are discriminating figure from ground. Visual following of a moving object also occurs at this early stage. By one month there seems to be more voluntary control, and movement of an object at the periphery of the visual field leads to eye movements which bring it to the centre of the field of vision. A question of considerable interest has been whether perceptual constancy is a function of learning, and recent evidence shows that it is present in very young babies, too young for them to have had much chance to learn it. The technique for studying constancy with babies between 40 and 60 days old has been developed by Bower (1966). The babies were placed so that a left turn of the head closed a microswitch, which in turn activated a counter so that the number of turns could be counted. The child was rewarded for turning his head to the left when the training stimulus was present by having the mother or experimenter pop up from behind a screen and say 'peek-a-boo'. With partial reward ('peek-a-boo' about every fifth turn) a child can emit about 400 such responses in a twenty-minute session.

In one experiment babies were reinforced in the presence of a twelve-inch cube at three feet. After training of this type the original stimulus and others differing from it in various ways (same or double the size at double the distance) are presented and the number of responses to each counted. It is argued that the baby will respond more to stimuli it considers most like the original stimulus. As a result of experiments with a variety of stimuli and observation conditions (monocular, binocular, with and without head movement parallax) Bower concluded that apparently the infants were responding on the basis of real size and distance rather than retinal size. The results from this and other studies indicate that by the age of eight weeks human infants have some capability for distance discrimination, size constancy, and shape constancy, although these abilities improve with age.

Infants possess more perceptual skills than was previously thought. They can detect 'depth' at four weeks old, show attending ability from two weeks, with preference for complex patterns, and perceptual constancy at six weeks old.

Summary

The neonate appears a passive and primitive organ but does possess many abilities and skills by which it makes contact with the world. Using these skills the infant is able to learn quite rapidly how to cope with its environment. Physical growth is irregular and individual in rate.

Changes in height are rapid in the first year but steady-off until adolescence. The nervous system develops substantially in the first three years with myelinisation of nerves and increases in neural connections. The cortex and cerebellum develop more slowly than the mid brain and brain stem areas. Body proportions change from infancy where the head is proportionately large through childhood when legs and trunk increase as a proportion of body length.

Much early development is controlled by maturation but a minimum environment is needed for normal development. Practice in a suitable environment is necessary to develop a skilled performance in a maturation feature. Critical periods for developing specific skills may not exist in humans though attachment behaviours may require particular conditions to occur in early childhood for them to develop.

Psychologists believe that a baby has some basic perceptual abilities which may be innate, though it is difficult to prove since learning begins from birth. Depth perception, preference for complex patterns, distance discrimination, size and shape constancy are all available in the first two weeks of life though, of course, these abilities improve with experience.

Activities

1. Locate a mother with an infant. Design a series of questions that will provide some information about the mother's recollections of the kinds of visual displays that attracted her infant's attention. List the questions and record the mother's answers. How do the answers relate to the information in this chapter.
2. In an experiment exploring the infant's ability to pinpoint the direction of sound, Bower found that infants less than six months old are fairly accurate in locating objects directly ahead of them but poor in locating objects to their right or left. With an infant less than six months old, test Bower's conclusions. Make a pleasant noise directly ahead of the infant, 30 degrees to the infant's right, and 30 degrees to the infant's left. Record whether or not the infant appears to reach toward the noise. Were your results similar to Bower's? If not, discuss how they were different.
3. For this activity locate an infant in your neighbourhood. Construct six different patterns on different pieces of paper, varying the colour and the amount of detail in each. Show the infant the patterns one at a time, each for one minute, and record

the number of seconds that the infant looks at each pattern. Describe the patterns that the infant looked at longest. Were certain colours associated with those patterns? Were more complex patterns looked at longer than simple patterns?

4. Question mothers about their attitude to potty training. Classify the mothers as 'strict' or 'permissive'. Did 'strict' mothers start training the infant well before it was mature enough to control the sphincter muscles? Did 'permissive' mothers leave training until the infant was capable of control? How quickly did the infants gain control? Did early training have positive or negative effects?

Questions

1. What do you understand by the term 'maturation'? Is the environment important in maturation? What developments in early childhood appear to be maturational?
2. To what extent do you consider perception in infants to be innate?
3. What is a 'critical period'? Do children pass through any such periods?
4. Growth is a highly uneven process. Discuss this contention in relation to height, weight, body proportion and brain in childhood.
5. In what ways might physiological development (e.g. nervous system, endocrinal system) affect behaviour in early childhood?

Further Reading

Bower, T.G. (1966) 'The visual world of infants', *Scientific Amer.*, *215*, 80–92

Bower, T.G. (1977) 'The perceptual world of the child' in J. Bruner and M. Cole (eds.) *The Developing Child*, Cambridge, Mass.: Harvard University Press

Carpenter, G. (1974) 'Mother's face and the newborn', *New Scientist*, *61*, 890

Davie, R., Butler, N. and Goldstein, H. (1972), *From Birth to Seven*, London: Longman

Sinclair, D. (1969) *Human Growth after Birth*, London: Oxford University Press

Tanner, J.M. (1979) *Education and Physical Growth*, London: Hodder

Wachs, T. and Gruen, G. (1982) *Early Experience and Human Development*, London and New York: Plenum

References

Atwell, W. and Albel, E. (1948) 'Reaction time of male high school students in the 14–17 year age group', *Res. Quart. Amer. Assoc. of Health, 19*, 22–9

Bower, T.G.R. (1966) 'The visual world of infants', *Scientific Amer., 215*, 80–90

Bower, T.G.R. (1977) *The Perceptual World of the Child*, London: Fontana

Carpenter, G. (1974) 'Mother's face and the new born' in R. Lewin (ed.) *Child Alive*, London: Temple Smith

Clarke-Stewart, K. and Hevey, C. (1981) 'Longitudinal relations in repeated observations of mother-child interaction from 1–2½ years', *Devel. Psychol., 17*, 127–45

Conel, J.L. (1939-1959) *The Postnatal Development of the Human Cerebral Cortex*, vol. 1–6, Cambridge, Mass.: Harvard University Press

Fantz, R.L. (1961) 'The origin of form perception', *Scientific Amer., 204*, 66–72

Gardner, L. (1972) 'Deprivation dwarfism', *Scientific Amer., 227*, 76–82

Gibson, E. and Walk, P. (1960) 'The visual cliff', *Scientific Amer., 202*, 64

Gray, P.H. (1958) 'Theory and evidence of imprinting in human infants', *J. Psychol., 46*, 155–66

Greulich, W. (1950) 'The rationale of assessing the developmental status of children from roentgenograms of the hand and wrist', *Child Devel., 2*, 33–44

Hubel, D.H. (1963) 'The visual cortex of the brain', *Scientific Amer., 209*, 554–62

Lorenz, K. (1955) *King Solomon's Rings*, London: Methuen

Maccoby, E.E. and Feldman, S. (1972) 'Mother attachment and stranger reactions in the 3rd year of life', *Monogr. Soc. Res. in Child Dev., 37*, No. 146

Marvin, R.S. (1977) 'An ethological-cognitive model of mother-child attachment behaviour' in T. Alloway, P. Pliner and L. Krames (eds.) *Attachment Behaviour*, New York: Plenum

Murphy, L.B. (1962) *The Widening World of Childhood*, New York: Basic Books

Rheingold, H. and Eckerman, C. (1971) 'Departures from the mother' in H. Schaffer (ed.) *The Origins of Human Social Relations*, London: Academic Press

Sperry, P.W. (1952) 'Neurology and the mind-brain problem', *Amer. Scientist, 40*, 291–312

4 HOW CHILDREN LEARN

Learning theory provides some of the most important, exciting and practical knowledge in psychology. To possess knowledge of how people learn is to possess power, for through that knowledge one can modify the learner's behaviour. The mother socialising her children, the teacher educating the pupils, the hospital staff member trying to modify an adolescent's attitude to his illness require an insight into the principles that govern learning.

Most people think of learning in the very narrow sense of acquiring a set of correct facts. But of course learning is concerned with more than knowledge. There is the equally important learning of social skills, i.e. how to get on with others, and the learning of attitudes and values. Emotional learning is vital too, i.e. learning to emit appropriate emotional responses to relevant stimuli, e.g. guilt, happiness, fear. Motor skills such as walking, riding a two-wheel bicycle, writing etc., are learned. So the range of learning is extremely wide and is involved possibly in every piece of behaviour.

Learning need not necessarily be correct either. We can learn incorrect facts, pick up 'bad habits' and respond maladaptively to situations. The fact that neurotic behaviour is learned is a major tenet of faith of the behaviour therapists (Chapter 15). We have never set out deliberately to learn most of our behavioural repertoire. Much of our learning has been going on surreptitiously through the processes of socialisation into our particular culture pattern. The child simply soaks up the norms of the family without any explicit teaching and may involve such things as learning: 'children are nuisances', 'boys don't cry', 'black people can't trust the police', 'I am considered clumsy (or noisy or unintelligent or . . .)' etc.

Pupils learn far more in a lesson that that which the teacher deliberately sets out to teach them. Through non-verbal and verbal cues the pupils learn about the teacher's attitude to each individual pupil and to the subject matter; they learn how to work together, to share, and to accept each other.

The earliest learning in a child's life is the most profound and long-lasting, for it consists of the only learning he has and is constantly reinforced. Although new behaviours are continually being learnt even through adulthood, these are more weakly held and will give way under stress to earlier forms of more childish behaviour (Freud called this regression). New Year resolutions are hard to keep if they involve new behaviours. The Jesuit claim 'give us a child for the first seven years and we will give you the man' reflects the power of early conditioning to programme a child's behaviour for life.

So in view of this wide ranging nature of learning, it is generally defined by psychologists as 'a relatively permanent change in behaviour'. Two major theories of learning, classical conditioning and operant conditioning, lie within the behaviourist approach to studying behaviour, in which the focus is on observable and measurable stimuli and responses. Another approach to the study of learning stems from the Gestalt cognitive approach, where man is seen as an active processor and interpreter of his environment, responding not mechanically and unthinkingly to it, but to his own experiencing of it. A further approach, social learning, links the previous two.

Classical Conditioning

The technique of classical conditioning was discovered by Ivan Pavlov while he was investigating the digestive secretions of dogs in 1909. He noticed that the dog eventually began to salivate at the approach of the attendant bringing the meat. Pavlov found that any stimulus, e.g. a bell, buzzer, metronome present at the same point in time as, or just immediately before, the presentation of the food stimulus would, after around 20 presentations, come to elicit the same response as the original food stimulus, even when the food was not given. This then was simple association learning or classical conditioning, effected by pairing a new stimulus with an existing stimulus-response (S-R) link.

The diagram below illustrates one of Pavlov's basic experiments.

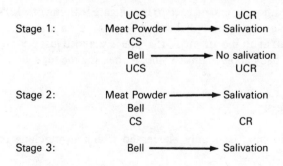

The meat powder as the original stimulus is termed the unconditioned stimulus (UCS) to which the dog responds by salivation or by the unconditioned response (UCR). The new stimulus becomes the conditioned stimulus (CS) to which the conditioned response (CR) is given. There must always be an existing S-R link available into which a new stimulus can be introduced for classical conditioning to occur.

After the CR has been established to the CS, other stimuli present in the context can also become attached to the response, for it is rare for one stimulus to exist in isolation. This is a form of generalisation. For example, a child visiting the dentist will probably respond with anxiety to the sometimes unavoidable odd throb of pain as a tooth is drilled. But also in the context are a variety of other stimuli; the dentist in his white coat, the 'smells' of a surgery, the whine of the drill, etc. These too can come to evoke the CR, so that as the mother goes into the chemist's shop on the way home from the dentist to buy some aspirin, the child clings tightly to the mother as the chemist appears in his white coat. Many of us still shudder on hearing a road-drill! Even though the pain-anxiety link of medical context is infrequent for most people, when stimulus cues of medical staff, equipment and disinfectant smells linked to the original S-R connection are met with at some later date, a sudden evocation of the original feelings can be manifested. Generalisation can occur with words so that the presence or uttering of a word in another context may evoke the original feelings which become attached to the new context. Volkova (1953) used some young children to illustrate this. Cranberry puree was delivered to the child's mouth by a tube and salivation ensued. At the same time the word 'good' was pronounced aloud by the experimenter. After conditioning of salivation to 'good' alone, Volkova tested for generalisation by repeating some sentences that communicated something 'good' and other sentences that communicated 'bad' or unpleasant thoughts. The children salivated to the former but not to the latter.

Classical conditioning can be used to investigate learning in week-old human babies. A baby will blink its eye as a natural reflex response to a puff of air blown into it. If a tone is sounded just prior to the air puff, the baby soon begins to blink on hearing the tone alone.

Emotional Learning

Classical conditioning is mainly concerned with the attaching of emotional and attitudinal responses to new stimuli, e.g. generalising fear or pleasure responses to a wide range of stimuli by the association of the latter with the original fear- or pleasure-producing situation. This is, of course, how some maladaptive or phobic responses can develop so that to understand an irrational fear (phobia) one can seek its origins in its association in the past with a rational fear-producing stimulus. Behaviourists believe that neuroses are all examples of learning inappropriate responses through conditioning.

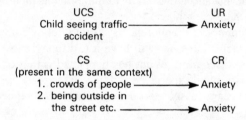

This simple set-up could lead the child to fear going out.

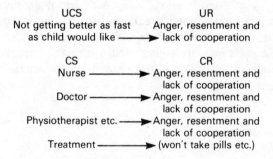

The classic experiment performed in the early days of Pavlovian conditioning by Watson and Raynor (1920) illustrated how fear could be learned and how easily such anxiety could generalise to other similar stimuli. In this experiment Albert, a stolid nine-month-old, was first exposed to a regular routine in which his reactions to the sudden presentation of a white rat, a rabbit, a dog and other 'stimuli' were examined. Watson noted that Albert never showed fear on such occasions but, on the contrary, often reached out for the animals. On the other hand, it could be easily established that a sudden loud noise did produce a fear reaction in the child. Watson's plan was to transfer, by a conditioning process, the fear of the loud noise to one of the preferred stimuli. Simply associating the noise with the concurrent presentation of the white rat did indeed have this effect, and Albert came to exhibit fear when the rat was presented without any need for the loud noise as an accompaniment after six pairings of the UCS and CS.

In short, Albert had acquired a conditioned fear. But this was not all, for Watson observed that the fear had shown generalisation or spreading to other stimuli which bore some resemblance to the white rat (such as a dog, a rabbit and a fur coat). Furthermore, these newly acquired fears were enduring and showed little diminution one month after the 'conditioning' had taken place.

Test anxiety, so common in children, is usually classically conditioned. When a teacher says 'we will have a test today' most children feel unease and discomfort. What has happened is that on some previous occasion the pupil experienced anxiety in the presence of the test and the two became associated. Every future occurrence strengthened the bond.

Much advertising on TV is based on classical conditioning, associating one thing with another. For example, soft drinks are linked with fun, youth and freedom; soap with social approval; toothpaste with sex appeal; and breakfast cereal with sporting prowess. The list is endless but children and adolescents constantly exposed to the associations are conditioned to demand particular soaps, cereals and drinks from harassed parents in the middle of shopping trips.

Operant Conditioning

At the beginning of this century, Thorndike (1911) was studying animal behaviour and discerned that the effect of successful behaviour is to increase the probability that it will be repeated in similar circumstances. This principle is formulated into his Law of Effect which is the major element in Skinner's (1951) theory of operant conditioning. Skinner has carried out comprehensive experimental investigations into operant conditioning using mainly pigeons and rats.

Basic Experiment

Operant conditioning differs from classical conditioning in the very fact that the S-R link is not already there and the experimenter has to wait for the responses to be emitted first. A basic sort of experiment

Skinner conducts runs as follows. A hungry rat is placed in a box in which there is a lever which, if depressed, will activate a mechanism to deliver a food pellet. The rat will tend to explore this box and by chance will press the lever and a food pellet will drop. It will begin to press the lever more and more frequently to obtain the food, which is reinforcement for the behaviour which is now under the control of the experimenter.

With animals, food is a major form of reinforcement as with the dog who gets a biscuit for performing some 'trick'. With humans, attention, praise, approval, success and money are major reinforcers. One of the problems with trying to eradicate the troublesome behaviour of a naughty child is that he gets his reinforcement from the attention the unwanted behaviour attracts. Such behaviour ought to be ignored so that it is extinguished while positive reinforcement is given for required behaviour. Of course some people feel they can only gain attention if they attract it by nefarious behaviour. For example, a child wanting to ask its mother something may have eventually to scream and shout to get her attention, which it does. So the child knows what to do next time it wants her attention.

The operant conditioning of autonomic responses in children is the basis of numerous psychosomatic complaints. For example a child's fear of going to school may cause him to have an upset stomach or headache. If this illness provides the required excuse for absence then the psychosomatic response is reinforced and will increase in frequency. The child has effectively learned to be sick in order to avoid school.

Extinction

So far the learning of a response thorugh its successful delivery of positive reinforcement has been discussed. What happens if the reinforcer is no longer given? As you would expect, the response is emitted less and less often, and finally extinction occurs as it ceases to be emitted at all.

Reward or Reinforcement

Many writers employ the term 'reward' when discussing positive reinforcement. There is nothing wrong with this, but it is important to remember that 'reward' is not synonymous with 'reinforcement'. For example, a reward could be given, without any effect on behaviour. By definition a reinforcer is only a reinforcer if it increases, or maintains at a high level, the probability of responding, i.e. it is reinforcing from the recipient's point of view. For example the reward of public verbal praise may not be regarded as reinforcing by a 15-year-old male pupil who does not want to be made to look a teacher's 'pet'. He is likely to work less hard in future to avoid the situation. For the learning mechanism to be efficient, it is necessary that the reinforcement must come immediately after a response for the probability of that response to be increased. There is always the danger, if reinforcement is delayed, of reinforcing some other behaviour which happens to be going on at that time. With increasing age the range of effective reinforcers widens. Food is a useful reinforcer in babies. Visual stimuli become important later in the first year of life and lead to social reinforcement developing into a potent reinforcer by the end of year one; it remains very potent for the rest of one's life.

Shaping

Before a particular response can be reinforced it must be emitted by the animal. This could mean a very long wait for an experimenter who wishes to produce a response which is rarely made by his animal. Because of this the technique of shaping is used. Shaping involves reinforcing responses which approximate to the one required. As the animal then performs these responses, a closer approximation is required before it is reinforced, until finally the desired response is emitted. Many behaviours can be shaped into an animal's behaviour which are so rare in normal life that they never occur. For example, Skinner trained pigeons to play table tennis. Shaping is common in human learning too. Tennis coaches, driving instructors, teachers, parents, all guide their clients to the desired performance whether it is in manual, linguistic, social or emotional behaviour.

Imagine a child learning to play the clarinet. The teacher shapes the behaviour by showing approval if she holds the instrument approximately correctly and makes any sound at first. Later the stakes are raised gradually. The correct fingering, suitable breathing, accurate counting etc., are all built in by shaping while errors and mistakes will on many occasions be ignored initially (extinguished) so that punishment which might cause dropping out is minimised.

Schedules of Reinforcement

The learning situations described so far involved the presentation of the positive reinforcer every time the response designated for reinforcement occurred. Although some real life situations are of this form, many are not. The 'right' responses may not always be followed by reinforcement. If you 'phone friends they will not always be in. The child working at arithmetic in the classroom is not praised by the teacher for every sum as it is correctly solved. There has been a considerable amount of research by Skinner and his followers into the effects of giving reinforcements following only some of the responses. Such a procedure is known as scheduling reinforcement. Skinner found that once a response has been established it will still be maintained even if reinforcements are given only after a number of responses, or after a predetermined time has elapsed. Different schedules lead to different patterns of responding.

(1)   The fixed ratio schedule occurs when the reinforcement is given after a set of responses, e.g. every tenth or every fifteenth. This keeps the response rate fairly constant and relatively high.

(2)   The fixed interval schedule occurs where the reinforcement is given after a set interval of time, e.g. every ten seconds or every thirty seconds. This results in a reduction of response rate just after reinforcement.

(3)   The variable ratio schedule provides reinforcement after a varying number of responses, e.g. after the third then the tenth, then the fifth. This produces a very high and steady response rate.

(4)   The variable interval schedule provides reinforcement at varying time intervals, producing a steady and high response rate.

The variable ratio schedule is the one which is most resistant to extinction because the subject never knows when he is ever going to be reinforced again. It is this irregular schedule that makes gambling so hard to eradicate since the gambler also feels he might be lucky next time. Haven't we all felt the same way in our little 'flutters' on the one-armed bandits of the amusement arcade until we have expended far more money than we meant to!

Children's tantrum behaviour is often reinforced on a variable ratio schedule for parents will from time to time give in to the child after ignoring it for a period. This simply encourages the child the next time round. So while continuous reinforcement is essential in initially establishing a behaviour, behaviour is learned and maintained strongly on a variable ratio basis.

Secondary Reinforcement

Most human behaviour cannot be seen as having developed through the sort of reinforcement used in the Skinner box. Much human behaviour is not directly reinforced by food or drink. The reinforcers used in most animal learning experiments are examples of primary reinforcers. A primary reinforcer is one which is naturally reinforcing to the organism without its association with other reinforcers. Food, drink and sex are examples. Primary reinforcement is contrasted with secondary reinforcement. A secondary reinforcer is a reinforcer which has derived its reinforcing properties from being associated with one or more primary reinforcers. Thus money is the classic example of a secondary reinforcer. A ten-pound note is just a piece of paper, not worth working for, until it has been associated with a whole variety of primary reinforcers. Secondary reinforcers develop their reinforcing properties from the primary reinforcer with which they are associated. In behaviour modification and procedures in school and hospital, tokens are often given to reinforce behaviour. These are secondary reinforcers too as they can be used to 'buy' privileges when enough have been obtained.

Negative Reinforcement and Punishment

The underlying principle of operant conditioning is that an individual's behaviour is governed by its consequences. People behave to attain desired ends and through experience learn that the goal is attained by behaving one way rather than another. There are three types of reinforcement possible:

(1) Positive reinforcement, as we have noted, increases the probability of the response being repeated, e.g. praise, money.

(2) Punishment decreases the probability of a response, e.g. verbal criticism, a smack, imprisonment.

(3) Negative reinforcement increases response probability as responding removes unpleasant conditions, e.g. pupils work hard to avoid failure rather than for the positive reinforcement of success. Truancy and recourse to drugs are escape mechanisms which are maintained by negative reinforcement. In these cases the pupil receives neither punishment nor positive reinforcement but by responding in those ways avoids what he regards as unpleasant things.

Spare the rod and spoil the child is a well known idiom reflecting folklore wisdom. However, the work of Skinner has revealed that positive reinforcement is far more effective than punishment in regulating behaviour. Positive reinforcement has advantages over both punishment and negative reinforcement in that the subject is less likely to feel hostile or anxious towards the agent of change and positive reinforcement actually forges a link between the act and its outcome. Punishment only tells you that you are wrong, not what to do to get it right, and an even more undesirable response might be substituted. The effect of punishment tends to be temporary too, involving only the suppression of the response, which can reoccur when the punishment is unlikely to follow.

However, research on punishment suggests that in certain circumstances, it may be a valid way of 'being cruel to be kind'. A short brief punishment may prevent suffering in the future. For example, lightly slapping a child's hand when he reaches for a saucepan of boiling water is much to be preferred as a way of teaching that saucepans of boiling water should not be touched than is the child's own discovery when the water pours over him.

The following general principles have been found to maximise the efficiency of punishment, while minimising its unpleasant side:

(1)   Punishment immediately after the undesired behaviour is by far the most effective. Delinquent behaviour is reinforced immediately through its success and the less probable likelihood of detection in the future is a very weak deterrent. The consequence must follow the response as quickly as possible. To delay punishing the child until its father comes home is ineffective in removing the undesired behaviour — the connection has been lost. This explains the paradox of the adolescent who, despite warnings about lung cancer, has another cigarette. If death from lung cancer was to be an immediate consequence of raising that cigarette to his lips then he would not smoke it, but the immediate pleasure of the smoke outweighs the distant worry of possible cancer.

(2)   It is best to administer sufficient punishment to stop the behaviour the first or second time the punishment is given. If punishments are given in a mild form at first, and then built up in strength because of their failure to suppress responding, the final level of punishment needed to eliminate the response is always higher than the level necessary to eliminate the behaviour at the start (with only one or two punishments). For example, a shouted 'Don't do that' using an angry voice may eliminate an undesirable response in a child. A quietly spoken 'Don't touch that' may have

little effect. If so, a later shouted 'Don't touch that' will also have little result, and it may be necessary to punish the child physically to eliminate the behaviour. Ideally then, the minimum level of punishment which eliminates the undesirable response after one or two punishments is the kindest technique for all concerned.

(3)   Most important of all it is necessary to provide an alternative source of positive reinforcement. The combination of punishment for an undesirable response and positive reinforcement for a desirable response is the most effective way of altering behaviour, if necessary using the shaping technique on the slightest approximation to desired behaviour.

Cognitive (Gestalt) Learning

The two types of learning so far considered stress associative learning of a rather mechanical and rigid form. They lay little emphasis on human ability to interpret and evaluate incoming stimuli and decide how or even whether to respond. They also tend to regard the S-R links as individual building bricks rather than look at the various types of buildings that can be constructed using the same elements in different ways. In fact we don't receive sensory input in neat packages, each stimulus tied inexorably to a discrete response. Life is a continuity of experience, a flow of subtle combinations of stimuli which can evoke a variety of responses depending on their interpretation.

For example, individual tones of sound can be put together in different musical pieces. As the Gestalt psychologists claim, 'the whole is greater than the sum of the parts'. Moreover, even one combination of notes making, say, Beethoven's Fifth Symphony will have a different meaning to a classical music scholar than to a Second World War French resistance worker. Man can interpret because not only does he possess a large cerebral cortex but he also stores there an organisation of past experience. Present experience is tested against this to determine appropriate behaviour. Meaningfulness becomes an important concept in cognitive learning, for by structuring our perceptions we learn particular meanings of events in a personal form.

Kohler and Insight

The Gestaltists' work connected with insight has proved to be their most important contribution to learning. It was Wolfgang Kohler's studies of learning in chimpanzees, described in *The Mentality of Apes* (1927) conducted on Tenerife while he was marooned there during the First World War that promoted a cognitive view of learning. A typical experiment is where a chimpanzee is confined inside a cage; outside the cage is a bunch of bananas just out of reach, whilst inside the cage are two sticks. The animal is required to join two sticks together in order to reach the fruit. The chimpanzee would try first one stick then the other. After many unsuccessful attempts, eventually in the handling of the two sticks the chimpanzee would accidentally join them together, and immediately he would take the joined sticks to the bars and drag in the fruit. Even if the sticks separated on the way, he would rejoin them. This represents the sudden or 'insight' solution of the problem which the Gestaltists claimed.

The following appear to be the main characteristics of insightful learning.

(1) Suddenness of solution.
(2) Immediacy and smoothness of behaviour after solution.
(3) Ability to repeat solution without error on successive presentation of original problem.
(4) Abilty to transpose the solution to situations exhibiting the same relational or structural features, but in a different context.

Kohler observed in his experiments that the behaviour of his chimpanzees was not mere blind trial and error but that there was purposiveness and insight into the whole problem and restructuring. This restructuring is an important concept in Gestalt psychology, in which the structure is the composition, the arrangement of component parts, and the organisation of a complex whole, forming units of learning.

Wertheimer (1945) has demonstrated restructuring and insight with children in a problem-solving situation. In one example he taught children how to find the area of any parallelogram after understanding how to find the area of a rectangle. He describes how he visited a classroom where the teacher was teaching the class to find the area of a parallelogram after revising the area of rectangles. This was taught by the conventional method of dropping the two perpendiculars as in Figure 4.1. With the help of this diagram and the usual explanation, the area of the parallelogram was established as the base multiplied by the perpendicular height. Examples were set and extremely satisfactory results obtained. Wertheimer then explains how he asked permission to set the class a similar example. He drew a parallelogram as in Figure 4.2. This confused a number of the class who attempted blindly to drop perpendiculars as in Figure 4.3 and became extremely puzzled.

Figure 4.1

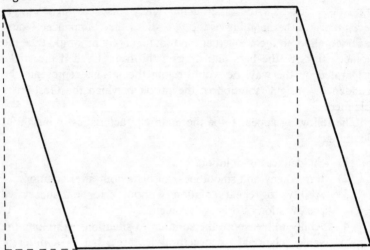

Figure 4.2

Figure 4.3

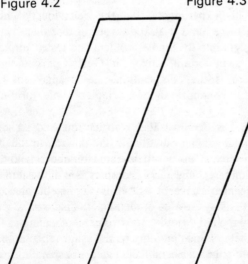
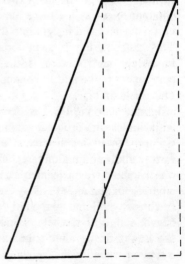

A minority realised that Figure 4.2 was similar to Figure 4.1, only it had been rotated. They therefore turned their pages through 45° as in Figure 4.4 and successfully solved the problem.

Figure 4.4

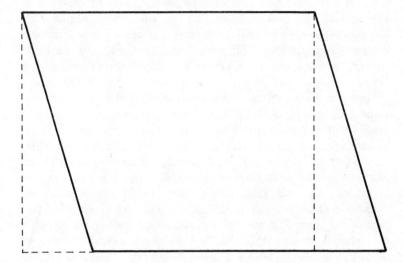

Wertheimer stresses that insightful solutions depend upon the structural features of the problem being presented in a variety of ways. Although the class had been taught a number of problems with different measurements they were all perceptually similar.

Learning Sets

The work of Harlow (1949) demonstrates that S-R learning and insightful learning are related. S-R appears to be dominant in the initial states with insight developing on the basis of this previous S-R learning. In his experiments, Harlow presented monkeys with a variety of discrimination tests. The simplest experiment of the series was the one in which the monkey had to select from two objects placed on a board. For each test the two blocks were easily distinguishable and clearly different in either size or colour. For example, one might be white and the other black, one cylindrical and one triangular, or one large and the other small. The monkeys were presented with a board on which were two different blocks, under one of which the experimenter had previously placed a reward, for example a raisin or some peanuts. The monkey was allowed to look under one block, and if correct he was given the reward. The experiment was then repeated with the same blocks in different positions on the board, and the reward was always under the same block. When the monkey was able to select the correct block first, in fact when he had learnt which one to choose, the blocks were changed. The trial was repeated with different shaped blocks until the monkey was again able to select the correct object each time. This in itself would be simple trial and error learning, or one could say that the monkey had learnt to respond to a certain perceptual cue only — either the size, the shape or the colour.

However, by presenting a long series of trials Harlow observed a distinct change in the behaviour of the monkeys, for the animals gradually developed a strategy to solve the problem. They learnt to switch their choice, if incorrect the first time, to the other object. They had, in fact, achieved two facets of learning. Firstly, they had learnt to discriminate; for example when two objects were presented, of a cylindrical and triangular shape, they would realise that the cylindrical object was the correct one and would choose this 100 per cent of the time. Secondly, when different objects or blocks were presented, they learnt that if their first choice was incorrect they must immediately switch choices. Harlow called this a 'learning set', or learning how to learn.

Harlow argued that this acquiring of learning sets, or 'learning how to learn', was the natural progression from the random trial and error learning to insightful learning. If we accept that one of the ultimate objects of learning is to solve problems, or to develop reasoning capacity, then to permit children to operate at the mere trial and error stage would be extremely wasteful; but one could not expect them to acquire insight unless they had previously acquired the learning set of any particular type of problem. There are of course areas in education where a learning set cannot be achieved, nor can insightful learning take place, e.g. a foreign language vocabulary or anatomical details of the body. There would thus seem to be a hierarchy in types of learning, those higher up founded on lower order ones. Content and context are needed before problem solving is possible.

Social Learning Theory

This approach involves a synthesis of the other theories. It integrates behaviourist processes of reinforcement with cognitive processes of observing others' behaviour and identifying with it, of self-evaluation, and of understanding what constitutes 'meaning' for different individuals. Social learning theory, whose main proponent is Bandura (1977), emphasises that many behaviours are learned by watching others, understanding the consequences and appropriately imitating the behaviour. Emotions can be learned vicariously by watching the emotional responses of others as they enjoy or endure some experience. Social and interpersonal behaviour is particularly susceptible to social learning. The role of a 'model' (child or adult) is vitally important in such an observation — imitation — reinforcement sequence. Social learning theorists have directed much research effort into discovering how modelled behaviour is transmitted, what types of models are most effective and what factors determine whether the model's behaviour will be followed or not. But much of what a child learns depends on the presence of other people.

What is felt to be rewarding is an individual matter, can often depend on the way the person perceives the situation and can often be self-engendered or internal. This is an elaboration of Skinner who saw reinforcement generally as external and made no real attempt to consider reinforcement from the perspective of the recipient.

Several learning theorists argue that children learn or become socialised into the culture by conditioning and shaping through the positive and negative reinforcements of parents and significant others; by imitating or modelling the behaviour of others; and by identifying with significant others and thinking about their behaviour and its meaning for them as they grow older. The work of Hebb (1949) on the physiological basis of intelligence suggests that early learning is very much a stimulus response type of associational process while later learning involves integrating the stimulus-response atoms into more complex thoughts. Harlow's work on learning sets suggests the same crude development, from trial and error to insight as learning progresses. Piaget's model of thinking commences with an almost behaviourist stimulus-response period in infancy which starts to modify into a more cognitive model by the end of the first year of life.

Bandura (1965) asked children to look at one of three different films. In each film a male adult 'model' exhibited a number of aggressive actions that were novel to the children. In one of the films the model's aggressive behaviour was followed by punishment. In the second film the model was rewarded, reinforcement taking the form of food and social approval. In the third film the model's aggressive behaviour had no apparent consequence.

After the children had watched the films a record was made of the number of actions made in imitation of the model. Most of the children imitated the model to some extent, demonstrating learning through observation, but the children who had watched the film in which the model's aggressive actions were punished produced fewer imitative acts than children who had watched either the film in which the model was rewarded or the film in which aggressive behaviour produced no reaction. There were some differences between the sexes, boys making more aggressive acts in imitation of the model than girls.

Following the experimental trials described above, the children were offered attractive rewards for reproducing the aggressive actions made by the model they had previously watched. The effect of providing these incentives was to eliminate the earlier differences in performance between the groups. This finding clearly shows that learning was equivalent in each of the three experimental groups, the previous differences being ones of performance only. The findings of Bandura's experiment make it clear that children can learn aggressive activities from observing models. The findings have clear implications for those who are concerned about the effects on children of violence shown on television.

Children who see their parents acting generously are more likely to learn that behaviour than children who don't see such behaviour and are simply told that generosity is a positive virtue. When there is a conflict between what a model does and what a model says, it is the behaviour that is copied and not the words. The old adage 'do what I say, not what I do' is invalid. If a parent doesn't want his children to smoke even though the parent is a 20-a-day man, giving them warnings on the evils of smoking will have little effect. They will be more likely to follow the parental behaviour.

Imitation of models occurs where there is a high level of warmth and nurturance shown to the child by the model (Mischel and Grusec, 1966). Imitation also occurs when it is rewarding to imitate (Bandura, 1965) i.e. if the model is rewarded or if the child is rewarded for imitating the model then imitation and social learning will be promoted. Children also tend to imitate others who have power status. 'Pop stars', sporting heroes, teachers etc., all fall into this role. But in all these aspects the most frequent models are the parents.

Role learning within the culture provides another basis for social learning. Different roles e.g. pupil, son, friend, provide different sets of expectations about behaviour. These distinctions are learned through reinforcement, imitation and identification, and this learning begins early in life, especially that concerned with the learning of appropriate sex roles and the behaviour expected from males and females. But it must not be forgotten that the child is far from being a passive recipient of reinforcement; he is actively involved in his own socialisation. The child perceives, evaluates and interprets events, and calculates outcomes, based on subjective expectation and experience so that only certain models are imitated and particular reinforcements are attended to with consequent appropriate responses made. The young child is quite a calculating individual. For example it can learn to play one parent off against another from an early age. Mischel (1973) has suggested that the variables that influence a child's behaviour in any given situation include his competences (intelligence, social skills, etc.), his ability to attend selectively, his expectations of outcome, the subjective value of such expectations and his level of conscience development.

Summary

Learning is a relatively permanent change in behaviour and may not necessarily be correct or deliberate. Learning covers social, emotional and motor aspects as well as the intellectual area. The earliest learning of a child is the most deeply entrenched. Pavlov's classical conditioning involves the attachment of new stimuli to existing responses through association with the original stimulus, and is basic to the child's learning of emotional and attitudinal responses to a wide range of stimuli, particularly through the process of generalisation.

Trial and error learning was a theory developed by Thorndike which maintains that an organism modifies its behaviour as a result of experience. His major law, the Law of Effect was later used by Skinner in operant conditioning.

Skinner's operant conditioning shows how responses that cannot be elicited by an identifiable stimulus can be brought under control by reinforcement scheduling and shaping. Positive reinforcement is far more effective than punishment in regulating behaviour, as it increases the likelihood of that response recurring on similar occasions.

Cognitive learning as exemplified by the laws of Pragnanz, and the work of Kohler and Wertheimer is based on the premiss that man responds to stimuli not in a mechanical way but by organising experience and making it meaningful. Harlow argues that 'learning sets' reveal a gradual progression from an initial trial-and-error learning to insightful learning through experience. Social learning theory elaborated by Bandura (1977) invokes imitation of models in conjunction with external and internal reinforcement, in addition to personal meaning, as a major approach to explain much of children's social and emotional learning.

All theories require that the child is able to pay attention in a selective fashion in order to learn. Attention becomes more selective as the child's age increases.

Activities

1. Psychologists have found that children can be reinforced vicariously; that is, children who watch other children receiving reinforcement for a behaviour may themselves be reinforced for that behaviour. To demonstrate the impact of vicarious reinforcement, arrange for two groups of preschool children, four children to a group. Working with only one group at a time, give each child paper and crayons and ask the group to draw a simple picture of the outdoors. While the children are drawing, approach one child in the group and with enthusiasm tell the child how much you like some particular part of his or her picture — the clouds, for example. When the drawings are finished, collect them. With the second group of preschoolers, follow the same procedure but do not provide the vicarious reinforcement. Keeping separate records for each group, count the number of times the vicariously reinforced object (i.e. the clouds) appears in the drawings of both groups. In which group of drawings does the vicariously reinforced object appear more often? Did the children in the first group respond to the vicarious reinforcement? Did the child whose picture you commented on with enthusiasm respond to the direct reinforcement?

2. Choose a young child playing with a variety of toys. Give the child strong and appropriate reinforcement for playing with *one* particular toy and provide no reinforcement for playing with other toys. Note the change (if any) that occurs in the play activity of the child. You may wish to quantify this activity by using a stopwatch to record the amount of time particular toys are played

with before your intervention, during the reinforcement period and after reinforcement has ceased.

Questions

1. Describe from your own experience or from observing a child, a situation where learning:
   (a) was inappropriate (i.e. an erroneous or maladaptive response)
   (b) was achieved but not meaningfully understood.
2. To what extent is reward more effective than punishment? Why do you think so?
3. Under what conditions is social learning most effective?
4. Explain the differences between trial and error learning and 'insight'.
5. Why is 'attention' important as a factor in learning?
6. The following examples represent different kinds of learning that you read about. For each example explain the kind of learning that is illustrated.
   (a) A young boy was playing with a toy train. While he was playing, a large crash of thunder occurred and scared him. From that day on the child did not want to play with his toy train because it frightened him.
   (b) Every time her mother refused to give Jan an extra helping of dessert Jan cried. Since her mother felt bad at the thought of making Jan cry, she always let Jan have more dessert.
   (c) Tommy was watching his favourite cartoon programme on television. The cartoon characters on this programme always used aggressive behaviours to obtain what they desired. One day when Tommy was playing with his friends, he remembered what his favourite cartoon characters did when they wanted to get their way, and he began behaving aggressively with his friends.
   (d) During the first week of school Joan's infant teacher taught the children that all four-legged animals that bark are called dogs.

Further Reading

Bolles, R.C. (1975) *Learning Theory*, London: Holt, Rinehart and Winston
Hilgard, E. and Bower, G. (1975) *Theories of Learning*, Englewood Cliff, NJ: Prentice Hall
Houston, J.P. (1976) *Fundamentals of Learning*, New York: Academic Press

Howe, M. (1975) *Learning in Infants and Young Children*, London: Macmillan
Piene, H. and Howarth, R. (1976) *Children and Parents: Everyday Problems of Behaviour*, Harmondsworth: Penguin
Stevenson, H.W. (1972) *Children's Learning*, New York: Appleton Century Croft
Thorndike, E.L. (1911) *Animal Intelligence*, New York: Macmillan
Volkova, V.D. (1953) 'On certain characteristics of conditioned reflexes in children', *Fiziologicheskii Zhurnal SSR*, *39*, 540–8
Watson, J.B. and Raynor, R. (1920) 'Conditioned emotional reactions', *J. Exp. Psychol.*, *3*, 1
Wertheimer, M. (1945) *Productive Thinking*, New York: Harper
Yussen, S. (1974) 'Determinants of visual attention and recall', *Dev. Psychol.*, *10*, 93–100
Zeaman, D. and House, B. (1967) 'The relation of IQ and learning' in R. Gagre, (ed.) *Learning and Individual Differences*, Columbus: Merrill
Zeaman, D., House, B. and Orlando, R. (1958) 'The use of special training conditions in visual discrimination', *Amer. J. Mental Def.*, *58*, 453–9

References

Bandura, A. (1965) 'Influence of models' reinforcement contingencies on the acquisition of imitative responses', *J. Pers. Soc. Psychol.*, *1*, 589
Bandura, A. (1977) *Social Learning Theory*, New Jersey: Prentice Hall
Harlow, H.F. (1949) 'Formation of learning sets', *Psychol. Rev.*, 56–61
Hebb, D.O. (1949) *The Organisation of Behaviour*, London: Chapman and Hall
Kohler, W. (1927) *The Mentality of Apes*, London: Routledge
Mischel, W. (1973) 'Towards a cognitive social learning reconceptualisation of personality', *Psychol. Rev.*, *80*, 258–83
Mischel, W. and Grusec, J. (1966) 'Determinants of the rehearsal and transmission of neutral and aversive behaviours', *J. Pers. Soc. Psychol.*, *2*, 197–205
Pavlov, I. (1927) *Conditional Reflexes*, Oxford: OUP
Skinner, B.F. (1951) 'How to teach animals', *Scientific Amer.*, *185*, 26
Volkova, V.D. (1953) 'On certain characteristics of conditioned reflexes in children', *Fiziologicheskii Zhurnal SSR*, *39*, 540–8
Watson, J.B. and Raynor, R. (1920) 'Conditioned emotional reactions', *J. Exp. Psychol.*, *3*, 1
Wertheimer, M. (1945) *Productive Thinking*, New York: Harper

5 COGNITIVE DEVELOPMENT

As adults we take a lot of facts for granted. For example we know that our hands are part of our body but the chair isn't; we know that when we turn to face away from an object it still exists even though we are not looking at it; we know that equivalent amounts of the same material weigh the same even though they might be of different shapes. But children have had to learn all this through experience with the environment. No knowledge is innate. The Swiss psychologists Jean Piaget (1952; 1955; 1962) and Inhelder and Piaget (1969) have made an intensive study of the development of thinking in children, and have delineated various stages as listed below:

Sensori-motor	Birth – 2 years
Pre-operational	2 – 7 years
Concrete Operational	7 – 12 years
Formal Operational	12 years upwards

According to Piaget, infants do not inherit any ready-made mental abilities but only a way of responding to the environment. This response consists of a drive to adapt to the environment as any living creature must if it is to survive. Intelligent behaviour is only one aspect of a general biological tendency towards adaptation and organisation.

The main forces in the child's mental growth, for Piaget, are (a) the essential part played by the child's own actions; and (b) the way this turns into a process of inward building, forming within his brain a continually extending structure corresponding to the external world. This developing structure is a set of schemas constructed through the complementary process of assimilation and accommodation.

Schemas (or Schemata)

Piaget suggests that from birth the infant starts to organise his activities in schemata. A schema is a pattern of activity which is coordinated and acts as an integrated whole, e.g. the individual responses made by the beginner learning tennis become integrated into one smoothly flowing action, or schema. Piaget also suggests that through varied experiences we build up schemata we can use in a variety of situations. We don't use identical responses in every given situation. He gives the example of a baby who through its experience of sucking different objects built up a schema of sucking so that it would adopt a different mouth and grasp position depending on whether it had a bottle, thumb or spoon. The schema has a common core into which many similar behaviours are integrated. This common core can be used in a variety of common situations.

Once the tennis player has built up a schema of returning service through repeated experience in different conditions he will, on any one occasion, use the basic core of this activity plus the more specific behaviours needed to cope with such things as wind direction, skill of opponent, position of opponent, etc. The examples so far are of motor schemas. We can consider mental phenomena in a similar light; these are cognitive schemas. They also have a common core which is relevant to many different situations. An integrated system of concepts is a cognitive schema operating as a unified system of thinking or understanding. A useful way of thinking about cognitive schemas is to consider them as concepts of a fairly general nature. Piaget believes that the schemas we acquire increase in complexity with age and experience. In the early stages, because of limited experience, the child's schemas will coordinate only a few responses. With more experience the schemas will be enlarged or restructured.

Assimilation and Accommodation

Through observing the schematic nature of the interaction of individuals with their environment, Piaget has described two processes at work which help to explain how schemas are formed and developed. He calls them assimilation and accommodation. Assimilation is the process by which an individual behaves towards the environment through the application of already existing schemas. Initially, for example, all the objects that come to the infant's mouth are assimilated into the sucking schema — everything has a single, simple meaning; it is 'to be sucked'. In assimilation, the individual behaves towards objects in terms of the familiar.

To take a further example, a child of three may have a schema for all four-legged things that move: he calls them 'dog'. Cats, cows and so forth, will be assimilated into this one schema by having the same label attached to them by the child.

The other main process Piaget describes is accommodation, i.e. that in every interaction schemas are not applied without recognition of the varying properties of objects and a subsequent adaptation. A schema modifies itself according to the particular characteristics of the object, e.g. a schema of reaching for and grasping something must accommodate to the distance of the object and to its size and weight.

As a result, no two applications of a schema, however simple, are exactly alike. Nevertheless, there is a basic similarity which gives the schema its organisation, permitting its repetition and consequent growth. By the very fact of having to accommodate to this variety, it becomes more differentiated and able to respond differently to the various objects it assimilates. In simple terms, whilst assimilation means that the organism has adapted and can handle the situation presented to it, accommodation means that it must change in order to adapt.

So, in summary, Piaget is suggesting that when a child is faced with a new problem of learning he brings his past experience to bear on it in the form of a previously elaborated schema. This schema is potentially adequate to solve the problem and is termed the anticipatory schema. If it coincides closely with the demands of the present problem the solution is attained (assimilation) but if there is less common ground the schema is restructured (accommodation). Hunt (1960) sees this restructuring possibility as the motivation for learning. The changed schema will now be more comprehensive and relevant to more problems and of wider application. Thus Piaget sees learning as advances by a series of schemas which increase in complexity as they assimilate new elements. Learning that does not involve schemas will consist of mere S—R linkages, rote learning with no understanding or possibility of transfer to other situations. Instead of learning in a situation impregnated with meaning the child learns isolated facts. Conceptual and schematic learning on the other hand can always be assimilated into existing understanding. The aim is an understanding of general principles so that application is possible in a variety of new situations.

Schematic learning is an important element in Piaget's theory, for it forms the basis for motivation. His view is that the existence of a schema is motivating in itself. He does not see individuals as sitting around waiting for stimuli to impinge, but as actively applying schemas to the environment. Humans are active in the development of their own thinking abilities. A brief outline of each of the stages as Piaget sees them now follows.

Piaget's Stages in the Development of Thinking

Sensori-motor Stage (Birth–2 Years)

In this stage the infant is restricted to sensing elements in his environment and responding to them through motor activities. He is unable at first to internalise a representation of an object so that, up to seven months of age, if some toy is hidden the child ceases to have any interest in it. To all intents and purposes it has gone forever, and no longer exists. Out of sight *is* out of mind. From nine months there is increasing activity and interesting results tend to be repeated. He does not yet relate stimulus patterns to objects and must learn what he saw yesterday is what he is seeing today. Even at ten months the child shows little interest in searching for objects temporarily covered up, but the ability to follow rapidly moving objects with the eyes is a sign that the permanent object and its displacement in space is becoming understood. At eleven months the child will search for something hidden under a blanket but if the toy is rehidden elsewhere the search will continue in the same place. Only at one year is a child capable of correctly locating the position of an object when its hiding place is changed each time. The child, of course, must watch the object being hidden. He does not react to invisible placement until 18 months old. But, gradually, the major task of this stage is learned, that of the permanence of objects. The child begins to realise that objects still exist even though not sensed. The infant, as part of this learning, comes to realise that he too is an independent object with a continued existence (cf. Chapter 10). This learning is slow and only gradually does an infant become able to differentiate thinking about an object from acting upon it. He can only solve simple problems by acting out his own responses to those objects. Piaget describes how his daughter, on dropping a rattle waved her arm more energetically apparently in an attempt to reproduce the rattling noise. During the second year the child moves toward internal representations which do not require this activity. Such an internalised process is termed a pre-operation. Pre-operational thought requires that the child forms some symbol which can represent an object in his mind. When such symbolism is becoming established Piaget concludes that the second stage has been reached.

Pre-operational Stage (2–7 Years)

Pre-operational thought is severely limited, yet it is a distinct advance on the previous stage. The child is able to represent the environment in symbolic form and to distinguish between himself and objects in the world around him. Both his language and his thought are characterised by egocentrism. In everyday language this term is pejorative, and denotes someone who is selfish and self-centred, but

Piaget uses it as a simple description. The child is 'self-centred' in the literal sense that he is unable to comprehend the view other people may possess. He acts and speaks on the assumption that what is known to him must be common knowledge to all. This is clearly manifest when a young child attempts to recount an episode which he has experienced. Usually he does not attempt to set the scene or describe the participants, but assumes the listener already knows these.

A classical experiment to illustrate this phenomenon is the 'three mountain problem'. The subject is shown models of three mountains. When a doll is placed in some position other than that from which the child views the scene, the subject is unable to identify which view the doll will have, and he cannot rearrange the mountains to reproduce the view which the doll has. The child too is still confused in the use of physical concepts and in evaluations of cause and effect. During this phase children make inappropriate generalisations and attribute their feelings to inanimate objects — assuming, for example, that clouds 'cry' to make rain.

The notions he builds up are termed pre-concepts by Piaget, for the three-year-old uses something that is between the concept of an object and the concept of a class. When playing in the garden he does not bother if he sees a succession of different worms or whether the same worm keeps reappearing. To him they are all worms. He argues from particular to particular, or what is termed transductive reasoning. He will say that if mummy is combing her hair, she must be going out because she combed her hair before she went out yesterday. Overall, it can be seen that, during the nursery years, the child's thinking is not very stable or internally consistent but, given good opportunities to interact with the environment by means of play and experimentation and good patterns of adult speech from parents and teachers who talk to children and answer their questions, the ground is being prepared for the changes in thinking that will come later.

The pre-conceptual stage shows the start of logical reasoning but it is unreliable as it is subjective and influenced by perceptual appearances. If the appearance or perception is favourable then the child is correct in his reasoning but, if not, he is misled. He cannot make due allowances for the subjective element and represent reality in objective terms. A child of six can give an account of his route to school. If he hurries there and dawdles on the way home, he will strenuously deny the route is equally long in either direction.

Conservation is Piaget's term for the idea that a property or attribute of an object remains the same despite some transformation that changes the appearance of the object. Piaget found that when pre-operational children are shown two identical balls of clay and then see one rolled into a sausage, they may claim that the sausage contains less clay because it is thinner than the ball. The child is taking only one aspect of the situation (shape) into account. By focusing on the end state without considering how the sausage was produced, the child arrives at the wrong answer. If the child remembered that the sausage came from a ball identical with the unchanged ball, a different answer would be arrived at. This inability of the pre-conceptual child to conserve is again vividly illustrated by the famous lemonade glasses experiment.

If two identical glasses are filled with equal quantities of lemonade so that the levels are equal, the pre-operational child will agree that there is the same amount of liquid in each glass. When the contents of one glass are then poured into a shorter, wider glass, so that the height of the liquid is less, he will say that the taller column of liquid is the greater amount even though the pouring was done in front of him. Again, he is being influenced by a single predominant attribute, the height of the column. He has failed to comprehend conservation of amount which is bound up with what Piaget refers to as the principle of reversibility. This principle, when it is mastered, enables the child to undo the process mentally. In this case, it would involve mentally recognising that if the water were poured back into the tall jar again, the heights would still be the same.

The child is overimpressed by visual impression or perception and fixes on one aspect. By not noticing more than one thing, the child cannot see the cancelling out of the differences. To be able to conserve, he must see that the two differences of taller but thinner together cancel out.

Pre-operational thinking is also limited to handling only one attribute of a stimulus at a time and these are usually very obvious physical attributes. For instance, if five coins and five sweets are laid out each in two rows, with a coin against each sweet, the child will readily agree that there are the same number of coins as sweets. If the coins are now spread out so that the row extends beyond the row of sweets, he is likely to declare that there are now more coins than sweets even though he knows that none were added and none subtracted. This is because he is influenced by one obtrusive dimension, the length of the row, and he uses this as an index of 'more than' and 'less than'. He is unable to master the idea that, if none have been added or subtracted, the number is still the same.

This experiment shows how counting in a young child is merely a verbal activity. Even when children had counted the number of items, they would still say there were more in the longer row. They believe what they see; counting is meaningless and they have no understanding of the conservation of number.

Concrete Operational Stage (7–12 Years)

Concrete operational thought is logical, rule bound and integrated. An operation is a mental activity that transforms or manipulates information; it is also an integral part of an organised network of related thinking. Imagine a ten-year-old preparing a snack for himself and his five-year-old sister. He pours the same amount of coke into two differently shaped glasses and counts out five biscuits each. The younger sister bursts into tears when she sees her 'little' glass of coke and her 'tiny' plate of biscuits. She will not stop crying until she switches plates and exchanges glasses, even though the ten-year-old counts the biscuits with his young sister and gets out a measuring flask to show they have the same amount of coke. The ten-year-old is in the concrete operational stage and knows that visual impressions are not a valid way of judging amount. He knows by principle that the coke and biscuits are not changed in amount by their container or by how they are spread out. He recognises that multiplication is related to division, that subtraction is the opposite of addition, that 'equals,' 'greater than,' and union intersection of sets are interrelated. When a child's thinking is able to manipulate information and is organised into an integrated system, it is what Piaget called operational (Inhelder and Piaget, 1969). The term concrete refers to the fact that the child can reason only about tangible objects, such as coke and biscuits. Recognition that certain manipulations of objects are reversible is a major advance of concrete operational thinking. Realising that coke poured from one glass to another can be poured back again is one example of this.

A second important aspect of concrete operation is the child's ability to decentre. Decentring is focusing on and coordinating two or more dimensions at once. When the elder brother poured coke for his sister and himself his equitable sharing depended on his ability to decentre, to coordinate the dimensions of width and height. The five-year-old concentrated only on one dimension at a time. She focused on the heights of the glasses and believed that she had less because her glass and the level in it were shorter. Had the elder brother pointed out that the tall glass was narrower the younger sister would not have understood what he was getting at.

So the emergence of operational thinking denotes yet a further emancipation from the here and now perceptions of a problem situation. The child is now released from the dominance of the senses. An operation is an action capable of being carried out in thought and undone again. The superiority of the concrete child over the intuitive one lies in this mental reversibility, for the child can now see the possibilities of potential actions without having to carry them out physically. But he is limited to considering concrete actions, not hypotheses. In the concrete operational period the child acquires and applies the notions of reversibility and identity across a wide variety of tasks. It is during this period that systems of classification and of number are learned. Arithmetic is much easier when it is realised that $2+3=5$ is the same as $3+2=5$. The ability to perform these mental operations in many different situations, with many numbers, in any concrete problem, eliminates the need for rote memorisation. The same rules are applicable across all situations. The child gives evidence of beginning to realise that arithmetic, as well as other disciplines, is based on a system of rules.

In his work on number Piaget tries to show the relation between these aspects and the conservation of number. If we consider the fact that any large number, e.g. 8, must contain any smaller number, e.g. 6, it is clear that the number series consists of a nesting set of classes. But at the same time, in counting, the number series presents the features of a transitive series in which the transitive relation is the order of their enumeration. One of the Piaget's key arguments is that number is a synthesis of the logic of classes and the logic of relations and to do number work children must master all these modes of reasoning.

The concrete period can also be illustrated by the growth of the child's capacity to classify into groups and put items into series. An understanding of time in the sense that equality of time intervals is not affected by their containing different happenings and that different events can occupy the same time intervals occurs in the concrete period. The concepts of God now become that of a superman rather than the pre-conceptual old man with a beard, and Jesus changes from being a good man to being a miracle-worker.

Lovell (1960, 1961) has replicated some of the basic Piagetian experiments in Britain. Over 300 seven- to eleven-year-olds were presented with two balls of plasticine which each agreed to be identical in amount. One was then drawn out to form a sausage. The pupils were then questioned regarding the amounts of material in the ball and sausage. Conservation of amount (mass) is reported by Piaget as starting by the age of 7. Three stages of non-conservation, transition and conservation were confirmed by Lovell (Table 5.1).

Table 5.1: Conservation of Amount

Age (years)	Number	Non-conservation %	Transition %	Conservation %
7	83	31	33	36
8	65	20	12	68
9	99	11	15	74
10	75	5	9	86

Source: Lovell (1960)

The conservation of weight followed the same age trend, though it occurs a little later than that of amount (Table 5.2).

Table 5.2: Conservation of weight

Age (years)	Number	Non-conservation %	Transition %	Conservation %
7+	57	91	5	4
8+	73	29	36	36
9+	66	32	20	48
10+	168	13	13	74

Source: Lovell (1961)

Can Training Speed up Development of Conservation? Piaget did not promote deliberate training or teaching as a way of encouraging children's development of concrete operations. At his most generous Piaget allowed that transitional children might benefit from training. But the training would be useful only if it were tailored to fit the child's existing mental capacities and offered information about concepts at the next higher stage. He did not believe that short-term training could create new mental capacities.

As soon as Piaget's work became popular in the United States during the 1960s, however, American psychologists undertook studies to find out whether children could be trained to understand concepts earlier than Piaget had suggested that they develop. The first training studies were generally not successful, but later ones have been.

A Conservation Training Study. In one training study Gelman (1969) demonstrated that five-year-olds could be taught to conserve number and length and that, later, many would be able to generalise from their training and conserve liquid quantity and mass. Gelman's results strongly suggested that by receiving feedback that helped them focus on the relevant relations, pre-operational children very quickly became concrete operational in conservation of quantities for which they were trained and were at least in a transitional state for conservation of other quantities. Moreover, even though they had been told only that their earlier choices were right or wrong, not why, they now gave explanations for their answers that showed they understood conservation principles. The results cast some serious doubts on Piaget's views about training.

Class Inclusion Training. Language has been shown to figure in class inclusion problems too. Researchers have wondered whether Piaget's manner of presenting these problems may have over-emphasised the subclass within the class as a whole. Thus if tulips are stressed more than flowers, the child may not consider them flowers. But if flowers are pointed out as a general category, more important than a specific type of flower, the child will focus on the whole class instead of on the tulips. Using this strategy, researchers (Markman and Siebert, 1976) have been able to get children to succeed on class inclusion problems earlier than Piaget had found possible.

Formal Operational Stage (12 Years Onward)

From about twelve onwards in very bright children, and from about 13 or 14 in ordinary children new thinking skills begin to emerge, probably because of the maturation of the central nervous system and also, of course, because of increased and continued social and cultural experience.

Formal operations consist of several new abilities. Whereas earlier thinking was concrete and earthbound, formal operations allow for greater abstraction and speculation (Inhelder and Piaget, 1958). Children with concrete operational thought are able to discuss the world as it *is*; formal operational thought allows adolescents to discuss the world as it *might become*. Adolescents are comfortable with hypothetical thinking and have a greater ability to imagine the logical consequences of existing states. They consider subjects of great moment and seriousness — love, morality, work, politics, religion and philosophy.

Having formal operational thinking is a necessary, but not sufficient, condition for achieving identity, formulating ideological goals and selecting an occupation. Adolescents will want to choose a job or career, a political candidate, a spiritual or religious mentor. Without the flexibility of formal thought that allows them to place their lives in a personal and societal perspective, they are not able to figure out their 'place' in the world.

Adolescents discuss endlessly self, sex, love, friendship, society, religion, justice and the 'meaning of life.' With their formal operational thinking they are better able to form general concepts and to understand the impact of the past on the present and the present on the future. The capacity to think about how one thing relates to another allows them to question social institutions and examine the limits and possibilities of personal and collective action. Their new thinking is full of challenges and daring, but it also gives them a greater capacity to evaluate the immediate and long-range costs and benefits of actions and events. Finally, with greater complexity of thinking, adolescents are able to envision the world not only as it might be but also as it ought to be.

This mature system of thought allows the mastery of complex systems of literature, mathematics and science. It also enables the development of abilities necessary for adult socio-emotional adjustment, such as the planning of future goals and the integration of past and present into a realistic self-identity. One major cause of student unrest and the espousal of courses alien to those of their elders has been seen as deriving from the ability of such young people to direct their new thinking to the realisation that existing forms of society and ways of organising life are only some of many possible options of doing so.

Piaget devised a number of tests of formal operations. In one the person is shown a pendulum consisting of a set of weights, which can be changed, and a string, which can be shortened or lengthened. The subject is then shown how to change the weights, change the string length, vary the height from which the pendulum weight is released, and vary the amount of initial push given to the weight. He or she is asked which of these factors, or a combination of them, determines the period of the pendulum, i.e. the time to complete one cycle. To solve the problem, the subject must begin by holding all factors but one constant at a time and vary each systematically. If the answer is not yet evident, the subject must then vary two factors at a time, and so on. Actually, one factor alone, the length of the string, determines the period of the pendulum (if friction and air resistance are ignored).

In another test the subject is asked to suppose that six people of a district are running for town council, and that the top three vote-getters will be elected. Then he or she is asked how many different combinations of three people could be elected. Obtaining the answer, twenty, depends on the ability to think and work systematically, say by combining symbols standing for the candidates in a methodical way.

Other changes have been noted by research workers. For example Goldman (1964) in his work relating to the growth of religious thinking shows that the adolescent's ideas of God and Jesus change. Now the pupil can think of God as non-physical and superhuman, in short, he has an abstract idea of God. Moreover, the 13- to 14-year-old thinks of Jesus not as a miracle worker as he did formerly, but in terms of his mission on earth, his nearness to God, of his part of the Godhead and Saviour of man. Unfortunately, some adolescents and adults, but we do not know exactly how many, never reach this stage of formal thought at all.

Acquiring Formal Operational Thinking

Piaget maintains that children begin to acquire formal operations at approximately eleven to twelve years of age and complete the process by age 15. In his theory this process is universal and invariant, and the order of thinking reached forms qualitatively higher stages of development. Empirical research done by other investigators, however, paints a different picture. For one thing, although it is true that children's performances on the tests Piaget devised improve with age, developmental curves generally appear to be continuous and gradual; they do not show the abrupt rises that we would associate with stagelike change. Unfortunately, however, too few longitudinal investigations have been of the developmental curves of individuals, rather than of groups of children, to establish whether formal operational thought is acquired in stages during adolescence.

For another thing, there is a question whether all people achieve formal operational thinking at this or any other age. In most studies only 40 to 60 per cent of adult subjects performed at a formal operational level (Niemark, 1979; Keating, 1980). Were the other individuals not capable of formal operations, or were the tests not accurately reflecting their abilities? It is likely that most adults make the kinds of everyday, ordinary, casual deductions and inferences of formal operational thinking. They plan for the future and make their plans contingent on unknown factors that may intervene. They evaluate the logic of the tales they are told. Thus their failure on tests may be explained by inadequacies in the assessment method or restrictions of the tests themselves. This is an issue that needs further research.

There are two questions of great importance to which the answers are in doubt. What are the factors that lead to development of formal thought and how does formal thought arise? It seems that the maturation of the central nervous system plays some part, but beyond that we do not know whether it is schooling or the more general quality of the culture pattern that is important, or both. Piaget argues that the age of the onset of formal thought is related to the kind of culture in which the child lives. Adolescents in so-called primitive societies appear to be unable to think formally at this level. Piaget believes, therefore, that the growth of formal thought is linked to the evolution of culture. So beyond an age of, say, twelve years, this level of thinking may develop because of the influence of education and culture. The 13-year-old in our society is not only dissatisfied with the gaps and uncertainties resulting from concrete operational thought but he is beginning to think beyond the present. This thinking ahead is likely to be determined by the experiences the adolescent receives at home and at school. The really determining factors are likely to lie in the social activities around him, the climate of opinion in which he lives, the kinds of expectations the adult world has of him. If certain kinds of concepts are made frequent use of in his particular society, these are the kinds of concepts which he will learn. In our society, thinking ahead is something which matters, and in thinking ahead the adolescent thinks in terms of the possible. In other words, he begins to build theories to make hypotheses, something which might not be the case in a culture of another kind.

A Critical Overview

Piaget reveals that children's thinking is not merely less knowledgeable than adult thinking, it is also qualitatively different. Children are often limited to their own perspective of the world, unable to free themselves from the senses' perception of how things appear to be. Arguing logically with a young child is a lost cause because his logic is that of a child, not of an adult. Children are not just small adults. This would be more obvious but for the very cooperative nature of children themselves. If we demand they do something they will try in fact to put up what Nathan Isaacs calls a verbal façade that may deceive us. Their thinking is more primitive because their internalised actions lack manoeuvrability. They cannot arrive back at the starting point and draw the necessary conclusions. Only maturation and experience can help a child to think, and experience must be in the form of doing. We must let the child do things before we can expect him to think about them. The thought material he needs can come only from the actions he has performed. Here is a major reason for activity methods in the primary school. A child cannot think before he acts. He must perform the fundamental process himself, not learn from adults.

Piaget's major contribution was to question the assumption that something which is obvious to an adult must be so to a child. If we give the child as much concrete experience as we can when his growing maturity demands it, we shall have given him the best possible climate in which to develop intellectually. Experience does speed up the process, as Piaget found that some children became conservers during the experiments as they 'twigged' what was going on. Despite some children proceeding faster and further than others, all children have in common the same successive stages that Piaget discovered.

He mainly uses a question and answer method of investigation but there has been much criticism of this interview technique, because the situations are highly verbal yet children are not skilled in the way they answer. Piaget may read too much into the answers. Each interview is unique and thus no standardisation or statistical analysis is involved. Further he uses very small numbers of children not selected by any accepted sampling procedure. Despite these criticisms his results have been replicated throughout the world, reflecting the ecological validity of his findings.

Replications, for example, by Lemos (1969) and Dasen (1974) with Australian aborigine children in the outback, and Price-Williams (1961) and Greenfield (1966) both using West African child subjects, reveal the main Piagetian stages quite clearly, though the stages occur a little later chronologically than in western cultures, are affected by the amount of schooling and degree of western acculturisation, and formal thinking is less frequently found. For example in testing unschooled Wolof children in Senegal, Greenfield (1966) found that when examining conservation of liquid the pupils gave non-conservation answers because they attributed magical powers to the tester. When they did the experiment themselves the proportion of conservers more than doubled — the 'action magic' reasons had disappeared. But another reason was that the child was 'free to solve the problem, rather than the experimenter'. She also found that by 11–13 years all her schooled Wolof subjects had achieved conservation of quantity in contrast to only 50 per cent of her unschooled sample. Price-Williams (1961) found that 100 per cent of his unschooled sample of Tiv (Nigeria) children by the age of eight years had achieved this conservation and voluntarily could even reverse the operation. Dasen found that aborigines did better on spatial concepts than on logico-mathematical ones — an 'ecological' effect.

Recent criticism has been voiced by Bryant (1972) of the method Piaget used to test for conservation of number. You will recall that Piaget laid out a set of items (e.g. sweets, coins, beads, eggs and eggcups as in Figure 5.1)

Figure 5.1: One to One Correspondence

then transformed the display into Figure 5.2

Figure 5.2: Transformation of One to One Correspondence

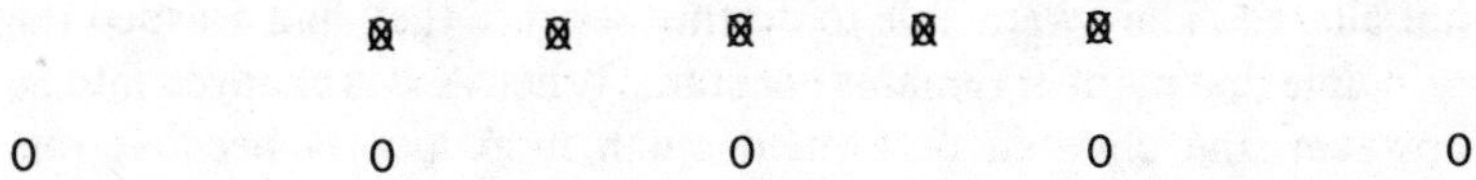

Even after counting, you will remember, the young five-year-old says there are more elements in the lower row.

Bryant contends that Piaget's results do not prove the child's lack of a concept of invariance because there is an alternative interpretation, i.e. that the young child does understand invariance, but he also uses the relative lengths of two rows as a useful cue as to which contains more objects and this, in many cases, produces the right answer. Thus, what the young child has yet to learn is not the idea of variance but that, in any situation in which the principle and the relative length are in conflict, it is the invariance principle that is correct.

Support for this contention was provided by reference to the behaviour of children in response to experimental situations indicated in Figure 5.3.

Figure 5.3: Three Experimental Situations (after Bryant, 1972).

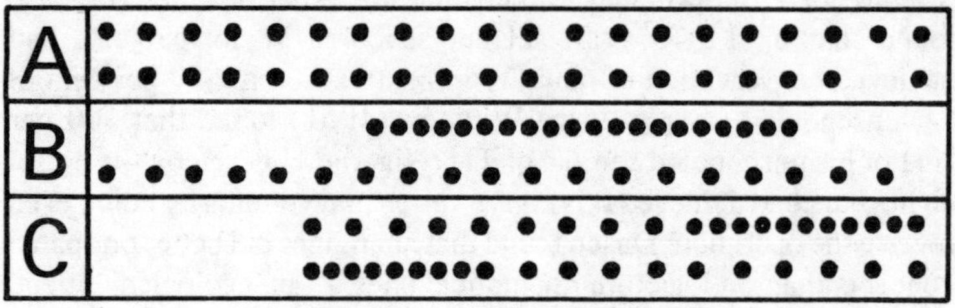

Bryant's research indicated that nearly all the children — even the three-year-olds — knew that the top row in A had more counters than the bottom row. They use a simple 'counting' method which is always correct: all the counters are paired off except one. With B, nearly all the children gave the wrong answer; they said the longer row had more counters. This time they were using a second method — 'longer means more' — which must have seemed equally valid to them because no one had told them it wasn't. With C, the children were completely foxed, roughly half of them saying that the top row contained more counters and the other half saying the bottom row. This time the children couldn't use any strategy to get the right answer short of counting up each row.

What Bryant found basically was that when pattern A was changed into pattern C, nearly all of the children knew that the numbers had not altered. They were able to do this because they had grasped the principle that number remains constant. When A was changed into B, however, the children performed much more poorly because this principle now clashed with another but stronger one that longer means more. When the children were taught that this was an unsatisfactory method of counting, they abandoned it and stuck to the principle that number stays constant.

The child's main problem is to learn which methods for estimating quantity are correct and which are not. Constancy, accordingly, is fixed in the child's mind all the time. An analysis of Bryant's work suggests that he has demonstrated that the main feature of development is thus not the acquisition of conservation, but rather learning when it is essential that the conservation principle should take precedence over less reliable length principles. However, the actual results in the classic situation are undisputed and have implications whatever theoretical description eventually achieves consensus. Evidently, if visual cues mislead the child then parents and teachers need to be aware of this.

More doubt has been cast by Donaldson (1978) on Piaget's claim that the young child's thinking is non-logical. She argues that, while children do make mistakes through failure to reason, such failure is caused usually by factors other than a lack of logical ability. She attributes much failure to the child's inability to understand mature adult language. The experimenter at the formal operational stage presents child subjects with problems often requiring skills of hypothesising imaginary states, e.g. when the child is asked to report what a person might see of a scene from another viewpoint (cf. experiment, p. 87). The child can think quite logically in daily activities but fails to solve such a hypothetical query since the language of the task prevents them understanding the nature of the problem. With subtle changes in wording Donaldson has shown that children can solve many Piagetian tasks far earlier than Piaget claims.

Donaldson also identifies the experimenter as an agent who determines the sort of response given by the child. Since adults are authority figures, the child is apt to believe that when an experimenter manipulates test materials (e.g. lemonade in glasses, or plasticine from ball to sausage shape) something strange or magical might have occurred (cf. Greenfield's observations in W. Africa). Thus the child suspends his rational beliefs and logic when the psychological 'conjuror' is presenting his 'show'. When Piagetian tasks are effected by the child himself or by a toy doll, the child argues quite logically about what has happened. So it may be that the specific format of Piaget's tasks constrained the thinking of the young child to what Piaget describes as pre-occupational thought. The experimental design determined the result and an underestimation of the child's mental capacities.

Piaget's theory, in one form or another, is similar to that held by many child psychologists. Bruner describes the intellectual development of the child in terms of the ways children can represent reality at various times in their lifespan. Bruner (1964) has identified three fundamental ways human beings convert the world of immediate experience into a cognitive or mental-world model. The first to develop is what is called the enactive mode and is based upon action or movement. Within this mode the world is constructed of bodily movements. The child knows no other way to 'think about' the world. This enactive mode is somewhat equivalent to Piaget's sensory-motor stage. At a later stage of development, in the iconic mode, knowledge of the world is based heavily on purely sensory information stored as sensory images. Think about the arrangement of furniture in your room or house. You can imagine the scene and 'read-off' your image. In so doing, you are using iconic knowledge. This mode is similar to the one used by the pre-operational child. The third mode involves the use of language, the symbolic mode. In this case, words and sentences are used as symbols of objects, events and states of affairs. Obviously, the chief milestone of cognitive development is the child's acquisition of language and his or her development of the ability to think in the symbolic mode.

Like Bryant, Bruner and his colleagues (1966) believe children adopt non-conservation approaches to Piagetian tasks because the arrangement of the experiment directs them towards non-conservation answers. Bruner contends that young children can employ the symbolic mode when necessary. He illustrates this with a conservation-of-volume task.

A five-year-old child is shown two identical beakers filled to the same level with water. When asked which contains more water, the child replies that they are the same. The water in one beaker is then poured into a third beaker that is taller and thinner so that the resulting water level is higher (Figure 5.4). Now, when the child is asked which beaker contains more water, he or she selects the tall beaker, as in the classic experiment. Perhaps, the child is limited to the enactive mode of knowing. ('What is involved in drinking from the containers? — taller things require more drinking.') Maybe, his or her thinking is bound by the visual stimulus and he or she focuses too much on the level of the liquid, the iconic mode.

Figure 5.4: Conservation of Amount

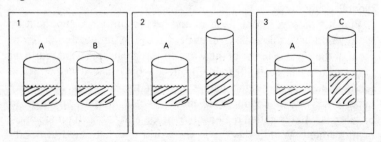

Source: Adapted from Bruner *et al.* (1966).

Bruner then placed a screen in front of the beakers so that the tops of the beakers could be seen and not the water level (the distracting feature). He studied the responses of children who were four to seven years old. Without the screen, almost all the four- and five-year-olds missed the answer and even up to half the six-year-olds and the seven-year-old children responded that the taller beaker contained more water. With the screen blocking the view of the water levels, however, almost all the five-, six- and seven-year-olds answered that the beakers contained the same amount and even about half the four-year-olds answered correctly. When Bruner removed the screen and presented all the children with the differing water levels, the four-year-olds who had answered 'equal' now changed their minds and chose the taller beaker. The older children, however, stuck with their original answers. By this procedure, then, five-year-old children, who almost always fail the test under ordinary circumstances, come to answer correctly and stick with their answers.

According to Bruner, five-year-old children are capable of symbolic thought but they are at a transition point between the iconic and the symbolic modes and feel unsure of themselves. They rely heavily on enactive or iconic information when available. The screen forces the child to use the symbolic mode and blocks the iconic by preventing distracting information about the different water levels. Four-year-olds are even less sure of their symbolic abilities and revert to the dominant iconic mode when the screen is removed.

Thus cognitive development is more plastic and less invariant than Piaget describes it. There are numerous reports of significant variations in cognitive development as a result of environmental influences too (e.g. Hunt, 1976). Piaget minimises the role of experience and environment, a position that is difficult to accept in the light of training experiments in concept development. Brainerd (1977) analysed the available data on concept training experiments and concluded that, contrary to Piaget's theory, children's susceptibility to conservation training does not depend on their developmental stage. Pre-operational children have learned the conservation concept and other concepts by such training procedures as simple feedback, learning set and modelling. Training studies suggest that the apparent invariance of concept formation which Piaget describes may be partially attributable to common child-rearing practices.

But, despite these critical points, Piaget's work is of monumental impact, importance and scope within the field of child development.

Some Educational Implications

Piaget has not directed his research towards education and teaching, but his theory of how children acquire knowledge and develop intellectually clearly provides much that is relevant to education.

Piaget claims that the sequence from sensori-motor through to formal operations is fixed. That being so, then the curriculum should be arranged with this changing cognitive status in mind. If what is being taught and how it is being taught do not take into account children's levels of conceptual development, learning with comprehension is going to be inefficient. Children will not learn (develop schemata) if they do not have the prerequisite cognitive skills. Readiness to learn is of particular concern to educators of elementary school children, though it should be of concern at all levels of education. According to Piagetian theory, a child is 'ready' to develop a particular concept when, and only when, he has acquired the schemata that are necessary (prerequisites).

Possibly the most important and most revolutionary implication of Piaget's theory is that children construct knowledge from their actions on the environment. Number, length and area concepts cannot be built up from hearing about them or reading about them. Experience at manipulating blocks, items and all sorts of materials is the only way children build up valid concepts. But it is not just experience but active interaction that is required.

Cognitive reorganisation resulting from assimilation and accommodation can only come about through the actions of the child. Thus actions, physical or cognitive, must occur if cognitive reorganisation is going to take place. It must also be remembered that, according to Piaget, assimilation and accommodation of actions are always under internal control (equilibration) and reorganisation of cognitive structures in a particular way can never be *ensured* by external organisation of experience. A child's reorganisation is always his own.

Through the period of concrete operations, manipulation of objects and materials dealing with concepts to be learned is most important. Seriation schemata ($A < B, B < C$ thus $A < C$) can best be developed in concrete operational children if they visually and manually manipulate objects employing the concepts to be learned. In a similar manner equivalence concepts ($A = B, B = C$, thus $A = C$) can best be learned if the child acts on objects that employ the concept. Reversibility in mathematical operations can be facilitated in children's learning if problems in multiplication and division are placed in opposition to one another (initially using concrete materials such as blocks) ($14 \times 3 =$ ____; $42 \div 3 =$ ____; $42 \div 14 =$ ____). The same principle holds true for reversibility learning in simple addition and subtraction. Problems placed in opposition demonstrate reversibility and help facilitate accommodation to the concept ($5 + 4 =$ ____; $9 - 4 =$ ____; $9 - 5 =$ ____). Through the concrete operational period, concrete experiences generate conceptual development.

Even the adolescent or adult with formal operations needs concrete experiences in order to develop *new* physical knowledge. Children are *motivated* to restructure their knowledge when they encounter experiences that conflict with their predictions. Piaget calls such an occurrence *disequilibration*, and the result, disequilibrium. Some have called it *cognitive conflict* or *conflict inducement*. To the extent that educators are interested in helping children acquire knowledge (as it is defined here) they must develop methods that encourage disequilibrium and permit children to carry out, in their own ways, the re-establishment of equilibrium through active methods (assimilation and accommodation). How can disequilibrium be recognised and encouraged by the teacher? Wadsworth (1978) suggests that children be permitted to explore many of their *spontaneous interests*. Such interests, frequently unique to the individual child, reflect disequilibrium and are sources of motivation. Teachers must find ways to permit children to follow their spontaneous interests. It is essential that teachers view such expenditures of time as valid from the point of view of intellectual development.

Peer interactions become important with respect to cognitive development when the child becomes able to assimilate the viewpoints of others when these are different from his own. This comes about when the egocentrism of pre-operational thought is dispelled around age six or seven. Accordingly, peer interactions are of cognitive importance from the time the child enters school. Children learn to evaluate their egocentric thoughts by comparing them to the thoughts of others. About the age of six or seven most children become able to accommodate to the views of others. Thus peer interactions can be a fruitful means of stimulating natural cognitive conflicts that can generate accommodation to the views of others and evaluation of one's own concepts.

Summary

Piaget shows from the beginning the child taking a hand in obtaining and organising all his experiences of the world into schemas. Assimilative processes constantly extend their domain as the child becomes more able to deal with his environment whilst at the same time accommodation steers them in ever more successful adaptations to the environment.

According to Piaget, cognitive development can be divided into four qualitatively distinct stages: sensori-motor (birth to two years), pre-operational (two to seven years), concrete operational (seven to eleven years), and formal operational (eleven years and beyond). In the first two years of life the young child develops a knowledge of the permanency of objects or the ability to represent internally stimuli that are not immediately present in the environment. From two to seven years, approximately, children's logic is often faulty and reasoning can be illogical, frequently based on perceptual experience. After seven the processes of conservation and reversibility allow the child to reason in concrete ways. By adolescence adult logic and reasoning begin to appear. Adolescents can solve complex abstract problems and deal with hypothetical questions.

Piaget's major stages appear to be universal but some studies suggest that many of Piaget's observations are seriously dependent upon Piaget's specific methodology. The heavy reliance upon children's language may lead to results that reflect language skills, expression and vocabulary more than limitations of reasoning processes.

Activities

1. *Conservation of Mass*

This activity is concerned with replicating in a simple fashion some of Piaget's work on conservation. You will carry out some procedures to test the understanding by four children of the conservation of mass (amount), weight and volume. You should choose two at one age and two at a different age, e.g. two six-year-olds and two eight-year-olds and two ten-year-olds.

Materials: Two equal balls of plasticine or its equivalent, at least 40 mm in diameter.

Procedure:
   (1) Hand balls to child, to enable him to determine that they are the same. Modify as required until child agrees.
   (2) Roll one ball into a long sausage (90 mm long approximately) and place it beside the other ball.
   (3) Ask, 'Will there still be the same amount of plasticine in each?' Record answer fully. Try to get child to explain his answer as fully as he can. *Score 2/1/0*
   (4) Ask child to make each piece into a ball and ask if they are still the same. Follow up answer as required. *Score 2/1/0*
   (5) Ask child to roll one ball out into a long thin sausage. Repeat 3 and 4.

Scoring
Clear understanding throughout, with reasons given   4 points
Partial understanding and/or only one correct   3, 2 or 1 points
No real understanding evident at all   0 points

You can try your hand at designing very similar experiments on the conservation of weight, using plasticine, with the children.

2. Spatial Reasoning

This activity looks at some aspects of spatial reasoning in children, i.e. understanding the concept of the horizontal.
   Choose the same sort of subjects as last time, i.e. four children, two each at two different ages (primary level).

Materials: A clear bottle with parallel sides, two-thirds filled with coloured water, and sealed; large cloth; paper and pencil for the child.

Procedure:
   (1) Show bottle in upright position and ask child to draw the water level. (Drawings of bottle outlines may be needed for younger subjects.)
   (2) Cover bottle with cloth and tilt bottle about 30°, neck showing. Ask child to draw bottle and level as it *would* be now.
   (3) Turn bottle on its side, neck showing, and again ask child to draw bottle and the level of water as it *would* be.

Scoring
Both levels are drawn correctly   2 points
One level drawn correctly (specify)   1 point
Both levels incorrect   0 points

3. *Understanding of Metaphor, Proverbs and Parables*

Procedure:

    (1) Tell the child a proverb, e.g. people in glass houses should not throw stones; or you can't make a silk purse from a sow's ear, etc.

    (2) Ask the child to explain what it means.

    (3) Record his response.

    (4) Scoring

Understands implicit meaning	2 points
Surface (concrete) meaning	1 point
No real understanding at all	0 points

    (5) Repeat with a Biblical parable (e.g. Good Samaritan) and/or metaphor (e.g. icy fingers of fear stabbed at her spine).

4. *Other Concepts*

Piaget conducted numerous experiments which illustrate in a wide number of concepts the difference in the thinking between pre-operational and concrete operational children. Examples are shown below and are often so simple that readers are encouraged to try them with some young subjects. The reality of one's own results is more potent than any text material read.

(1) Distance. Two toy trees of equal height are placed 50 cm apart. A screen is set up between them and the child is asked if the trees are still as near (or as far apart) as they were before. Five- to seven-year-olds suggest the distance is shortened by the thickness of the screen and the distance may be regarded as greater from R-L than from L-R. From approximately seven years of age, the children are able to answer the questions correctly.

(2) Length. In the case of a straight stick with a length of wavy plasticine underneath it so that the ends of both are in line, a child has to say whether the length of the stick is the same as that of the plasticine or whether it is different. Children under four-and-a-half years of age are mostly positive that the lengths are the same even after tracing them with their fingers. They are considering only the end points. After reaching seven years of age the children can often straighten out the wavy one in their minds.

In another demonstration two sticks of equal length were placed together so that one projected beyond the other. Children below six formed the opinion that the projecting one was longer even when the sticks were swopped around. Length is identified with 'reaching further'. From seven years of age the children pointed to the unoccupied space, etc.

(3) Area. Two sheets of cardboard of equal size represented two fields. A toy cow was placed in each field and the children recognised that each cow had the same amount of grass to eat. A toy house was then placed in the middle of one field and in the corner of the other. The children were asked if the cows still had the same amount of grass each and the five-year-olds said not. The six-year-olds began to fail only when a few houses were put into each field and at seven it was agreed that the grass left was equal.

(4) Speed. Dolls were passed through two tunnels of unequal length. The time of starting was the same as was the time of arriving and the children were asked if the one went faster than the other. The five-year-olds insisted that because they arrived together the speed must have been the same but the seven-year-olds worked out correctly the time and space relationship.

Questions

1. Compare the cognitive abilities of the pre-operational child with those of the concrete operational child according to Piaget.
2. Critically evaluate the work of Piaget on cognitive development.
3. Explain the relationship between assimilation, accommodation and schema formation.

Further Reading

Beard, R.M. (1969) *An Outline of Piaget's Developmental Psychology*, London: Routledge and Kegan Paul

Boyle, D.G. (1969) *A Student's Guide to Piaget*, London: Pergamon

Brown, G. and Desforges, C. (1979) *Piaget's Theory: A Psychological Critique*, London: Routledge and Kegan Paul

Cohen, D. (1983) *Piaget: Critique and Reassessment*, London: Croom Helm/New York: St Martin's Press

Donaldson, M. (1978) *Children's Minds*, Glasgow: Collins

Flavell, J. (1985) *Cognitive Development* (2nd edn), Englewood Cliffs, NJ: Prentice-Hall

Wordsworth, B. (1979) *Piaget's Theory of Cognitive Development*, New York: Longman

References

Brainerd, C.J. (1977) 'Cognitive development and concept training', *Psychol. Bull.*, *84*, 919–39

Bruner, J. (1964) 'The course of cognitive growth', *Amer. Psychol.*, *19*, 1–15

Bruner, J., Olver, R. and Greenfield, P.M. (1966) *Studies in Cognitive Growth*, New York: Wiley

Bryant, P.E. (1972) 'The understanding of invariance by very young children', *Canad. J. Psychol.*, *26*, 78–96

Dasen, P.R. (1974) 'The influence of ecology' in J. Berry and P.R. Dasen (eds.) *Culture and Cognition*, London: Methuen

Donaldson, M.C. (1978) *Children's Minds*, London: Fontana

Gelman, R. (1969) 'Conservation acquisition', *J. Exp. Child Psychol.*, *7*, 167–87

Goldman, R.J. (1964) *Religious Thinking from Childhood to Adolescence*, London: Routledge

Greenfield, P. (1966) 'On culture and conservation' in J. Bruner *et al.* (eds.) *Studies in Cognitive Growth*, New York: Wiley

Hunt, J. (1960) 'Experience and the development of motivation', *Child Devel.*, *31*, 489–504

Hunt, J. McV. (1976) 'The utility of ordinal scales inspired by Piaget's observations', *Merrill Palmer Quart.*, *22*, 31–45

Inhelder, B. and Piaget, J. (1958) *The Growth of Logical Thinking from Childhood to Adolescence*, New York: Basic Books

Inhelder, B. and Piaget, J. (1969) *The Psychology of the Child*, New York: Basic Books

Keating, D.P. (1980) 'Thinking processes in adolescents' in J. Adelson (ed.) *Handbook of Adolescent Psychology*, New York: Wiley

Lemos, M.M. (1969) 'The development of conservation in aboriginal children', *Int. J. Psychol.*, *4*, 238–47

Lovell, K. (1960) 'A study of the conservation of substance in the Junior School child', *Br. J. Educ. Psychol.*, *30*, 109–18

Lovell, K. (1961) 'A study of the conservation of weight in the Junior School child', *Br. J. Educ. Psychol.*, *31*, 134–44

Markman, E. and Seibert, L. (1976) 'The facilitation of wholepart comparisons', *Child Devel.*, *44*, 837–40

Niemark, E.D. (1979) 'Longitudinal development of formal operational thought', *Genetic Psychol. Monogr.*, *91*, 171–225

Piaget, J. (1952) *The Child's Concept of Number*, London: Routledge

Piaget, J. (1955) *The Child's Construction of Reality*, London: Routledge

Piaget, J. (1962) *Play, Dreams and Imitation in Childhood*, New York: Norton

Price-Williams, D.R. (1961) 'A study concerning concepts of conservation of quantities among primitive children', *Acta Psychologica*, *18*, 297–305

Wadsworth, B. (1978) *Piaget for the Classroom Teacher*, New York: Longman

6 LANGUAGE DEVELOPMENT

Language is man's supreme achievement. Many essential human activities spring from this unique characteristic. Without language much of what constitutes our civilisation would not be possible since culture depends on communication between individuals.

The acquisition of language is an achievement unique to human beings and the speed with which it occurs is remarkable. A child starts to speak intelligibly at about one year of age and goes on to master the fundamentals of language in about three years. By age four the child has a vocabulary of well over a thousand words and can understand and produce most of the grammatical structures used.

Initial Speech

The baby's first sounds are merely accidental byproducts of the business of living–breathing, digestion, crying in distress. Such sounds are called speech sounds.

Mothers have often claimed that their child 'doesn't talk, but she understands everything.' In a study of the extent to which 'everything' is understood, Huttenlocher (1974) found that children as young as ten months do indeed comprehend many language expressions, but that mothers have been guilty of a very common parental error — reading much more into the child's behaviour than was probably intended by the child. The children studied understood a great deal more than they could say, but they used cues other than words to determine mother's meaning. Mother might point to the ball at the same time that she said, 'Where is the ball?' Or the ball itself would serve as a cue when mother said, 'Roll the ball to me'. What else would the baby do with a ball? By asking children to locate certain objects — 'Where is the ball?', or to perform certain actions — 'Give the ball to Mummy', without giving them gestural cues and in contexts that were essentially ambiguous, Huttenlocher was able to trace the beginning of language understanding. She found that proper names and object words were the first responded to, and that the very first word understood was often a pet's name. She also found that children have, to some degree, an understanding of the meaning of words, the semantic component of language, before they begin to use words.

Babblings are the first sounds of infants that resemble speech. By repeating syllables, infants experiment with, and practise, many of the sounds that will eventually be put together into meaningful words. But some of them are sounds that they have not heard and will not use later. The fact that during the first year the babblings of infants the world over are the same — whether or not particular sounds will find their way into later speech — has been taken as evidence that each human infant possesses the potential to master any language. At about nine months the babblings of babies whose language will be English start to lose their German gutturals and French nasals. This is an environmental effect. Certain sounds are not made by the parents and thus imitation may be one of the major features of infant speech development.

The vowels a baby produces exceed the consonants by 5:1 at two months but gradually this discrepancy reduces until, after the first year, consonants predominate and the adult vowel: consonant ratio of 1:1.4 is achieved. This changing ratio can be used as a measure of speech development in the child. The earliest consonant sounds are those made at the back of the throat (h etc.), and there is a gradual move to labial and post-dental consonants (p, b, t, d). This forward shift is due to the development of greater control of the tongue, lips etc., due to practice with sucking, swallowing, spewing and growth of teeth. Posture changes on learning to sit alter the shape of the oral cavity and enable the lungs to be used to capacity. The voice also sounds stronger in a vertical than in a horizontal position.

Consonants and vowels are combined into one-syllable utterances ('Ma') and, at about eight months, children begin to imitate their own speech and the speech of others, producing repeated syllables like 'di, di, di, di'. Some of the syllables heard in babbling are associated with objects or events, resulting in the child's first words at about one year of age. Babbling is thought to be inherent in humans because deaf children also babble.

Miller and Dollard (1941) and Mowrer (1950) have produced similar theories to explain why babbling occurs. The theory also explains the occurrences of the first spoken words near the end of the first year, which are usually rough imitations of what they have heard. The theory suggests that when a child is being fed, washed, handled and fondled, the mother speaks and coos to it. The baby will associate seeing parents and hearing speech with the happy satisfying situation where all its needs are satisfied and cared for. Parts of the baby's own self-initiated sound play will by accident sound like something it has heard from its mother. These sounds associated with the happy, satisfying situations of being cared for will themselves recreate these satisfying feelings.

Thus, the child when alone or bored will obtain satisfaction and continue to repeat the babbling or his first few words — the sounds have a reward value. This theory is simple, parsimonious and most likely, as it does not depend on instinct nor is it done to please the parent but merely because the child pleases himself. Once a child babbles, it is encouraged by adults who will repeat certain words.

Dore (1978) has found that before the end of the first year, in this period between babbling and words, infants use the same short speech sounds repeatedly in specific contexts. That is, sounds are chosen and uttered for a particular purpose.

The First Words: One to Two Years

All of language development for the child can be regarded as a gradual decrease in dependence on context for communication and a gradual increase in the child's reliance on the tools that an abstract language system provides. This movement away from context does not happen all at once. Children's first clearly intelligible words, said near the end of their first year, are usually uttered in conjunction with some action. 'Hot' which may come out 'ah' is said while touching bath water, or the child may notice the front door swinging open and say 'ohpn'. The first words usually name an entity that has in some way changed. Things that have appeared, disappeared, opened or closed in the immediate surroundings are commented on first — 'Daddy' when the child's father appears at the door, 'Mama' when mother is leaving.

First words, such as 'mih' for milk, 'bah' for ball and 'puh' for apple, may bear only a vague resemblance to adult speech. But children use them in a context that helps their parents understand. And they continue to make the motions — pointing, reaching and other physical clues — that helped them communicate before they could utter words. They may point to the refrigerator or to the chocolate syrup as they say 'mih', thereby requesting that milk be poured and chocolate be put in it. Even though children have very few words and say only one of them at a time, with word and gesture, actions and facial expression working together, they possess a much greater ability to communicate. They can name objects or persons, make requests and demands, describe actions and, with intonation, express emotional states of joy, displeasure and surprise at encountering something unusual. These single-word utterances have been called holophrases. In the light of the accompanying gesture or intonation or both, they seem to do the work of a whole sentence.

Which Words?

The first words children learn include names of objects. These are quite similar from child to child. They cover the same general categories, such as foods, animals and toys. Nelson (1973) conducted a longitudinal study of 18 toddlers, using mothers' reports of children's vocabularies and tape recordings of their speech. She found that between 15 and 24 months, children have obtained a vocabulary of 50 words or more.

Nouns for basic categories are acquired first, rather than nouns at a higher level of generality or nouns that are very specific. So, for example, 'flower' is much more likely to be in the child's early vocabulary than either 'plant' (general) or 'rose' (specific) and 'dog' more likely than either 'animal' or 'collie' (Rosch, 1976). Mothers usually choose nouns at the basic level when naming things for their toddlers.

Other early words are closely tied to actions, actions which involve first the children themselves and later other things and then people. The first action words are rarely full-fledged verbs but rather are the prepositions that appear with verbs, for example, 'up' as in 'pick me up'; 'down' as in 'put me down' or 'I get down'; or 'on' as in 'put on me'. Next, children use intransitive verbs, verbs with no object of the action, such as 'dance' or 'go'. Later they add transitive verbs, verbs that do have an object such as 'eat' and 'take'. Children talk about unchanging states, or non-actions, with words such as 'dirty' or 'green' even later yet (Greenfield and Smith, 1976).

Children often use their early words to cover much more than the conventional adult meaning. The 'larger' meanings that children have for words have been called 'overextensions'. They are usually based on perceptual properties of the object or actions, such as shape, movement, size, sound and texture. Thus, for the child, 'fly' may mean all very small objects including raisins as well as insects; 'bow-wow' can signify all furry animals, 'ball' all objects that are round and 'dance' any kind of turning around. Anglin (1975) has also documented children's underextensions of words. They may think that 'dog' applies only to their family's dog and not to dogs on the street or dogs on television or in picture books.

The one-word stage lasts from about 12 to 18 months. During this period, children are gradually building up a vocabulary, one word at a time. Their words, as indicated, name objects — 'ball', 'car', 'cat', and make requests — 'more', 'up', 'down', and they also perform social rituals — 'bye-bye', 'hi', 'go'. Through enthusiasm for communication on the child's part and willingness on the mother's, conversations can also be held, one word at a time.

After the child has acquired some 50 words, at around 18 to 20 months, language undergoes an 'explosion' propelling the child to the next stage of language development, two-word combinations.

Two-Word Sentences: Two to Three Years

Although children's two-word sentences prevail in their language from two to three, they continue to use one-word utterances and will also occasionally put three words together. During the two-word phase children use their small but growing vocabularies and their limited two-word utterances with remarkable ingenuity. They find many ways to combine the few words that they have mastered.

Between the ages of two and three, as children switch from predominantly two-word to longer utterances, they do begin to acquire the inflections of adult speech (Dale, 1976). In this period children extend the meaning of one of their favourite words, 'no'. In Bloom's (1970) examination of negation, she found that children first use the word 'no' to indicate non-existence, as in 'No milk' when a cup is empty. Next, they use it for rejection of an offer, as in 'No ball' when the child is pushing a ball away, and 'No down' when they do not want to be put down and, third, they use it for denial of a statement, as in 'No bottle' after the child has been given a cup and told it is a bottle. During the age period when language is increasing in complexity, children became able to coordinate two or more ideas in a single utterance using relative clauses (Clark and Clark 1977).

Children discover that they may also link two ideas together with 'and' to form a coordinate sentence: 'Mummy took me to the store and I bought a coke'. Other coordinators or conjunctions used very often by three-year-olds are 'if', 'when' and 'because'. Until about five years of age, children describe two events in the temporal order in which they actually occurred: 'We went to the zoo and then we had ice cream'. 'We brushed our teeth and then we went to bed'. Coordinate constructions are easier for children to comprehend if the order expressed mirrors the real order of events. Mothers should remember this when they are giving their children directions. Some sequences they consider irreversible are not so to children. If children are told 'Before you come to the table, go comb your hair', they think that they can tend to their hair later (Kavanaugh, 1979).

Growth in the acquisition of elementary meaningful forms of our language, as in the formation of plurals and tenses has been extensively studied. At seven most children can cope with a plural formed by adding 's' but experience greater difficulty when other changes are required (thief – thieves) or none (sheep – sheep). Likewise, in the formation of the past tense, 'ed' is not found to be too difficult to apply but where a change such as 'sing – sung' is required, only one-third of seven-year-olds can manage.

Templin (1957) investigated four aspects of language amongst children of three to eight years of age. These were (i) articulation and discrimination of speech sounds; (ii) sentence structure; and (iii) vocabulary size. In articulation skills, the three-year-old was found to be making, on average, 50 per cent errors, whilst at eight years he is accurate 90 per cent of the time. In five years the child reaches close to articulatory maturity. Boys usually take about a year longer than girls and children from working class homes about a year longer than those from middle class homes. In speech sound discrimination Templin found a consistent increase in the ability beyond five years of age. At the lower ages there does not appear to be any significant difference in the ability between boys and girls but at eight girls are better than boys. Children from middle class homes used longer and more complex remarks than working class children. About half the remarks made by three-year-olds were grammatically accurate and this improved to about three-quarters at age eight. The vocabulary count presented Templin with problems. The estimates of basic vocabulary for the six-to-eight-year-olds ranged from 13,000 to 23,000 in Templin's work.

The Language and Thought Issue

A long-standing theoretical issue concerns the relation of language and thought. Language emerges in an interactive context and is not spoken spontaneously in isolation but language is also intimately connected with thought. Within the time frame of the child's development, the growth of language and thought overlap. Whether acquiring or using language, children certainly are thinking. They are remembering words and associating them with meanings. They are figuring out rules about putting words together. And they are using words and sentences to express their thoughts. But the question is, do children first have a thought and then try to express it in words, or does the language they have first shape their thoughts?

Jean Piaget

That language is not entirely necessary for cognitive development has been suggested by Piaget. His research on sensori-motor intelligence in the first 18 months of life clearly demonstrated that children have thoughts about objects before they can name them. Children need a firm mental representation of an object before they can connect a word to it. In Piaget's view thought can affect language, but not having language does not prevent the individual from thinking. But can learning words help children to think? Piagetian researchers have examined that possibility. In one study children were taught the verbal expressions used by youngsters who had been able to describe how two pencils, two balls of clay and two quantities of beads differed. The training sessions, which exposed the children to comparatives such as 'long' and 'thin', 'short' and 'fat' and 'more' and 'less' proved largely unsuccessful (de Zwart, 1967). Although children appeared to understand the language instructions and how to use the words, it was concluded that their level of mental maturity prevented them from solving the Piagetian tasks, such as conservation, correctly. In an early work Piaget (1926) suggested that 'dialogues' of preschoolers with their peers, as opposed to with adults, were more accurately termed collective monologues, since neither child really listens to or responds to the words of the other. Young children do engage in 'private speech' talk about what they are doing, repeat themselves, and play with words to a greater extent than older children and adults. It is 'egocentric' speech since the child behaves and talks as if all points of view were his own. He seems unable to appreciate another's point of view, or to conceive things from another position. The egocentric monologue is a running commentary on the child's present situation and frequently acts as a means of self-regulation and direction. At three years of age about half a child's utterances are egocentric (the rest are socialised) and this reduces rapidly to 25 per cent by age seven.

Egocentric speech is not meant to be secretive. It is a half-way house as thought is not mature. The child is saying aloud to himself what he is doing: only later will he do this internally as thought. Thought is internalised action. The gradual decline of egocentric speech is considered a sign of the development of a more sophisticated mental world model, one that is not centred exclusively on the child but allows for other perspectives.

But more recent research suggests that conversations of preschoolers are focused more than half the time, and that children do respond appropriately to each other's questions and replies. Moreover, they are more likely than older children to clarify any misunderstandings and to express reciprocation of feelings (Gottman and Parkhurst, 1977).

Benjamin Whorf

Even more strongly than Piaget, Benjamin Whorf (1897–1941) believed that language affects thought. From his observations of Western languages and of American Indian languages, he developed two related hypotheses about the relation between language and thought, linguistic determinism and linguistic relativity. The hypothesis of linguistic determinism holds that the structure of language determines the structure of all higher levels of thinking — language determines thought. According to the hypothesis of linguistic relativity, the forms of the particular language affect the individual's perception of the world. A strong version of Whorf's hypotheses, then, claims that language determines both our perceptions and thoughts about the world.

For example, Eskimo language has a number of terms to indicate the texture, recency and fall of snow. Whorf would claim that not only does this multiplicity of words reflect the Eskimos' greater dependence on snow in their surroundings and their consequent need to make finer distinctions than we, but it also enables speakers of the Inuit language to see better these distinctions. Just as distinct languages have been examined to find out about their influence on the thought patterns of the people speaking them, so have dialects in the United States and Great Britain been investigated.

Lev Semenovich Vygotsky

According to Russian psychologist Vygotsky, thought and speech have separate roots but later coincide. Vygotsky proposed a period when thought is not touched by speech or speech by thought. When children are approximately two years of age, these two lines of development, thought and speech, meet; speech begins to serve the intellect, becoming rational, and thoughts become verbal. The child seems to have discovered the symbolic function of language. The union of thought and speech is marked by the child's curiosity about words and requests for names, and by a rapid increase in vocabulary. Thereafter children talk more and more to themselves. At first they may describe what they have just done. Angie may take off her mittens and then say, 'Take off mittens'. Then she will describe what she is doing as she does it. 'Put kitty in the doll cradle. Pull up the blanket. Rock the cradle . . . .' Eventually, at about four, language will help her form ideas, and she will say aloud or to herself what she is going to do.

According to Vygotsky, private speech branches off from social speech, becoming more and more abbreviated and internalised, and is referred to then as inner speech. Inner speech is critical to the organisation of thought. Words children have acquired and their associated meanings, for example, influence how children classify unfamiliar items. They know that a hat is 'clothing' because it is placed on the body, or that a celery stalk is a 'vegetable' because it is green and not sweet to taste. Intellectual growth in Vygotsky's theory depends on the development of both inner speech and social speech. In Vygotsky's view children retain a certain amount of non-linguistic thought and non-intellectual speech, non-linguistic thought being used initially in solving problems and only later becoming embodied in words, non-intellectual speech being used, for example in memory, when only language forms need be retained. But in most intellectual activities, speech and thought, once developing along separate pathways, are inextricably bound together.

Language Acquisition Theory

Do children imitate what they hear and then receive reinforcement, or are they physiologically predisposed to communicate using language? Two psychologists Skinner and Chomsky take issue over these questions.

Skinner

As a behaviourist whose research on learning is detailed in Chapter 4, Skinner (1957) views language acquisition as the inculcation of verbal skills, through trial and error and imitation, by reward (or extinguished by non-reward).

Skinner's aim is to attempt to apply to verbal behaviour his theory of learning. He claims that adults, through their systematic reinforcement of the behaviour of children, can cause them to acquire all new skills, including language. In 1957 Skinner published a book, *Verbal Behaviour*, in which he attempted to explain how children are conditioned to talk by their parents. When babies babble 'babababa' as Skinner's argument goes, their parents are delighted and talk back; the babies, so rewarded and pleased, make the same sounds again. When they say 'mama' mothers give them even more excited attention. Later parents hand biscuits to toddlers who managed 'bik'. And later still they help their children with grammatical constructions by understanding and responding to their attempts at sentences and by repeating their words in the correct form and order. Through this process children's words and sentences gradually converge with the adult forms of speech. Note how imperative is the presence of other people. With no-one around to show approval or test the accuracy of verbal utterances, they would soon be discarded, since extinction would operate (p. 67).

Not all psychologists are satisfied with this paradigm of Skinner's. To begin with, verbal responses quickly take on much wider meaning as indicated by the range of usage, than can be explained by operant conditioning. Again, there are many words which do not 'name' objects (they have no referents). Learning such articles as 'the' or 'a' is difficult to explain in Skinnerian terms. Add to this the phenomenal vocabulary count of young children accumulated in a comparatively short time, and Skinner's theory does not appear to provide the whole explanation. In no conceivable way could the many thousands of individual words, the subtleties of expression, and the complexities of grammatical structure be learned item by item as conditioning of the S–R model necessarily implies. Life would not be long enough to learn more than a simple vocabulary. Also children use constructions found nowhere in adult speech — 'foots', 'runned', 'breaked' and 'allgone wet'. On the other hand, children with Down's syndrome and autistic children, who do learn language only through imitation, do not have normal speech. Clearly, children do not learn language through imitation alone, the issue is more complex.

This is not to deny that some verbal learning is the result of reinforcement particularly that in early childhood where the toddler learns the 'names' of particular objects in his environment like 'cup', 'potty', 'mummy' and is rewarded by verbal and non-verbal forms of adult approval. Skinner does not consider the structure of language regulation, because he restricts himself to a descriptive set of laws. He does not consider them relations between learned elements in terms of syntax and grammar. The result is a tendency to regard the longer sentence as no more than the summed result of putting smaller elements end-to-end. But we do not just string words together. There are rules which once grasped enable the child to generate sentence forms he has rarely heard using particular words which have not been associated together in his past history of reinforcement. Such novel behaviour is explained by Chomsky (1972).

Chomsky

Chomsky argued that no theory of language learning could be practically based on operant conditioning principles: parents simply did not go to such ends to correct their children's uses of language. Chomsky also argued that the language of adults heard by children is so degenerate, so riddled with 'false starts' and structural errors, that it would be surprising indeed were children to acquire language merely by listening to this speech.

Chomsky admitted that reinforcement, as well as imitation and motivation, played roles in the child's acquisition of language, but he did not consider reinforcement sufficient to explain the child's propensity for learning language. He called attention to the 'remarkable capacity of the child to generalise, hypothesise and "process information" in a variety of very special and apparently highly complex ways which we cannot yet describe, or begin to understand, and which may be largely innate' (1957, p. 158). Chomsky has described this innate capacity of the human brain as a sort of 'black box' for understanding regularities of speech and the fundamental relationship of words. He calls it a language acquisition device (LAD), to emphasise its automatic nature. The speech heard by the child enters the LAD and, by the processing that goes on there, the child unconsciously gathers ideas about language rules. Through this generative neural capacity children acquire rules for under-standing and constructing their native language. He proposes that language has two levels, a surface structure and a deep structure. The surface structure of the sentence consists of the actual words in it and the order in which they occur. The deep structure has to do with fundamental syntactical relationships underlying these words, for example, those between nouns and verbs, and also with the intended meaning — the thought to be conveyed. The following sentences will help to illustrate the differences between these two levels.

Arnold kicked the ball.
The ball was kicked by Arnold.

The two sentences clearly have different surface structures, yet they have, in Chomsky's view, the same deep structure. Sentence 1 is an active direct statement, sentence 2 is in the passive voice. The sentences have two different syntactic forms, yet as children acquire language they seem to recognise that these sentences have the same meaning. They also know the meanings of sentences that they have never heard before. After hearing a thought expressed in the passive voice, they will recognise the same thought expressed in the active voice. Such recognition is possible, in Chomsky's opinion, because the deep structure is identical for both active and passive forms of a sentence. Both sentences have certain basic constituents, the noun phrases 'Arnold' and 'the ball' and the verb 'kick'. Through a set of transformations, which are the several possible syntactical ways of arranging these constituents, children can take the basic or deep structure and put it into different surface structures. The syntaxes of all known human languages are strikingly similar. From this fact Chomsky derived his idea that deep structures are somehow innate to the processes of the human brain and give us our special capacity to learn language.

Greenberg provides evidence from a survey of 30 languages of certain common characteristics so that a child who had an innate knowlege of them could acquire any natural language merely by finding out how his particular language expressed these universal concepts common to all languages. What universal concepts are there? Every language employs consonants and vowels, syllabic structure, subject–predicate and verb–object. These are characteristics of the abstract underlying structure of sentences.

Language and Home Environment

Children can only learn the language in the early stages of their development if, and when, they hear the language spoken. Different linguistic environments have a startlingly variable effect on language usage, not just as a regional accent or dialect, but in the systematics of the language. Mother is a particularly important figure in the early language development of her children. The frequency and content of her conversation with her babies and toddlers significantly affect their progress. Mothers who provide simple explanations in answer to the many questions which children pose, lead a dialogue or describe the host of objects surrounding the child, play games involving language usage, read stories and buy toys which develop language skills are more likely to raise the linguistic standards of their children. Mother and child often share the same experiences. During play they share toys, during meals they share food, and in many other contexts they focus on the same objects and are affected by the same events — and mother talks about them. The stage is set for a basic understanding of reference, the recognition that words refer to things and events.

Although adults do not directly teach grammar they do greatly modify their speech when talking to children (Slobin, 1975); the younger the child, the greater the modification. Adults speak to babies in what has been called baby talk or motherese, using first sounds that the infant babbles and later concrete nouns in short, simple sentences, which they repeat for emphasis. These sentences, compared to adult-speech, contain more commands and questions, fewer pronouns, verbs modifiers, and conjunctions, fewer past tenses and fewer false starts. In talking to children, parents are given to whisperings and exaggerated intonations and to redundancy — there is little variation in wording. They enunciate clearly, and they stick to the 'here and now' (Slobin, 1975; Furrow *et al.*, 1979).

Mothers also use simplified, more basic words when talking to children, the same words that the children understand. For example, when the child has just learned the word for cat, mother will call all felines — tigers, lions, and panthers — 'kitty cats', overextending her use of the term, just as the child is likely to do (Mervis and Mervis, 1982).

Do children benefit in any way from the motherese modification of the speech that they hear? Shorter utterances very likely ease comprehension, for the memory abilities of young children are limited. Simplification of sentences probably helps children pick out the most important words. But although some modification of adult speech to a simpler level is probably beneficial, or adults would not all do it, it does not follow that the simpler the language, the beter. A study by Alison Clarke-Stewart (Clarke-Stewart and Hevey, 1979) determined that within the normal range of motherese — in this study mothers' sentences to their 30-month-olds ranged from two and a half to six words long — the longer the mother's sentences were than the child's, the more advanced was the child's spoken language. Apparently children are not encouraged to advance linguistically if the language they hear is reduced all the way down to their level; it should be somewhat more complex. For example, when children are at the one- or two-word stage, adult sentences should probably be a word or two longer.

Simplifying, shortening, repeating and emphasising their own speech is only one thing mothers do when talking to children. They may also extend the child's speech.

Child: Doggy out?
Mother: Doggy wants to go out?

Correlational studies have found that children have greater language ability the higher the level of their parents' education. Being exposed to adult speakers other than members of the immediate family relates positively to acquiring a vocabulary of 50 words at an earlier age. The number of peers the child comes in contact with appears to have no effect on learning language, but spending too much time with these other children rather than with an adult does slow down the process (Nelson, 1973). Firstborn children, who interact primarily with parents, acquire language faster than later-born children, who spend more time speaking to other children.

Children who spend considerable time watching television acquire language later than those who do not (Nelson, 1973).

Bernstein (1959; 1971) an English sociologist, has identified in an oversimplified way two speech patterns, the elaborated code of the middle class and the restricted code of working-class speakers of English. Middle-class speakers tend to use longer sentences, which are more grammatically complex and precise. The sentences may communicate feelings and emotions and intentions, but they are also more independent of immediate context in their wording and interpretation. Working-class speakers tend to use short, grammatically uncomplicated sentences referring primarily to concrete objects and immediate events. Their sentences are less flexible and more dependent on the assumption that the listener shares the same knowledge and background information as the speaker. Starting a conversation with the sentence, 'He gave me this,' when the listener does not know for certain who and what 'he' and 'this' are, is one example of a restricted use of language. A person using an elaborated code would begin the same conversation with 'My friend Harry gave me this car.' Bernstein has suggested that a restricted code of expression does restrict thinking.

Bernstein believes that language is 'one of the most important means initiating, synthesising and reinforcing ways of thinking, feeling and behaviour which are functionally related to the social group'. Children from more articulate backgrounds, generally found in middle-class homes, not only display marked differences in the vocabulary they use as contrasted with children from working-class homes, but also organise and respond to experience in more sensitive ways. A middle class child understands the veiled innuendo of 'I'd rather you made less noise' but 'shut up' is more meaningful to working-class children. The school works on the elaborated code and thus is more readily understood by the middle-class child.

Bernstein does not conceive of restricted code speakers as being deficient in certain basic structures or vocabulary: rather, that working-class jobs, community life and, in particular, family relationships normally constrain their linguistic choice. So that while the working-class child will rarely, if ever, use the elaborated code, the middle-class child will be more practised at being flexible, able to use both codes and switch easily between them.

In a longitudinal British study Newson and Newson (1970) found that the major differentiations in language were socioeconomic class based.

Summary

Language is a unique achievement of man and is acquired rapidly in childhood. Infants first babble, eventually they shorten some of their syllables and combine particular ones with gestures and intonation to get the attention and assistance of adults.

A child's first intelligible word near the end of the first year usually exclaims on something that is especially noticeable or changing in the immediate surroundings. Between 12 and 18 months children acquire a vocabulary of nearly 50 words, many of them being names of objects; others are connected with actions. Children are able to extend the meaning of their single words with gestures and intonation so that a word acts as a whole sentence.

Between 18 and 24 months children begin putting two words together, in regular 'telegraphic' ways of their own creation that make combinations unlike those in adult speech. They may be able to communicate with gestures.

From two to five years of age, children add morphemes to their speech, expand their negatives, lose their irregular past tenses and plurals, and then regain them; learn more specific adjectives and prepositions, question words and word order; add relative and coordinate clauses.

The relation between language and thought is a controversy; Piaget believed that in infancy thought certainly precedes language. Later, however, children's conversations with their peers are a way of advancing their thinking. Benjamin Whorf believed that language determines our perceptions and thoughts about the world. Lev Vygotsky held that thought and speech have separate roots, but that at two years of age children discover the symbolic function of language. Thereafter their words help them to think.

Skinner maintains that children acquire language in the same way that they learn other behaviour through systematic reinforcement. Chomsky claims that parents do not pay this amount of close attention to their children's speech and that children have an innate ability to gather notions about the rules of language.

Language in Chomsky's view has a surface structure, which consists of the actual words spoken or written and their order, and a deep structure, which has to do with the underlying meaning of the words and their syntactical relationships.

Conversations with adults help children acquire language. Adults tend to adapt their utterances to the age of the child, motherese gradually becoming more complex as the child's language advances. Social class influences language codes which in turn affects ways of thinking and organising the environment according to Bernstein.

Activity

Tape some monologue and dialogue of children at different ages. Analyse the material for evidence of:

(a) egocentric speech
(b) virtuous errors
(c) restricted and elaborated codes.

Questions

1. Outline the theories of Piaget and Vygotsky with reference to the language-thought relationship.

2. What criticisms would you make of Skinner's approach to language learning?
3. Briefly outline the development of speech in the pre-school child.
4. In what ways might social class membership influence language development and use?

Further Reading

Gillham, B. (1979) *The First Words Language Programme*, London: Allen and Unwin

Greene, J. (1975) *Thinking and Language*, London: Methuen

Herriot, P. (1971) *Language and Teaching*, London: Methuen

Lock, A. and Fisher, E. (eds.) (1983) *Language Development*, London: Croom Helm

Nelson, K. (1978) *Children's Language* (vols. 1 and 2) New York: Halstead Press

Piattelli-Palmarini, M. (1983) *Language and Learning*, Henley, London and Boston: Routledge & Kegan Paul

Tough, J. (1978) 'The development and use of language' in D. Fontana (ed.) *Education of the Young Child*, London: Open Books

de Villiers, P. and de Villiers, J. (1979) *Early Language*, Cambridge, Mass.: Harvard University Press

References

Anglin, J.M. (1975) 'The child's first terms of reference' in S. Ehrlich and E. Tulving (eds.) *Bulletin de Psychologie*, Special Edition

Bernstein, B. (1959) 'Some sociological determinants of perception', *Br. J. Social.*, *9*, 159–74

Bernstein, B. (1971) *Class, Codes and Control* vol. 1, London: Routledge

Bloom, L.M. (1970) *Language Development*, Cambridge, Mass.: MIT Press

Chomsky, N. (1957) *Syntactic Structures*, The Hague: Mouton

Chomsky, N. (1972) *Language and Mind*, New York: Harcourt Brace

Chomsky, N. (1975) *Reflections of Language*, New York: Pantheon

Clark, H. and Clark, E. (1977) *Psychology and Language*, New York: Harcourt Brace

Clarke-Stewart, K. and Hevey, C. (1981) 'Longitudinal relations in repeated observations of mother child interaction', *Dev. Psychology, 17*, 127–45

Dale, P.S. (1976) *Language Development*, New York: Holt

Dore, J. (1978) 'Conditions for the acquisition of speech acts' in I. Markova (ed.) *The Social Context of Language*, New York: Wiley

Furrow, O., Nelson, K. and Benedict, H. (1979) 'Mothers' speech to Children', *J. Child Lang., 6*, 423–42

Gottman, J. and Parkhurst, J. (1977) 'Development may not always be improving', paper presented at annual meeting of Society for Research in Child Development, New Orleans

Greenfield, P. and Smith, J. (1976) *The Structure of Communication in Early*

Language Development, New York: Academic Press

Huttenlocher, J. (1974) 'The origins of language comprehension' in R. Soso (ed.) *Theories in Cognitive Psychology*, Potomac: Erlbaum

Kavanaugh, R.D. (1979) 'Observations on the role of logically constrained sentences in the comprehension of "before" and "after"', *J. Child Lang.*, 6, 353–7

Mervis, C. and Mervis, C. (1982) 'Leopards are kitty cats', *Child Devel.*, 53, 267–73

Miller, N. and Dollard, J. (1941) *Social Learning and Imitation*, New Haven: Yale University Press

Mowrer, O.H. (1950) *Learning Theory and Personality Dynamics*, New York: Ronald Press

Nelson, K. (1973) 'Structure and strategy in learning to talk', *Monogr. Soc. Res. Child Devel.*, 38, No. 149

Newson, J. and Newson, E. (1970) *Four Years Old in an Urban Community*, Harmondsworth: Penguin

Piaget, J. (1926) *Language and Thought of the Child*, New York: Basic Books

Rosch, E. (1976) 'Cognitive representations of semantic categories', *J. Exp. Psychol.*, 104, 192–223

Skinner, B.F. (1957) *Verbal Behaviour*, New York: Appleton

Slobin, D.I. (1975) 'On the nature of talk to children' in E. Lex, (ed.) *Foundation of Language Development*, New York: Academic Press

Templin, M.C. (1957) *Certain Language Skills in Children*, Minneapolis: University of Minnesota Press

Vygotsky, L.S. (1962) *Language and Thought*, Cambridge, Mass.: MIT Press

Watts, A.F. (1950) *The Language and Mental Development of Children*, London: Harrap

Whorf, B.L. (1956) *Language, Thought and Reality*, New York: Wiley

de Zwart, H.S. (1967) 'Developmental psycholinguistics' in D. Elkind and J. Flavell (eds.) *Studies in Cognitive Development*, New York: Oxford University Press

7 INTELLIGENCE

Introduction

Why do some people seem to be brighter than others? Are the differences between individuals actually differences in how much they know, in their styles of thinking, or both? Are the differences the result of genes, of family interactions, of nutritional or other environmental factors or of school instruction? Just how flexible is 'intelligence,' and what is it anyway? Is intelligence one thing, or is it many things?

Most psychologists would be hard-pressed to come up with definite answers or even with a definition of intelligence that would be acceptable to everyone. The most quoted one is 'intelligence is what I.Q. tests measure' (Boring, 1929) and that is patently a circular definition. Eysenck prefers merely to state that it is a useful concept for describing human conduct for intelligence is an inanimate, intangible concept on a par with such concepts as honesty, charity etc. Some definitions consider intelligence as the ability to carry out abstract thinking (e.g. Terman, 1916). Does this then imply that 'concrete' thinkers (i.e. many adults and most children below 11 years) are of low intelligence? The most accepted definition of intelligence is one based on Spearman's views that intelligence is the capacity to discern relationships.

Assessment of Intelligence

Most intelligence tests, whether verbal or non-verbal in content, use Spearman's theme of seeking relationships as a basis for their test items. Look at the principle behind the following:
Examples of verbal IQ items:

(1) *Underline the correct alternative*
Every book has (a shelf/pictures/a book-mark/an index/pages/a story).
(2) *In the following question the three words in capital letters are alike in some way. In the brackets there is ONE word which is*

like these three words in the same way but different from all the others. Underline this one word.
PLUM, PEAR, ORANGE (lettuce/wheat/grass/apple/onion)
(3) *Underline two words, one in each set of brackets*
WHEN is to TIME as (now/where/there) is to (then/place/watch).

Examples of non-verbal items:

1. Which of the following completes the square?

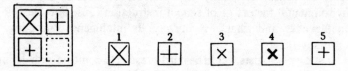

2. Which is the one that doesn't belong?

The Work of Galton

Galton was the first person to attempt to define and measure systematically individual differences in intelligence. Believing that people inherited different intellectual capacities, Galton established a laboratory in London in the 19th century and developed the technique of statistical correlation in order to study intelligence. He expected that intelligence would be correlated with the ability to make subtle sensory discriminations. Therefore he measured subjects' abilities to discriminate among blocks that differed only slightly in size or weight. Galton's tests were not designed to identify intelligence *per se* but to identify intelligent people.

Binet and the First Intelligence Test

Binet in 1896 criticised the Galton laboratory for its narrow focus on simple sensory and cognitive processes and for neglecting higher mental abilities. His criticism and subsequent test designs changed the direction of mental testing. In 1905 Binet and Simon constructed their objective test identifying mentally impaired children who would be unable to profit from traditional classroom instruction. The test that they developed has since served as a model for almost all mental tests.

Binet and Simon believed that the core of intelligence was judgment and knowledge. They suggested that the brighter the child the earlier he or she would be able to answer items on the test correctly. The test items were at progressive levels of difficulty and could be answered correctly by the majority of children at each chronological age. For example, a three-year-old was expected to be able to name the objects in a picture, repeat a sentence of six syllables and repeat two digits. A twelve-year-old was expected to interpret the meaning of a picture, repeat a sentence of 26 syllables and repeat seven digits.

In 1916 Terman defined intelligence as the ability to think abstractly and to use abstract symbols, especially verbal symbols. He added 36 items to the Binet-Simon test. These modified it to reflect his theory and extended its use to children aged two to 16. Since revised, Terman's Stanford-Binet test is the instrument by which the validity of most subsequent mental tests have been measured.

Wechsler's Scales

A widely used series of intelligence tests has been developed since 1938 by Wechsler. His Intelligence Scale for Children (WISC) was revised in 1974. All Wechsler's tests have the same basic format. They are individually administered and contain *verbal* and *performance* sections. The verbal sub-tests rely heavily on language skills. As a general rule, the performance tests are considered to be less culture-bound and a more valid indication of aptitude for people who are not native speakers of English. The verbal tests, on the other hand, are a better predictor of school performance.

The British Ability Scales

Another test, the British Ability Scales (BAS) has more recently been devised, standardised and issued (1978). It contains a wide range of test items grouped into 23 scales which can be selected by the psychologist according to the nature of the problem he is investigating. Such areas as moral reasoning, Piagetian tasks and memory are included, as well as the usual verbal, non-verbal and performance items.

The British Ability Scales can be used with children from two and a half years to 17 years old. It is an individual rather than a group test and combines coverage of all the ground in more traditional test batteries with innovations in test content, scoring and profiling. The scales can be used in a flexible way, individually or in combination as appropriate, for diagnosing and analysing children's learning difficulties, providing valuable information which can be used to initiate remedial treatment, and also for assessing change in ability over time. A new revised edition has recently been published (1983).

The BAS is a mixture of performance and ability tests ensuring that children's interest is kept over a long period. The scales are not based on a single model or theory of human ability, but have been constructed with a number of models or theories in mind. At least four of the types of abilities — speed of information processing, formal operational thinking, social reasoning and verbal-tactile matching — are not covered in any other major individual test battery. Scores can be easily analysed in a number of ways to suit different assessment requirements.

Standardisation

A fundamental concept in the administration and scoring of IQ tests is standardisation. The standardisation of intelligence tests means that there are standard conditions of administration, scoring, and interpretation.

Test situation. If scores obtained by different children are to be comparable then the testing conditions must be the same so that the only variable affecting the score is the ability of the person to do the test. All testees must have the same time limits, instructions, adequate lighting, ventilation and freedom from discomfort or distraction. Certain subtle differences between pupils cannot be standardised, e.g. health, fatigue, motivation. In individual tests, rate of speaking, tone of voice, inflection, pauses and facial expression must be kept standard or else the test will become a different one for each pupil.

Scoring. This enables test scores to be interpreted. On many tests there are no predetermined standards of failing or passing. A person's score can only be evaluated by comparing it with the scores obtained by other like persons. Such scores are called norms; they can be national, group or local. Before tests are issued they are administered to a large representative sample of the type of subjects they are designed for. This groups establishes the norms which indicate not only average performance but also the relative frequency of the varying degrees of deviation above and below it. If the test is for secondary pupils, or nine-year-olds it must be standardised on these specific groups. It must also be a random sample with the same relative balance between social classes, IQ age, sex, town and country etc. as in the total population. An eight-year-old can only be compared with other eight-year-olds. The norms of many American tests may be inaccurate here.

Binet and Simon administered their test items to many children and thus established a 'normative' age at which most children could answer the item correctly. By comparing a child's actual answers to this norm, the administrator of the test could determine a child's 'mental age' (MA). One problem with an MA score, however, is the difficulty in comparing the relative intelligences of children of different ages. For example, who is more intelligent, a six-year-old with an MA of nine or a ten-year-old with an MA of thirteen? The second child certainly 'knows more', but is he or she an intelligent person who knows more or can do more at an earlier age than the other child? In 1912 Stern developed the concept of the intelligence quotient (IQ) to resolve this issue. An individual's IQ was defined as mental age divided by chronological age multiplied by 100. Thus a child of average intelligence, performing at the normal level for his or her chronological age, would receive an IQ of 100. For example, the six-year-old just described has an IQ of 9/6 x 100, or 150. The ten-year-old has an IQ of 13/10 x 100, or 130. Thus, although the ten-year-old definitely knows more, the six-year-old is comparatively more intelligent.

In order to make comparisons of ages more consistent, IQ today is computed so that the mean score for each age is adjusted to IQ = 100 with a *standard deviation* of fifteen points. This means that two-thirds of all people fall within the 'normal' range of IQ between 85 and 115, and 96 per cent fall within the range of IQ between 70 and 130 (Figure 7.1). This use of 'deviation' IQs assumes, without evidence, that intelligence as measured is 'normally distributed'.

The value of standardised tests, i.e. norms with a mean of 100 and a standard deviation of 15 as in IQ tests, is that comparisons can be validly made between individuals' performances on the same test or between those of individuals on different tests, i.e. an IQ of 115 implies, whatever the particular test, that the child scored one standard deviation above the mean or, alternatively, only 16 per cent of children score higher. Children with IQs of more than 130 are exceptionally bright, while those with IQs less than 70 would be considered to be educationally sub-normal or ESN.

Figure 7.1: Normal Distribution Curve

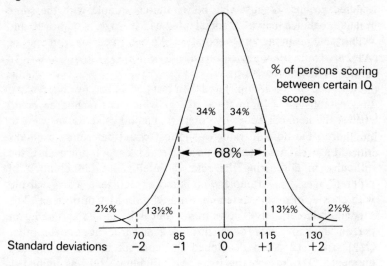

Individual and Group Tests

Group tests are paper-and-pencil tests which can be given to many individuals at the same time, whereas individual tests such as the Stanford-Binet and WISC are given individually by a trained and qualified practitioner.

There are important differences between group tests and individual scales with regard to administration. Group tests are often timed. On the other hand, individual scales have no overall time limit, though some of the sub-tests may be timed (e.g. the WISC performance sub-tests). In practice, an hour to an hour and a half is sufficient in most cases. Moreover, group test administration requires only the ability to read out simple instructions to the subjects and to keep the timing accurately. The scoring is typically more objective and can be carried out by a clerk or a computer. In contrast, individual test administration requires extensive training and experience. Group tests give little or no opportunity for direct observation of the examinees' behaviour or for establising rapport, gaining cooperation and maintaining interest. However, the one-to-one situation in individual testing allows the tester to observe the subject's behaviour closely which may provide clues about difficulties he is experiencing. Some practitioners would go as far as to say that they gain as much (sometimes more) from their observation of the subject as they do from the final test scores. The quality of the relationship that the tester is able to establish with the client is of primary importance, especially in the case of younger children who are often very easily distracted.

The most used group IQ tests in Britain are those by Alice Heim (AH2, AH3, AH4, AH5 and AH6), which include verbal and non-verbal items, Raven's Progressive Matrices (entirely non-verbal) and the wide range of tests produced by Moray House and the NFER.

Criticism of Testing

Intelligence testing is increasingly criticised now. The major criticisms are discussed below.

(1) IQ was used to uncritically make decisions about the academic potential of children despite the fact that such tests do not have scientific precision nor can they predict with great accuracy.

(2) IQ can only tell us what a child's status is in relation to all the other children of a similar age, social class and ethnic group who have taken the test.

(3) The normal distribution of IQ is an artificial creation of test makers who assume this distribution. We have no evidence on this point.

(4) The selection of items for IQ tests has been based on statistical criteria rather than on well researched accounts of how children learn and what items are developmentally significant at some particular age. The items included can therefore be, and appear, trivial causing lowered motivation in those having to answer them.

(5) Simon (1971) argues that IQ testing can produce self-validating teacher expectations in that if a teacher knows the IQ of a pupil the teacher will expect the child to function at that particular level and is unlikely to encourage the child to rise above it. The child then works to that level and the teacher's expectation is fulfilled.

(6) Intelligence test scores can give a mistaken impression of fixed inherited level of functioning. In fact IQ varies within an individual from time to time according to life circumstance and current experiences, and is influenced by environmental factors. Donaldson (1978) argues that few children are developed intellectually to their 'limit'. Most children have much unused potential. Thus an IQ score should never be used as the only piece

of data in assessing the academic potential of a child. A variety of other factors including motivation, self-concept, personality and home background are also implicated.

(7) The test items contain material that is culture and even sub-culture bound, because the language used is middle-class and the cultural matrix from which the questions are drawn is 'white Anglo-Saxon' in the main. If working class and non-white children perform badly on an IQ test it may be because the material is 'foreign' to them and not because they are deficient in intellect. This point is taken up later.

(8) The validity and reliability of intelligence tests are questioned. Validity asks the question 'is this test measuring intelligence?' Since we cannot define intelligence in an acceptable way how do we know what we are measuring? Reliability asks the question, 'are the scores obtained today accurate and would each child score exactly the same another day?' While reliability of IQ tests is very high (higher than any other educational tests), it is not perfect hence no score is a perfect 'hit', and each child could obtain a slightly different score another day.

One Intelligence or Many Specific Abilities

Writing at approximately the same time as Galton and Binet, Spearman was the first psychologist to articulate a coherent theory of the nature of intelligence and to develop the statistical methods by which to test his theory empirically. Spearman (1904) proposed that intelligence was a unitary trait, rather than a collection of separate abilities. In Spearman's theory intelligence consists of *conceptualisation*, the ability to induce general laws and relationships from particular instances, and *abstraction*, the ability to deduce particular relationships from general laws. Spearman maintained that intelligence consists of two factors, *g* and *s*. Factor *g* represents the true and general intellectual ability applied in all intellectual tasks, *factors* the several specific or idiosyncratic abilities required for particular cognitive tasks. The goal in designing a mental test is to measure as much *g* as possible.

Burt (1940) and Vernon (1950) argued for a hierarchy of abilities with general intelligence *g* at the apex. Below this were major group factors which Vernon identified as a verbal/educational factor (*v:ed*) associated with attainment in most subject areas, and a spatial/

mechanical factor (*k:m*) the spatial part of which underlies attainment in advanced mathematics and science. At a lower level Vernon described minor group factors and then a wide range of factors specific to particular tests (see Figure 7.2).

Figure 7.2: Diagram illustrating hierarchical structure of human abilities (from Butcher, 1968)

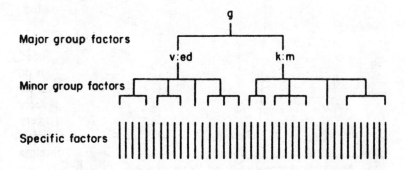

Such a hierarchy helps us to understand the sense in which it is valid to argue for the idea of general intelligence, and yet also accept several contributory, specific abilities.

Most British psychologists supported Spearman's view of one over-riding factor of general intelligence, but the American psychologists were more impressed by the differences between tests than by their similarities. For example Thurstone (1938) considered that he had good evidence for the existence of some seven distinct 'primary mental abilities' — perceptual speed, memory, verbal meaning, spatial ability, numerical ability, inductive reasoning and verbal fluency. More recent American research has, on the whole, continued the search for correlated specific abilities. Guilford (1967), for example, has argued that it should be possible to produce tests measuring as many as 30 distinct abilities, exhibited with four distinct types of content — 120 tests in all. Guilford's 'Structure of Intellect' model is shown in Figure 7.3.

Developmental Approaches

Another approach towards the understanding of intelligence has arisen out of the developmental psychology of Hebb & Piaget.

Figure 7.3: Guilford's Scheme of Ability Factors (from Butcher, 1968)

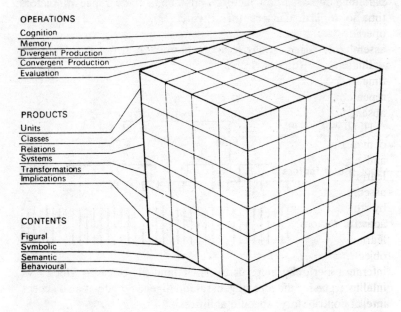

OPERATIONS
Cognition
Memory
Divergent Production
Convergent Production
Evaluation

PRODUCTS
Units
Classes
Relations
Systems
Transformations
Implications

CONTENTS
Figural
Symbolic
Semantic
Behavioural

Both emphasise,

(a) the gradual building up of more and more complex intelligent and complex behaviour, and
(b) the importance of a stimulating environment with which the child can interact to create this behaviour.

Both Hebb & Piaget are concerned to show how the infant comes to perceive a world of objects independent of himself. Hebb provides the physiological basis for Piaget's theory on the sequential development of the stages of thinking.

Piaget, as we have seen, regards intelligence as a process of adaptation, with simple adjustments in the early years facilitating the more complex adaptations later. The more intelligent the organism the more able it is to cope with imbalances in its environment utilising the reciprocal processes of assimilation and accommodation to develop required schemas.

Hebb (1949) argues that perception, sensation and experience build up patterns of electrical discharge or cell assemblies in the cerebral cortex. The cell assembly is thought of as a collection of neurons arranged in reverberatory circuits, but so arranged that parallel and alternative pathways keep the circuit operating for a long time so that damage to one part of the circuit will not prevent the operation of other parts. The synapse explains the growth of the assembly and constitutes learning.

Phase sequences are a result of the association of cell assemblies in time so that assembly 'a' is followed by assembly 'b'. In the course of repeated experience 'a' will more readily lead to 'b' and 'c' even in the absence of the sensory events originally associated with them.

Hebb draws a distinction between the learning of infancy and that of maturity. The former has nothing to build on and perhaps is the trial and error learning propounded by the behaviourist school. Later learning, the combining and associating of early learning or cell assemblies, is the characteristic of insightful learning, as propounded by the Gestalt psychologists. Insight is therefore the sudden activation of an effective link between assemblies, or concepts. Early learning, then, determines the sort of behaviour possible and the objects to which the organism can respond. It depends on the interaction of environmental experience with heredity to form intelligence (Chapter 2). Later learning attests to the operation of intelligence recombining familiar perceptions and patterns to form new. All school learning would be mainly a case of late learning. The absolute necessity of a rich, stimulating environment during infancy to build up the basic assemblies and during early schooldays to enable recombination for insight is indicated. Poverty of early experiences may underlie differences in functional intelligence between the middle and working classes. As Vernon says 'intelligence cannot be taught directly, but intellectual stimulation will provide the best climate for its growth'.

Studies of persons born blind and then given sight in adulthood shows what difficulties they have in building up an intelligible visual impression of the world. They have to learn how to see. Hebb gives examples of how little effect brain injuries, both their size and location, seem to have on intellectual functioning on verbal tests. One person had an IQ of 160 after the removal of one prefrontal lobe; another one of 115 after hemidecortication. He suggests that an important part of intelligence that is a product of experience, i.e. verbal tests, is not directly correlated with brain tissue integrity. This is because, as the patterns of electrical discharge have been built up, many alternate pathways come into existence, so that removal of some does not radically affect intellectual behaviour, though new learning would be seriously hampered. Problems requiring a new attack are not likely to be solved. Removal of brain tissue seems to be the same in effect as poverty of experience in the young child. There then seem to be two components to intelligence performance. One is immediately diminished by brain injury and amounts to the factor of inheritance. The other is related to experience and consists of permanent changes in the organisation of pathways in the cerebrum. Thus intelligence has two meanings. Intelligence A refers to innate potential. Individuals will differ with respect to this but we can never measure these differences. Intelligence B is the actual mental efficiency or functioning of the brain and determines the level of performance. It is the total sum of a person's developed intellectual skills. Although it is theoretically possible to assess it would be a mammoth job as every situation within which intelligent behaviour can be manifested would have to be sampled. Much disagreement over the nature and definition of intelligence has arisen because of the confusion between innate potential (i.e. 'A') and level of functioning (i.e. 'B'). Vernon has carried this distinction one stage further and invokes an Intelligence C which is what tests actually measure including the effects of anxiety, motivation and other social and situational factors, i.e. 'C' is the score on a particular test on a specific day. Intelligence scores do give a good index of the extent to which development has occurred but say nothing as to how much potential there is left. Hypothetically, intelligence will rise to the limit set by heredity or that set by environment whichever is lower.

Heredity and Environment

Most modern psychologists now agree that functional intelligence is the one that is important and that the role of environment in determining the level of functioning is vitally important. We need to clarify more precisely which specific environmental variables affect intelligence. The early insistence on the all-pervading, all-powerful role of heredity on intelligence summed up perhaps by Burt's definition of intelligence as 'an innate, general, cognitive ability' has now, with the contemporary generation of sociologically inclined minds, gone to the opposite pole in reaction and overstresses the role of environment. Halsey, Floud and Martin suggest that 'intelligence is largely an acquired characteristic.' The true answer lies no doubt between the two extremes.

What is it that determines the capacity of any individual brain or

Intelligence A? Certain basic features of the system, its 'wiring diagram', are genetically specified and laid down at birth. This ensures that, in general terms, the right parts of the brain are connected with one another, and it is probably in this very wide sense that functions of the brain, such as intelligence, may be said to be hereditary. But a significant amount of brain growth and development occurs after birth, in the first months and years of life. In this period, while only a few nerve cells are produced, much more importantly a vast number of new connections between cells are made. Anything which adversely affects these processes of connection-formation is likely to affect the proper development of the brain and hence intelligence. Severe malnutrition, for example, during certain vulnerable periods of infancy can result in permanent brain deficits.

The secret of the brain's powers probably lies in the way new possibilities for coding information are provided by the formation of new sets of connections between cells. In theory, any new connections — called synapses — could involve the cells which make them in unique new circuits; and any one such circuit could perhaps code for — or represent within the brain — a specific piece of information. Within the 10,000 million cells, each with its 10,000 separate synapses, this would provide ample potential for coding all the information the brain is likely to need to store over a 70-year lifespan.

In childhood, new connections may be made by the actual growth and development of new cell processes and new synaptic junctions. As the brain reaches full development, however, it loses the capacity for further growth — partly, no doubt, because all the available space within the system is used. Yet one still goes on learning, sorting memories and showing adaptive behaviour in new situations until old age, because new synaptic links and complex 'circuits' or pathways are possible. In this way, each day of our lives, more and more cell connections are opened up to store yet more information. Almost certainly, no-one has ever even remotely approached the theoretical limit set by his brain store. What sets the limit is not the wiring diagram of the system but peripheral blocks which prevent the information ever arriving, or the irreversible deficits introduced by a socially, emotionally or physically deprived childhood. Only when environment, prenatal and postnatal, has been optimal, can one genuinely say that brain capacity is even given a chance of being stretched to its theoretical limit. Until then, our brains will remain to a substantial extent the prisoners of our society.

The greater part of the development of Intelligence B occurs in the earliest years of life. Bloom (1964) has estimated that 50 per cent of measurable intelligence at age 17 is already predictable by the age of four. In other words, deprivation in the first four or five years of life can have greater consequences than any in the following twelve or so years. And the longer the early deprivation continues, the more difficult it is to remedy.

The most important factors in the environment necessary for full intellectual development are those concerned with language and with psychological aspects of the parent-child relationship. Much of the difference in measured intelligence between 'privileged' and 'disadvantaged' children may be due to the latter's lack of appropriate verbal stimulation and the poverty of their perceptual experiences.

Although these findings have far-reaching consequences one must add a note of warning. If we have in the past stressed the genetic component of intelligence too much, we must be careful not to swing the pendulum too far the other way and reject it altogether. Children do *not* all inherit the same potential for developing intelligence — if they did, how could we explain the differences in children from one family? These research findings, however, have led to a revision of the concept of intelligence. Instead of it being some largely inherited fixed power of the mind, we now see it as a set of developed skills with which a person copes with any environment. These skills have to be learned and, indeed, one of them — a fundamental one — is learning how to learn. From birth a baby learns from his environment, and how to react with it. He learns from one experience how to cope with other, at first similar and then different, experiences. Moreover his early learning is concrete. He will never develop a concept that he does not experience at first hand. He will not know what a book is unless he sees at least one; nor will he know what a gift is if he never receives one. Only from a variety of perceptual experiences will he build up a store of concepts — the 'bricks' with which we build up our knowledge of the world.

But having appropriate perceptual experiences is not enough. A developed concept is of little use without language. A child would be severely handicapped for further learning if the concept of, for instance, 'higher than' always had to be demonstrated.

Poverty of perceptual experiences will inevitably retard a child's learning. But, more than this, the lack of appropriate stimulation — particularly in language — may also hinder the development of his ability to cope with further experiences. Without this ability — that is, without intelligence — further experiences may 'bounce off', with no learning taking place. Indeed, for a child who has been denied the appropriate early learning experiences, no amount of bombardment with perceptual stimuli (television, for example) at a later age will be effective, unless steps are taken first to build up the missing 'coping mechanisms'. And the use of language is the most important of these. The child who, by the age of five, can still only speak in monosyllables and has no sensible sentence structure, is handicapped not only by being unable to communicate with others but by being unable to communicate with himself. In other words, he will be unable to think about the things he sees and hears.

Important though language is, it is not everything. Motivation must also play a part in any intellectual development. Children are inherently motivated to explore, manipulate and master their environment. We have only to watch the first weeks and months of a baby's life to be sure of this. But it seems equally certain that any built-in mechanism for learning needs to be sustained and encouraged or it may fade. An environment that fosters learning motivated only by fear of failure or desire for external reward may soon stifle any natural wish to learn. It is clearly important in the early developing years that a child's natural motivation to learn should be encouraged, possibly by involving him more and more in the learning process itself. As Piaget has revealed, a child must play an active part in regulating his own development; he must be allowed to do his own learning because full intellectual development will not occur if his role is a passive one.

Factors Affecting the Development of Intelligence

Genetic Factors

An individual's score on an IQ test is generally considered to be a function of both heredity and environment. It would be surprising if genetics had no effect, since it plays a role in many other attributes. Certainly, a defect in an individual's genetic make-up can lead to impaired intelligence: a genetic defect that affects one in every 2000 babies born to women in their twenties but one in 50 babies born to women in their forties is Down's Syndrome. This condition is often called Mongolism because of the babies' slightly Eastern appearance. 47 chromosomes are present instead of the usual 46. The condition is always associated with severe mental handicaps.

The role of the environment is also of consequence since genes provide only a potential for growth and do not determine its course independent of the environment. The importance of genetics in height, for example, is clear, but the general population in Western countries has been becoming appreciably taller over the last generations. This seems to be due to a better diet and living conditions. Specific gene mutations that affect IQ highlight the complexity of the inter-relationship between nature and nurture. Children born with phenylketonuria (PKU) used to suffer brain damage owing to the build-up of phenylalanine in toxic quantities in the bloodstream. Now, however, every infant is routinely tested a few days after birth (the Guthrie test), and in the rare cases in which the condition is detected, amelioration is possible by the provision of a special diet, largely fruit and vegetables and as low as possible in phenylalanine. Galactosemia is similar; a single gene defect leaves the patient unable to metabolise galactose. If not detected, this can lead to mental retardation. Once identified, the treatment is again mainly dietary. In both cases, by providing the right environment, the potentially damaging effects of the individual's genetic make-up are averted.

The effects of a wide range of environmental circumstances on intellectual ability (again, as measured by IQ tests) have been studied, including the prenatal environment, family, social class and education. Environment is taken to mean physical as well as social influences. The effect of specific environmental factors are difficult to disentangle in practice.

Children from multiple births often have lower IQs, though this could be due to diminished parent-child interaction through having to share the attention of parents, rather than to prenatal factors. During the birth process itself, the infant's brain is extremely susceptible to damage. Lack of oxygen during birth (anoxia) is estimated to prevent one baby in 1000 from reaching a 12-year-old level of functioning.

Family/Social Class

Numerous studies have shown clear relationships between parental social class and both the IQ and scholastic achievement of their children (e.g. Douglas, 1964). Part of this social-class influence may be related to differences in the quality and quantity of language used in the home. In residential nurseries, it has been shown that the quality of children's verbal environment and the richness of their activities were significant determinants of early cognitive develop-ment. Many studies have found marked social-class differences in the language used by parents to their children, which put working-class children at a disadvantage on traditional IQ tests compared to middle-class children. A review by Rutter and Madge (1976) of children reared in isolated or poor communities concluded that the longer the privation, the more intellectual development was impeded. The quality of the parent-child interaction and the range of experiences available to the child were among those aspects of the environment that were most important in this connection. Further, they point out that it is not the amount of stimulation, but rather the quality, meaningfulness and range of experiences available to the child that are important.

Parental attitudes to learning and education and the literacy of the home may also be part of the social-class-related influences, as, indirectly, are poor material circumstances such as poverty, overcrowding and lack of basic household facilities. More important, there is a high correlation between large family size and low attainment, larger families also tending to be those with less financial and material resources (Nisbet, 1953). The different forms of social disadvantage all tend to affect the same group of families. Verbal skills are particularly affected. McCall (1973) comparing pupils whose scores increased over time with those whose IQ scores decreased, found the former had parents who stressed intellectual tasks and achievements more. Additionally, there is some evidence that first-born children (particularly boys) tend to have higher IQs and to achieve more than later-born children. A study was made by Fraser (1959) of a representative sample of 408 twelve-year-olds in Aberdeen secondary schools, where a large amount of home data were collected by interview and correlated with IQ and a measure of school progress. The main figures are shown in Table 7.1.

'Parental encouragement' gives the highest correlations. It is clear that several other indices of socioeconomic status, of parental educational level and attitudes, and of an emotionally secure home, are also substantially related to general intellectual level at this age, and even more strongly to actual attainment.

Wiseman's (1964) investigations in the Manchester and Salford conurbation found very significant correlations in the .3 to .7 range between backwardness and such variables as birth and death rates, mental deficiency, illegitimacy, infant mortality and juror index. Much the same factors correlated with intelligence as with attainment quotients and, rather surprisingly, most of the IQ coefficients were higher.

On the basis of the results and of an extensive survey of the literature,

Table 7.1: Correlations of Background Factors with Intelligence and Achievement of School Children (Fraser)

	IQ	Achievement
Parents' education rating	.423	.490
General book reading in home	.280	.329
Newspaper and magazine reading	.381	.398
Income	.350	.444
(Small) family size	.404	.458
Living space	.363	.447
Occupation (not correlated but significant at .001 level)		
Abnormal or broken home environment (not correlated but significant at .01 level)		
Parents' educational and vocational aspirations	.297	.391
Parental encouragement	.604	.660
General family atmosphere	.393	.460
Mother at work	N.S.	N.S.

Wiseman concludes that the most crucial factors in intelligence test scores are the parents' own intellectual level, and their attitudes to education and aspirations.

Education

Education has been shown to affect IQ but to account for much less of the variance than features of family and home, perhaps because there is less variation between schools than between homes. There have been various attempts to help children from disadvantaged homes by means of compensatory education, generally at preschool level.

More specific compensatory programmes have focused on developing learning experiences in very young children within the community. During the earliest period there tends to be an emphasis on providing stimulation and interest. At around the age of two years, the emphasis usually changes to more structured teaching approaches which are designed to provide the development of basic educational skills. These programmes work best when the parents are involved and where the children can continue to develop their new skills at home. The results from some of these studies are quite impressive in that the children involved have been found to outscore control children by approximately 10–15 IQ points, which provides considerable justification for such early compensatory programmes. There are also indications that slightly later intervention can be successful if it is structured appropriately. For example, the provision of intensive individual tutoring in basic problem-solving and specific educational skills for groups of three-to-five-year old children from very poor backgrounds has been found to produce effective IQ and scholastic gains. The authors of one study noted that one important gain which resulted was a growing pleasure in learning and an increased feeling of mastery. They noted that mere exposure to a school environment did not provide the necessary basis for learning but that 'both mastery and enthusiasm for learning will only come when the child can be shown how to become actively involved in the learning process' (Blank and Solomon, 1968).

These results are important because they do indicate that compensatory intervention can be effective if it is early and intensive, focused on specific deficits like language. Involving parents with such intervention programmes also seem to have measurable, beneficial effects.

Age

Studies on the effects of ageing do not fall easily into either the genetic or environmental categories. Since growing involves both maturational and experiential influences, both factors apply. Although IQ tests assess current intellectual functioning, the underlying assumption is that they imply something about future performance. Many studies have looked at the stability of IQ over time. Before one year of age, test results bear little relation to results a year later, not because the tests are particularly unreliable (an infant will be likely to respond to a moving light or the sound of a bell in the same way on successive testings in the short term), but because these early tests sample a different, and greatly reduced, range of behaviours compared to tests for older children. Indeed, before one year of age, parental IQs provide a better predictor of the child's future IQ than infant tests. Differing test content is a source of change over time in all child IQ tests, but the older the child becomes, the more likely it is that similar items will be sampled. Even by two years, IQ results do correlate with those obtained say a year later, though they still bear little relationship to adult functioning.

Even when correlations between successive testings are quite high, this can mask quite substantial changes in IQ over time. Hindley and Owen (1978) point out that with a correlation as high as 0.76 from age five to eight years, the median change is still expected to be 9 IQ points. Between three and 17 years, half of their sample changed by more than 10 points, a quarter by 20 points or more. They concluded:

In the primary school period alone, a quarter will change by at least 15 points. Moreover, the tester cannot know towards which end of the spectrum any child will fall. Thus selecting children for different types of school at eleven years, though perhaps administratively convenient, is very hazardous from the standpoint of the educational welfare of the individual child. (p. 346)

Table 7.2: Correlations between Stanford-Binet IQ during the Pre-School and Middle-Childhood Years and IQ at Ages 10 and 18 (Wechsler-Bellevue)

Age at first testing	Correlation with IQ at age 10	Correlation with IQ at age 18
2	.37	.31
4	.66	.42
6	.76	.61
8	.88	.70
9	.90	.76
10	–	.70
12	.87	.76

Source: Adapted from M.P. Honzik, J.W. Macfarlane and L. Allen, 'The stability of mental test performance between two and eighteen years', *Journal of Experimental Education*, 1948, p. 17.

Table 7.2 illustrates the changes in IQ through correlations, between tests taken at different ages.

Intercultural Differences in Intelligence

Most of the debate and investigation of inter-ethnic differences in intelligence has taken place in the USA, the major controversy being the alleged differences in the intelligence of members of the white and black races. At one extreme are those who maintain that intelligence tests are accurate measures of intelligence and that group differences reflect genetic differences. At the other extreme are those who maintain that intelligence tests are culturally biased and that the differences in IQ either are invalid because of defects in the test itself or reflect the many social, economic and cultural differences between groups. The finding that whites as a group outperform blacks is not disputed by anyone (Brody and Brody, 1976; Jensen, 1980). There is, however, considerable disagreement over how to interpret this finding. According to Arthur Jensen (1980), even when blacks and whites of equivalent socioeconomic status are compared, whites still outperform blacks by 12 points. This difference, Jensen maintains, is too large to be explained by environmental factors alone.

Even the staunchest supporters of the heritability of IQ would not deny that the environment has some influence on intellectual development. Jensen himself (1973) has claimed that there are cumulative effects of deprivation on IQ so that the gap between disadvantaged and advantaged children widens as the children become older. A study of black children reared in white families further substantiates the importance of environmental factors in intelligence. Scarr-Salatapek and Weinberg (1976) studied 176 children, most of whom were black and all of whom had been adopted into white, upper-middle-class families. The adoptive families were all very well educated and held professional jobs. The natural parents of the adopted children had high school degrees. The mean IQ score of the adopted children was 106, above average. Although lower than the mean IQ score, 116, of the natural children of these adoptive parents, it was higher than would have been expected had the children remained with their biological parents, who had IQ scores of less than 100. Children who had been adopted in infancy scored an average IQ of 111; children adopted later scored an average of 97.5. The study did not refute the importance of heredity, but it indicated that IQ scores could be increased by 10 to 20 points by living in better circumstances, and the earlier the better.

Often forgotten in the emotion of the debate is that the outcome is of little practical application. First, even if IQ tests are assumed to be valid, the variation in scores within a race is three times larger than the difference in IQ scores of blacks and whites. Knowing a person's race is therefore virtually useless as a predictor of that person's intelligence. Second, if people's IQ scores are within the normal range, they do not by themselves indicate how well individuals will do when they apply intelligence to everyday matters. If the goal is to eliminate social and economic injustice, many more practical steps can be taken than to debate endlessly the validity or bias of mental tests.

Another controversy is the use of 'Western' IQ tests with children from other cultures. This is questionable since the concepts sampled will tend to be ones not always culturally valued, and in any case skill with the English language is a major prerequisite to taking most tests.

While verbal reasoning tests do emphasise reasoning rather than knowledge, content-free reasoning is impossible. Prior knowledge, particularly of the exact meaning of words, is essential before high scores on these tests are possible. In an attempt to overcome this problem, 'culture-fair' non-verbal reasoning tests have been developed in which logical relationships are described in terms of pictures or patterns. Scores on these tests are less affected by home background and previous schooling, but they are still not entirely 'culture-fair'. They still have inbuilt assumptions about the relative importance of different types of reasoning which are not valid, for example, in primitive cultures. It is difficult to appreciate the problems faced by children from primitive tribes, or even from some 'educationally disadvantaged' subcultures of industrial societies. There are many ways of thinking that we take for granted, but which are alien to them. Furthermore, performance on the test can be affected by such extraneous factors as cultural attitudes to test-taking, test sophistication, naîveté, competition, expectations of failure, etc. No test can ever be culture-free. Most Western children are used to tests and develop a knowhow which helps them to tackle more difficult items than when they first met this type. In much the same way the crossword addict becomes familiar with the style of clues set by the crossword compiler in his daily newspaper, but finds greater difficulty in tackling the puzzles in another paper.

In other ethnic groups, particularly when testees have not been exposed to schooling, the culture pattern may be entirely different, and the whole test situation meaningless. Competition for personal gain may be frowned upon. Important problems are discussed cooperatively with the elders of the tribe, not left to individual initiative.

Elements in the test materials can easily stimulate different associations in different cultures. A word or phrase, diagram or picture, may carry unintentional meanings. For example pictorial representation as such is discouraged among Moslems, so that even apart from the unfamiliarity of most Arab children with pictures, there may be inhibitions against recognising the objects portrayed. Africans, Arabs, Asians and Australian aboriginals are particularly likely to have ingrained attitudes of distrust for whites, which must interfere with their cooperation in test situations.

Intelligence as we define it and measure it is the capacity to cope with, and adapt to, a verbally and technologically sophisticated society. Other forms of society would regard possession of other capacities relevant to their survival in their environments as the criteria of being intelligent. The Australian aboriginal would certainly appear quite unintelligent when measured by conventional Western

IQ tests yet it would be the wise aboriginal who would survive in the desert, knowing how to obtain food and water while the 'intelligent' white man dies of thirst and exposure! Even within cultures, the performance of children from different socioeconomic strata will be influenced by such variables as motivation, self esteem, expectations, test sophistication, etc. Test constructors also seem to assume that middle- and working-class children all have equal familiarity with the content of a verbal test e.g. the understanding of the word 'malevolent', knowing what a novelist does, and being interested in working out a family tree. It is the specific verbal and cultural material that favours the pupils of professional classes but it is not part of the natural experience of the working-class child. There is also the difference in motivation, for the working-class ethos is less competitive than the middle-class one; solidarity and cooperation are set against individualism and competition.

Intelligence and Learning Skill

Most intelligence tests attempt to measure the ability of children to 'think' intelligently — that is, to comprehend, to make judgments or to reason. In answering a test a child has to do three things; he must first read or 'perceive' each item, then 'operate' upon what is given in the way instructed, and finally indicate his answer. It is the middle process, involving judgement or reasoning, that largely constitutes the 'intelligence' being measured, and yet it is clearly dependent upon previous learning or upon how well the early environment has allowed a child to develop the required skills. Any single test only measures a sample — and often a biased sample — of the skills which we describe as 'intelligent'. And the skills we regard as intelligent in our modern Western society may not be so regarded in other cultures. In view of these considerations it might be safest to assume that the IQ is an underestimate for *all* children, although clearly, the more a home is known to have provided appropriate cultural and educational stimulation, the more likely it is that the IQ does reflect innate potential.

The association of the concept of intelligence with that of the ability to learn is not, of course, a new one, although a new meaning has been given to it in recent years by the work of Jensen and Bloom. The latter, for example, has expounded the view, based upon a model for learning postulated by Carroll, that most children will master any task or solve any problem provided they are given sufficient time. Bloom admits that a few children, probably less than 5 per cent, may need an impossibly long time to learn some tasks. But for most it is time and not just 'brain power' that is required. The greatest gains from this new view of intelligence must come, however, for the disadvantaged child, since there can be no doubt that we have in the past underestimated his potential. Not only must we train him in the skills of learning but if necessary we must make our education system more flexible to give him more time for learning if he needs it.

Summary

Intelligence has been defined in many ways, none of which is fully satisfactory. The work of Binet, Spearman and Wechsler aided the development of the measurement of intelligence and attempted to produce understanding of what intelligence is.

Many early tests treated intelligence as a unitary concept but more recent ones have seen it as a mixture of many specific abilities. It is still impossible to decide whether or not there is a general factor in intelligence as Spearman suggested. Guilford's model suggests 120 unique abilities.

Most intelligence tests assess the ability to discuss relationships in verbal and non-verbal materials. IQ is usually measured in deviation scores on a normal distribution which allows comparisons to be made between subjects and tests.

IQ tests are strongly geared towards white, middle-class culture despite attempts to develop 'culture-fair' tests. Although predictive of the future average performance of groups of people, there are often large changes in particular individuals, indicating that caution is necessary in the interpretation of test results.

Piaget and Hebb provide an understanding of intelligence in a developmental perspective. Hebb's concept of Intelligence A and B plus Vernon's C aids the conception of intelligence as a developed potential requiring both genetic and environmental influences to interact.

Although intelligence undoubtedly has some genetic basis, the importance of heredity has been fiercely disputed. There are major environmental influences, such as the prenatal environment, a person's family, social class, race and education. Tests assessing intellectual performance can identify particular problems, such as mental handicap, though intelligence should only be regarded as one of the criteria influencing treatment and intervention programmes. Creativity or divergent thinking is promoted as a means of encouraging children to avoid rigid stereotyped thinking. The relationship between IQ and creativity is not clear.

Questions

1. What do you understand by the term 'intelligence'?
2. Can we measure 'intelligence'?
3. What factors influence the development of intelligence?
4. How do intelligence tests differ from creativity tests?
5. Explain the differences between Intelligence A, B and C.
6. What factors might affect the performance of children on intelligence tests?
7. To what extent is the knowledge of a retarded child's IQ of value in deciding how to help him?
8. What criticisms would you make of IQ testing?

Further Reading

Broman, S.H., Nichols, P.L. and Kennedy, W.A. (1975) *Preschool IQ: Prenatal and Early Developmental Correlates*, Hillsdale, N.J.: Lawrence Erlbaum Associates

Butcher, H. (1968) *Human Intelligence*, London: Methuen

Jensen, A.R. (1969) 'How much can we boost IQ and scholastic achievement?' *Harvard Educ. Review, 39*, 1–123

Lewis, M. (ed.) (1976) *Origins of Intelligence: Infancy and Early Childhood*, New York: Plenum

Lyman, H.B. (1971) *Test Scores and What They Mean*, 2nd edn, Englewood Cliffs, NJ: Prentice-Hall

Pyle, D. (1979) *Intelligence*, London: Routledge

Sattler, J.M. (1974) *Assessment of Children's Intelligence*, Philadelphia: W.B. Saunders

Sternberg, R. (1983) *Handbook on Human Intelligence*, Cambridge: Cambridge University Press

Vernon, P. (1979) *Intelligence: Heredity and Environment*, San Francisco: Freeman

Zajonc, R.B. (1975) 'Birth order and intelligence: dumber by the dozen', *Psychology Today, 8*, (8), 37–43

References

Blank, M. and Solomon, F. (1968) 'How shall the disadvantaged child be taught', *Child Devel., 40*, 47–61

Bloom, B.S. (1964) *Stability and Change in Human Characteristics*, New York: Wiley

Boring, E.G. (1929) *A History of Experimental Psychology*, New York: Appleton Century Crofts

Brody, E. and Brody, N. (1976) *Intelligence: Nature Determinants and Consequences*, New York: Academic Press

Burt, C. (1940) *The Factors of the Mind*, London: University of London Press

Butcher, H.J. (1968) *Human Intelligence*, London: Methuen

Donaldson, M. (1978) *Children's Minds*, Glasgow: Collins

Douglas, J. (1964) *The Home and the School*, London: MacGibbon and Kee

Fraser, E.D. (1959) *Home Environment and the School*, London: University of London Press

Guilford, J.P. (1967) *The Nature of Human Intelligence*, New York: McGraw Hill

Hebb, D.O. (1949) *The Organisation of Behaviour*, New York: Wiley

Hindley, C.B. and Owen, C.F. (1978) 'The extent of individual change in IQ for ages between 6 months and 17 years', *J. Child Psychol. Psychiat.*, *19*, 329–50

Jensen, A.R. (1973) *Educational Differences*, London: Methuen

Jensen, A.R. (1980) *Bias in Mental Testing*, New York: Free Press

McCall, R.B. (1973) 'Developmental changes in mental performance', *Soc. Res. in Child Dev. Monogr.*, *38*

Nisbet, J. (1953) 'Family environment and intelligence', *Eugenics Rev.*, *45*, 31–42

Rutter, M. and Madge, N. (1976) *Cycles of Disadvantage: A Review of Research*, London: Heinemann

Scarr-Salapatek, S. and Weinburg, R.A. (1976) 'IQ test performance of black children adopted by white families', *Amer. Psychol.*, *31*, 726–39

Simon, B. (1971) *Intelligence, Psychology and Education*, London: Lawrence and Wishart

Spearman, C. (1904) 'General intelligence objectively determined and measured', *Amer. J. Psychol.*, *15*, 201–92

Terman, L.M. (1916) *The Measurement of Intelligence*, Boston: Houghton Mifflin

Thurstone, L.L. (1938) 'Primary mental abilities', *Psychometric Monogr.*, *4*

Vernon, P.E. (1950) *The Structure of Human Abilities*, London: Methuen

Wiseman, S. (1964) *Education and Environment*, Manchester: Manchester University Press

8 SOCIAL DEVELOPMENT AND CHILD REARING

Introduction

The emphasis of this chapter and the succeeding chapters is on social and emotional development. Babies appear to be socially responsive from birth and are far more than a mass of clay to be moulded by human hands into a socialised individual. It is remarkable how the newborn child develops so quickly and efficiently into a socially aware and competent individual. Socialisation is the term applied to the process whereby the individual becomes reasonably predictable to others and other people become predictable to him. Child psychologists are now concentrating on the patterning of early relationships since such have a long term effect on the child and it is becoming clearer that the child takes a more positive role in its interactions with parents right from birth. Most research, however, still concentrates on child–mother relationships to the relative neglect of the child–father interactions.

The process of socialisation was, up to a few years ago, couched entirely in terms of what parents and other agents of society did to the young child, shaping it into an effective participant of its society. Emphasis was focused solely on external influences impinging on the child, which was a sort of inert, passive recipient of such forces. Now we perceive socialisation as something far more complex. The very individuality of each child determines its response to parental treatment and even determines the quality and quantity of the parental response itself.

The neonate in psychological terms is a far more competent organism than it was previously given credit for. We do not think of the baby any longer in such purely negative terms as the 'blooming buzzing confusion' with which William James once characterised the baby's consciousness, nor do we see him merely as an assembly of reflexes or as random mass activity. We regard him rather as a being with considerable powers to gather and process information from his surroundings, even in the earliest weeks of life, and though his capabilities are obviously limited by adult standards his orientation and responsiveness to the environment are nevertheless a marked feature from birth. It seems that from the start he is already structured in such a way that he will help to determine his own experience, and the adults who care for him must take into account and respect the particular kind of inherent mental organisation with which he arrives in the world.

Early Learning Is through Persons, Not Objects

Most of what a human infant learns is learned in the context of an ongoing, dynamic social interaction process. The inanimate environment, in and of itself, provides the infant with only the most impoverished stimulus towards an understanding, in human terms, of the world in which he finds himself.

While the work of Bower (1974) reveals perceptual ability of a higher quality in infants than was previously thought, such object interaction is not as well developed as person interaction. Newson (1974) suggests that the infant is biologically tuned to respond to person mediated events, as these are the only events that can be reciprocally timed by parents to coordinate with the infant's own spontaneous and unpredictable behaviour. As Newson claims,

> pre-programmed with some kind of sensitivity towards reciprocal social interaction, the human infant undoubtedly is; but the very nature of this pre-programming implies that within weeks — and perhaps within days or mere hours — after birth he is embarked upon the never-ending programme of social intercommunication with other self-conscious, intelligent, and above all, communicating human beings, (Newson, 1974, p. 251).

A mother's activity is thus by no means random with respect to the infant's own actions, and it is this simple fact of contingent reactivity that makes her an object of absolutely compelling interest to her baby.

Human babies only become human beings because they are treated as if they already were human beings. Whenever grown-ups react sensitively towards a human infant, they do so by monitoring the moment-to-moment shifts in the child's own apparent interests. They make the assumption that the infant is attempting some form of meaningful communication and out of this assumption the communication of shared meanings gradually begins to take place.

Trevarthen's work also supports this view that infant behaviour is not simply an unpatterned or random event sequence. It is, on the contrary, articulated and punctuated into a pre-verbal two-way communication with others. Trevarthen *et al.* (1975) argue that most mammals are biologically pre-tuned to produce, and to respond to, expressive movement patterns or gesticulations which conform to certain basic biological rhythms such as the rhythms that underlie the saccadic movements of the eyes within the head. Some form of 'biological metronome' regulates such pre-verbal social interaction.

Just as in any relationship there is a two way process, a sort of ping-pong in which the move of each player is to some extent determined by the previous move of the other. Only recently have child developers begun to look at this two-way flow and turn away from their previous concentration on artificially isolated one-way units.

A high percentage of mother–infant interactions are initiated by the latter and not by the adult, with the adult being synchronised into the infant's tempo. For example mothers undertake what would be deviant behaviour if it occurred with another adult, e.g. the slowed speech tempo, the highly repetitive nature of vocalisations, the exaggerated facial expressions and gestures — all these look like supernormal stimuli which Stern (1977) has suggested mothers adopt in order to match the infant's limited tolerance of stimulus change. The duration of the mother's gaze at her infant is very much longer than that found in a comparable situation with another adult, approaching only that found between two lovers. Again, whatever the explanation, we have some useful descriptive data here to show just what is involved in that otherwise rather elusive term 'mothering'. The mother lets herself be paced by the infant and conforms to his initiated requirements. The human baby both responds to, and responds with, actions which are synchronised in accordance with basically shared rhythms.

The looking behaviour of neonates — when viewed in slow-motion action replays — is very delicately coordinated with certain hand and arm movements, and even with facial and mouthing movements, all of which are integrated together in such a precisely coordinated rhythmic sequence that the total response can be most aptly designated 'pre-speech'. These and other phenomena, such as social smiling, may best be viewed as only parts of a more general complex responsiveness to the social approaches we make to babies: reciprocal social responsiveness which is the end product of a biological selection process aimed at the important biological goal of making human communication with babies feasible. It is possible, almost from birth, for the interacting adult to take his or her cue from the spontaneous actions performed by the baby and to weave these into the form of a dialogue with him.

Schaffer (1971) reports several experiments in which babies elicit behaviour from mother and not the other way round, and events in which the role of the adult (the social aspect) is as important as the role of the toy object (the perceptual aspect). For example the baby, presented with novel toys, looks at the various toys in turn; the mother then closely and often most sensitively visually follows him. In other words, she will keep an eye on the baby, find him looking in a particular direction, and then also look there. In this way mother and baby share by visual means an interest in some feature of the environment — an interest that is instigated by the baby but that shows interactional synchrony thanks to the mother's activity. The mother, moreover, does not only visually follow but may also elaborate on what the baby is looking at by pointing and, in particular, by verbal means — naming the object, talking about it and so on, and in this way linking word to action. The mother–baby interaction is not analogous to the following response of the young gosling. It seems on the contrary that, in this sense at least, a mother may follow the baby.

If the mother then tries to take the initiative and attempts to draw the baby's attention to a toy he is not looking at, she tends to be rather unsuccessful, at least up to six months of age. 'Mothering' then can be regarded as a specialised communication skill, a very sensitive social responsiveness towards infants. What caretakers need to do, then, is to respond to young children in the same way as they are able to respond to other humans by crediting the infants with human qualities and sensitivities from the outset and reaching to them as human beings. This principle can be followed by men as well as by women.

The social programming to which normal infants are ordinarily subjected, because it occurs as a natural consequence of the care which is necessary for the infant's biological survival, is both massive and continuous. The importance of social mediation in conveying to the infant meaningful dimensions about which it might be possible for him to communicate with other persons is, however, sadly underrated, not only by Piaget but by most other contemporary theorists in developmental psychology who emphasise perceptual and cognitive experience.

Infant Social Attributes

Neonates possess a number of attributes that permit them to attract the attention of others, leading to social interaction, and gradual learning about their environment. Smiling and crying are two powerful social signalling systems, with the former the first truly social response. Smiling as an elicited response appears at about two months of age, elicited usually by the presence of the relevant stimulus, as a human face, often of course the mother's. However, Emde and Harmon (1976) have established that smiling as a spontaneous, non-elicited activity can be seen from birth on. It appears in regular rhythms or bursts with an average eleven smiles per 100 min., no matter where it is observed in the 24-hr cycle, and is generally found in association with particular EEG patterns and specific arousal states. It bears, in short, all the hallmarks of an endogenously organised response which becomes evident only if the investigator is prepared to stand back and observe what happens when the child is left to his own devices. As long as it was believed that an infant's responses appear only when the adult happens to let loose on him a stimulus and that on all other occasions the baby is more or less inert, a partial and somewhat misleading view of the response system was obtained. In due course endogenous smiling diminishes and by the fifth or sixth month it becomes a rarity. By that time smiling has become closely linked to certain classes of environmental stimuli. Since adults find smiles attractive, smiling may be an evolutionary advantage. It is present in blind infants and in all cultures, suggesting that it is innate. Such smiling, whether produced autonomously by the child or elicited when another face appears in view, reciprocally elicits care giving and other pleasant social interaction for the infant.

The crying response is also a powerful social attracter, which is also controlled by internal neural activity. Wolff (1969) demonstrated that the cry has a complex time sequence controlled by brain mechanisms. The cry patterns determine when and how much attention the infant receives. There are three distinct cry patterns which evoke various forms of adult care giving and which mother distinguishes easily. The pain cry has an arousing characteristic that ensures attention is obtained. The other two forms of crying are an angry cry and a rhythmical cry.

Other forms of early communication devices available to an infant are eye gaze (eye contact) and pointing gestures. Hearing, too, has important social consequences. Neonates are able to locate sounds and attend to them visually. Further, they will not only attend preferentially to human voices over impersonal clicks, but also to a female voice rather than to a male one. An infant who can respond, even in such a rudimentary way, is likely to prove rewarding for the care giver. The infant's appearance, particularly the eyes, may also be important to survival and social interaction. Sight and eye contact appear to have a significance greater than the purely cognitive. Infants as young as three weeks look at human faces and objects resembling faces more than other stimuli.

The research discussed above suggests that infants possess several attributes that increase the probability that adults will take an interest in and care for them. Neonates are able to learn quickly, are able to signal their needs and are visually attractive. With the growth of sociability much of the new-borns's behaviour comes to be predictable to the adults who care for him or her. An infant's level of activity before feeding is a case in point. Individual infants also exhibit reasonably stable patterns of crying, perhaps making it easier for adults to interact with them.

However due to brain damage some infants may not be able to direct required signals to others autonomously in order to initiate social interaction. Vice versa, some mothers through personality defects, stress or their own upbringing (Chapter 9) are unable to respond to their infant's deliberate attempts to communicate preverbally. In both situations the partner capable of interacting will be frustrated and such attempts will gradually extinguish through lack of rewarding response. Lack of parental care is a result of the failure of parental attempts to engage a socially unresponsive infant in human interaction.

Prechtl (1963) indicated that mothers of brain-damaged children tended to reject their infants more than mothers of normal children. Robson and Moss (1970) conducted retrospective interviews with mothers in their third postnatal month, and concluded that a mother's feelings of attachment with her child decreased if crying, fussing and other demands did not lessen. They describe one woman who was enthusiastic about her pregnancy but later wanted little to do with the child. The child did not respond to holding, smiled infrequently and showed little eye-to-eye contact. The child was later found to have brain damage. When mutual predictability between care giver and child is difficult to establish, their relationship may be unsatisfactory.

In the reverse situation where infants met (in an experiment) a still, mask-like mother's face, the infants initially looked and smiled, but then became quiet and looked away. Several cycles of looking, smiling and then looking away were reported. Eventually, when repeated attempts failed to achieve a response, the infant withdrew into 'an attitude of helplessness, face averted, body curled up and motionless' (Brazelton *et al.*, 1975, p. 143). When the mothers returned to their more usual form of behaviour the infant, after an initial period of 'puzzlement', began to smile and return to its usual pattern.

Infant Behavioural Styles

Although infants all possess such commonalities as we have discussed above, such as smiling, crying, reciprocal pre-verbal social interaction, they also vary in a variety of ways. A variety of infant behavioural styles was discerned by Thomas, Chess and Birch (1963) with infants displaying individuality in style soon after birth. In this study mothers were asked to describe their infants' behaviours, and observation of the infants was also undertaken by the researchers. Thomas and his colleagues were able to identify nine characteristics of infant behaviour that differentiated children as early as three months of age, such as activity level, rhythmicity, adaptability, approach/avoidance mood, attention.

As a consequence of their work Thomas *et al.* (1963) identified three patterns of behaviour:

(a) The 'Easy Child' pattern applied to about 40 per cent of the children and consisted of high Rhythmicity, positive Mood, Approach, high Adaptability and low Intensity.

(b) The 'Slow to Warm Up' Child pattern (about 15 per cent) manifested low Activity, low Intensity, high Withdrawal, low Adaptability and negative Mood.

(c) The 'Difficult Child' pattern (about 10 per cent) showed negative Mood, low Rhythmicity, low Adaptability, high Intensity and high Withdrawal.

About 35 per cent of the infants did not fit into any classification.

The presence of these individual differences so early in life suggest that underlying metabolic factors have considerable influence. You may recall from Chapter 2 that identical twins had similar personality characteristics which pointed to affective and social behaviour having a genetic basis. Additionally, such individual differences would argue for a variety of child-rearing practices since each pattern has different requirements from, and responses to, the environment. Some care givers may constantly be faced with a lack of predictability and responsiveness in the child or be unable to adjust to the degree of stimulation the infant needs or can cope with. These issues are particularly salient where physically handicapped are involved. For example, comparison of the communication patterns between mothers with normal infants and mothers with Down's Syndrome infants found several differences. Although the Down's children were involved in as many interactive sequences as normal children, they took the initiative less often and their mothers tended to be more directive.

Similarly, infants born prematurely differ from full-terms in their need for stimulation and are less interactionally responsive, even when their families are similar. Pre-term infants are more likely to break off the interaction than full-terms and to look less at their mothers and their environment. Several studies have indicated that prematurity has an effect on the way mothers interact with their infants. They have found to issue more directive commands and to poke, pinch and rock more frequently when their children are pre-term. They are also more likely to initiate communication than mothers of full-terms, who share this responsibility more equally with their infants. The lack of cues from children with cerebral palsy and the excess of cues from hyperactive children have been shown to affect the mother–child relationship.

Parental Practices in Child Rearing

The behaviour and adjustment of children appear to depend on their families' treatment of them to a considerable extent. This seems particularly true in relation to the preschool years which are crucial in providing a basis for future development. However, psychological research in this area does not produce completely consistent results because parental practices differ subtly between families yet psychologists have to lump together variations to form a basic classification system of child-rearing practices. Again researchers often have to ask parents to remember how they dealt with their offspring so that this material can be related to the characteristics of the child in the present. Such recollections of the past can be hazy — distorted, or as seen through rose-tinted spectacles — rather than what actually was the case.

The Early Years

The preschool years seem crucial for shaping later development in all its aspects. Of all influences on the child, human relationships are the most pervasive and the major human relationships of the child are those of the family. A child's adjustment to life depends on his subjective interpretation of his family's treatment of him and conditions within the family. These early relationships and the feelings developed from them act as prototypes for the future.

The family is the organ within which the child is first socialised — his first social contacts. He discovers how people react to him and how in return he acts to them and to various family situations. Also within the family the child learns and trains in his first human activities and skills. His parents' attitudes to his success and failure, his interpretation of these attitudes, his feelings of adequacy and acceptance are all created here. There may be modifications later but the essential basis is laid down early. Naturally the same personality or behaviour will not develop out of similar family conditions since human individuality can produce an infinite variety of reactions from an infinitely varied set of subjective interpretations of the family context, but certain broad patterns do emerge.

There is in Erikson's work the underlying theme that the mother's loving care helps the child to develop a basic sense of security and trust. This occurs especially during the first year when mother has the responsibility of satisfying the child's basic needs. The period between two and five seems crucial for working out a satisfactory relationship between dependence and independence. The development of a sense of trust, love, acceptance and security is essential if a child is to have an adequate adjustment later on in life. These first human relationships set prototypes for the future enabling the child to consider what can be expected later in similar dealings and contexts with others. The period before five is so vulnerable because of:

(a) the intensity of dependence and emotional attachment to the family group, especially mother,
(b) a limited capacity to tolerate frustration,
(c) limited understanding of cause and effect,
(d) high rate of adjustment to new experiences required,

(e) high rate of failure,

(f) desires countered by parents.

The mother's handling of her child has an unremitting influence on it as she satisfies or fails to satisfy its desires for food, comfort and security. The child begins to feel the world either benign and to be trusted, or hostile and not to be trusted. If the mother responds to the infant warmly and rewardingly he will feel accepted and confident, but if the mother's reaction is cold, stunted and rejecting then the child's emotional and social development is also stunted. The family attitude towards the young child helps to create the child he is, his view of himself and his pattern and style of adjustment to life, his friendliness or his isolation, his aggression or his timidity, his sense of trust or his feeling that the environment is unreliable. If a child's first relationships give him the wrong view of life at the outset what hope is there for the future?

Early Feeding Practices and Potty Training

A considerable amount of research effort has gone into attempts to discern the psychological effects of various approaches to feeding and toilet training in infancy. However, the advice of experts from the results of these studies tends to change from one generation to the next. The basic argument with regard to feeding is whether the baby should be fed on demand, i.e. when he appears to need it (say by crying), or on schedule, i.e. sticking rigorously to a feed, say, every four hours. The best conclusion from the research is not that one of these practices leads to better psychological adjustment than the other, but that mothers who are relaxed and who provide security and acceptance for the infant in the feeding context, an atmosphere the baby interprets empathically as such, obtain more placid, contented and adjusted infants. Feeding problems, tension and anxiety in the infant are more related to tension, coping worries and difficulties in accepting the child, i.e. parental adjustment, attitudes and personalities rather than to any specific feeding routines adopted. Good child care provides a double diet; not only is there the provision of adequate food and warm, dry clothing, but also a menu of love, security and acceptance through the way the care taking is effected, through the way the infant is held, cooed to, smiled at and interacted with.

Feeding activities are also seen as important particularly by Freudian psychoanalysts because through such activities the infant develops attachment (bonding) to the mother (Chapter 9). Behaviourists would talk about the presence of mother having a reward value. However the experiments with rhesus monkeys conducted by Harlow and Harlow (1962) produced results contrary to this theory. Baby monkeys when frightened sought refuge by clinging, not to an uncomfortable wire frame dummy mother from which they had been fed, but to a terry-towel-covered frame dummy mother from which no food had been obtained. The infant monkeys had their anxiety reduced and security increased by tactile comfort. Food provision is not, for these animals at least, a force for the development of attachment behaviour. Of course in real life, human infants hopefully receive food, tactile comfort and security at one and the same time, though the first may not be as vital a consideration as some psychologists previously thought.

With regard to potty training, there would generally seem to be little reason for starting too soon. Few children can control themselves during the day until 18–21 months old, when postural control, sphincter muscle control and the ability to give some verbal warning signal about impending needs are present. Generally children whose training begins later learn more quickly. Early toilet training takes longer to reach a successful conclusion and because this early training is adopted by mothers who tend to be anxious, who stress other demands such as quietness, neatness and orderliness, it causes upset and anxiety to the child. Mothers who are rigid in this concern are rigid in other concerns and the emotional problems of a child faced with these demands are related to the whole set of demands rather than just to toilet training.

Many workers suggest that there is a general distribution of mothering behaviour along a restrictiveness–permissiveness dimension. The most successful mothers over toilet training were those who employed mild training procedures, and who showed warmth and acceptance to their children (Sears *et al.*, 1957). So the child-rearing practices adopted would appear to reflect the general outlook, personality and attitudes of the parents. Toilet training is a social and emotional situation as well as a physical one. For besides these physical controls there are two important attitudes which must be learnt in connection with toilet behaviour.

(a) Cleanliness. This is the first contact children have with this concept and Freud was perhaps right in seeing this experience as the basis of cleanliness, neatness and orderliness. Children do learn attitudes of disgust towards the texture, odour and colour of excrement from a mother who expresses these attitudes herself. (b) Modesty. Elimination requires exposure. If mother places a high premium on modesty then elimination is done in the strictest privacy. Definite rules are often made, e.g. don't speak about it in public, no member of the opposite sex to be present during toileting. Feeding and waste elimination were a major part of the basis of personality development for Freud.

According to Freud, a child's development is marked by a series of phases (oral, anal, genital) during which he is especially sensitive to certain kinds of experience. During the oral phase, for example, the baby is mainly concerned with activities like sucking, chewing, swallowing and biting, and the experiences that matter to him most thus include the manner of his feeding (breast or bottle), the timing of feeding (schedule or demand), the age when he is weaned, and so on. When these experiences are congenial to the child he passes on to the next developmental phase without difficulty; when they are frustrating and stressful, however, he remains 'fixated' at this stage in the sense that, even as an adult, he continues to show characteristics, such as dependence and passivity in his personality make-up, that distinguish babies at the oral stage.

The satisfaction, security and pleasure derived from early feeding activities can be reactivated. It is a means of getting satisfaction which can be recollected in dreams, and one may see a baby continuing with sucking movements when falling asleep. It is a sensation which can be reproduced by self-stimulation when a baby sucks the thumb, or the stimulation can be provided by someone else who puts a dummy teat in the baby's mouth. Sucking gives the sensation of love which can be experienced with another individual, or as something deriving from the stimulation of recollecting it. This capacity to derive sensual satisfaction with the mouth becomes partly superseded, as people grow, by other satisfactions, but it remains with us as an essential core. We celebrate important occasions with meals or with drinks; and we give ourselves comfort when we smoke or when we continue to suck our thumbs, our pipes, or our pencils, or when we chew gum which has no nutriment. The word 'companion' implies someone with whom one has shared bread.

This oral phase lasts from birth to around 18 months when, according to Freud, the anal stage commences. He argues that certain adult character traits derive from this stage depending on the degree of importance given to the toilet care during this period of training. Cleanliness is next to godliness, and dirtiness is sin; and the close anatomical association of bladder and bowel with sexual organs connects the sin of dirtiness with sexual guilt (and, incidentally, links sexuality with the toilet). Some people react to this so strongly that cleanliness and orderliness become their chief virtues. They are tidy in their appearance and in their work, and often put these characteristics to good use. Sometimes individuals carry the tidiness and carefulness into every field of activity and become miserly, or the same process may take more abnormal forms when the individual is so fearful about the power to damage people by dirt or untidiness that he or she develops obsessional rituals to protect others from the consequences of hidden powers of evil.

There are milder degrees of these processes that find justification in various cults concerning food and the control of movements of the bladder and the bowel. Many people regard regularity as a sign of health and go to great lengths to ensure it for themselves and their children, and, as mentioned above, the more that attention is paid to the activity, the more it can become an activity in which battles are fought between child and parent. Thus, bladder and bowel activity can succeed oral activity in providing individual gratification. The anal personality is thus one who is frugal, obstinate, excessively tidy and rigid in beliefs. The importance of sensations and fantasies over elimination together with parental demands for cleanliness and modesty lead, according to Freudians, to this personality type. In this way Freud's theory suggests that there are definite links between particular kinds of infantile experiences on the one hand, and adult personality characteristics on the other.

However, this theory has not been borne out. A large number of investigations have compared breast-feeding with bottle-feeding, self-demand with rigidly scheduled regimes, early with later weaning, and other aspects of the child's early experience that could be expected to produce lasting after-effects. No such effects have been found. Whatever their impact at the time, there is no reason to believe that these early experiences mark the child for good or ill for the rest of his life. And just as well, otherwise we would all be at the mercy of some single event, some specific parental aberration, that we happened to have experienced at some long-distant point in our past.

Freud's theory made little allowance for the ameliorating influence of later experience.

Some Specific Studies of Child-Rearing Practices

Psychologists have attempted to classify rearing practices and their effects on the personalities of children. What follows is a summary of some major studies.

Coopersmith's study

Coopersmith's (1967) study showed that the children's social development and self esteem are strongly related to parental practices, particularly parental warmth and the sorts of rules and disciplines imposed by the parents.

The parents of high self esteem boys manifested warm interest in the child's welfare, and gave other signs that they regarded him as a significant person. Such parents also tended not to be too permissive, demanding high standards of behaviour and enforcing rules consistently. They used reward rather than punishment and the child felt he was dealt with firmly but fairly. Thus, definite and consistently imposed limits on behaviour were associated with high self esteem. Such clear limits meant that less drastic forms of punishment were needed and that children knew where they stood, able to make decisions about their own behaviour within clear limits. Those parents who were cold, withdrawn, inconsistent or rejecting reared a child characterised by withdrawal, displaced hostility, dependence and passivity.

Such a child interprets the inconsistent parental restrictions as indications of rejection, hostility and lack of acceptance. Only if a child is loved, accepted and is aware of this will he interpret discipline as an expression of parental care. The existence of limits provides the child with a social world in which he can be successful when the chosen limits are suitable. Without limits or with inconsistent limits the child never really knows what is expected, or what is right. This situation is anxiety-provoking and prevents successful achievement of known and expected tasks. Self esteem thus appears to grow out of parental warmth and acceptance, and success in required demands that lie within the child's capabilities. Basking in favourable appraisal the child comes to evaluate himself in a similar favourable light.

The findings from Coopersmith's studies suggest that positive social development is more likely to emerge if children are treated with respect, provided with well-defined standards and provided with reasonable expectations of success. The development of the ability to respond constructively to challenge seems essential to becoming a person who evaluates himself as of some worth. On the other hand, the freedom to explore the environment in an unrestricted and unguided way, coupled with consistent permissiveness, appears to engender anxiety, doubts about self worth, low expectations of success and an inability to develop sound social relationships based on mutual respect.

Baumrind's Study

Baumrind (1967) found that children who were happy, self-reliant and able to meet challenging situations directly (pattern I) had parents who exercised a good deal of control over their children and demanded responsible, independent behaviour from them, but who also explained, listened and provided emotional support. The parents of withdrawn children (pattern II) tended to be somewhat less warm than parents of the immature children (pattern III). The parents of the immature children were moderately nurturant but conspicuously low in exercising control. These findings are, of course, based on very small samples of children who clearly fit a particular behavioural pattern.

The Baumrind research group has since extended its work to new samples of parents and children (Baumrind 1971, 1973). The original findings have been supported in almost all respects. Three patterns of parenting were identified: authoritarian, authoritative, and permissive. No parent fits a given category all the time — no-one was always permissive or always authoritarian. These categories are simply dominant patterns that reliably distinguish certain parents from one another. These three types of parents can be described as follows:

(1) Authoritarian. Parents who fit this classification were likely to: attempt to shape, control and evaluate the behaviour and attitudes of their children in accordance with an absolute set of standards; value obedience, respect for authority, work, tradition and preservation of order; and discourage verbal give and take. These parents sometimes rejected their children.

(2) Authoritative. Parents who fit this classification were likely to: attempt to direct the child in a rational, issue-oriented manner; encourage verbal give and take, explain the reason behind demands and discipline but also use power when necessary; expect the child to conform to adult requirements but also to be independent and self-directing; recognise the rights of both adults and children; and set standards and enforce them firmly. These parents did not regard themselves as infallible but also did not base

decisions primarily on the child's desires.

(3) Permissive. Parents who fit this classification were likely to: attempt to behave in an accepting, positive way towards the child's impulses, desires and actions; use little punishment; consult the child; make few demands for household responsibility or order; allow the child to regulate his or her own activities as much as possible and avoid the exercise of control; and attempt to use reasoning but not overt power to achieve objectives.

Children of these types of parents differed behaviourally in a number of ways, especially:

(1) Authoritarian parents had children who showed little independence and who obtained middle-range scores on social responsibility.
(2) Authoritative parents had independent and socially responsible children.
(3) Permissive parents had children who conspicuously lacked social responsibility and who were not especially independent.

While these general outcomes held true for boys and girls, some sex differences in the effect of parenting patterns were observed.

Authoritarian parenting seems to be more damaging to boys than girls, in the sense that the sons of these parents were less likely than the other children to have developed independent, self-reliant behaviour; also they were more likely to be angry and defiant. Authoritative parenting seemed to be more strongly associated with self reliance and achievement orientation in girls than boys, and these girls were often resistive toward parents and domineering toward age mates. In boys, authoritative parenting seemed to be associated with being friendly and cooperative.

The same theme is evident as with Coopersmith. Children reared in a democratic style, allowed independence within a defined framework, and subject to reasoned rules and constant discipline tend to be the more adaptable, balanced and self-reliant persons.

The Forgotten Father

Discussion of childhood socialisation and child rearing in Western society focuses generally on mother–child interaction but with increasing unemployment it is no longer uncommon to find families in which a complete role reversal has taken place: mother, having found a job, goes out to work, leaving her unemployed husband in charge of home and children. Fortunately, there is no evidence to indicate that the biological make-up of men makes them unfit for this task or even necessarily inferior to women in this respect. Parenting is unisex; the reasons for the traditional division of labour (such as the need to breast-feed the child and the importance of using men's greater physical strength for hunting and tilling the fields) are no longer applicable.

Children brought up without a father are more likely to encounter difficulties than those in a complete family. There are various reasons for this. One is that in any single-parent family the remaining parent must cope with a great multiplicity of stresses — financial, occupational or emotional — and the strain felt by him or (more often) her is very likely to have repercussions for the child too. Again, a fatherless boy has no model to imitate, and the developmental tasks of acquiring sex-appropriate behaviour may be more difficult. And, finally, the child isolated with his mother and caught up in one all-encompassing relationship does not have the same chance of learning from intriguing and complex interactions with a wide range of others.

Summary

Childhood socialisation is very complex. Even at birth the neonate is a far more competent organism than was previously thought and is capable of reciprocal social interaction. Infant behaviour is not random but has purpose, with the infant initiating adult behaviour towards it. Mothering can be regarded as a sensitivity in social responsiveness towards infants. The smiling and crying responses of babies are social responses involving communication patterns. Infants also display individual behavioural styles from birth.

Patterns of child rearing appear to influence social, emotional and intellectual development. Toilet training and feeding practices in infancy appear to be less important as determinants of later behaviour than originally believed by Freud. The broad principles that stand out from parental practices are:

(a) extreme attitudes on the part of parents lead to extreme behaviour in children;

(b) a balancing of behaviour between the extremes by parents results in adjusted children; and

(c) parents who are consistent, involve children in rule making, punish justifiably and provide acceptance and warmth for their children produce the most adjusted young person. But in all this work the father is a forgotten and ignored influence.

Activities

1. You are going to conduct a survey of at least ten families. At least five of these families are to have children five years or younger. Ask the mother and father of each family what they do when they discipline their children. Write exactly what each parent tells you. Then classify all of your responses into categories, e.g. power assertion, love withdrawal. Which category was used most often? Did mothers and fathers use the same strategies? Were different strategies used with younger children than were used with older children?

2. Invite a panel of mothers and fathers to class or interview them elsewhere. Have them discuss their initial reactions to their newborns. Give them the following list of issues to consider:

   (a) How did you feel when you first saw your newborn?
   (b) Did you react the way you had expected you would?
   (c) Did your baby look or act differently than you had expected? In what ways?
   (d) How did you expect your newborn to act? What did you expect the infant to look like?
   (e) Did your baby have bouts of colic?
   (f) How did you react to these bouts?
   (g) Is there anything that could have helped you cope with these bouts?
   (h) How does the reality of parenting match up with your expectations?
   (i) What social supports did you use in helping you adjust to your new role?
   (j) What additional social supports would you have liked to have used? Why didn't you use them?
   (k) Did you ever have regrets over your new parenting role? When?
   (l) Were there particular events associated with these regrets?

What were they?

(m) How did you cope with the feelings of regret?

(n) How did you cope with the events that precipitated these feelings?

(o) Were there ever times when you wanted to hit the baby or give the baby away? If so, what were the circumstances associated with these feelings and how did you cope with the feelings?

(p) What advice would you give to prospective parents?

You should provide the parents with a covering letter explaining that feelings of regret and wishes to hit or give away their child are very common. Assure them that it would be extremely helpful to the students to be made aware of these feelings. Too many young adults have an idealised view of parenting and little understanding of what newborns are actually like. An open discussion of these issues with new parents would prove very educational.

3. Describe the regime under which you were reared and socialised. What sort of demands and limits did your parents place on you? What sort of reinforcements and punishments were employed? Did both parents use the same strategy? To what extent do you think your personality and behaviour has been affected by your parents' practices?

4. Observe several infants if possible. Make notes on the differences between them with reference to activity level, approach–withdrawal, intensity, threshold, mood, attention, distractability. (Refer back to Thomas, Chess and Birch's work in this chapter.) Do the infants differ?

Questions

1. Discuss the major adjustments the newborn must make very shortly after birth. The 'birth without violence' movement advocates birthing in a very quiet, dark room and immediate immersion of the infant in a warm water bath. Do you think these practices will help or hinder the newborn's adjustment? Why?

2. William James described the world of the newborn as blooming, buzzing confusion. He was referring to what he felt were the limitations of the newborn's sensory capacities. Do you agree with his description? Why?

3. Which of the infant's sensory systems seems to be the most developed at birth? Is there any evolutionary significance to this developmental phenomenon? Discuss what this significance might be.
4. What behaviours and capacities yield consistent individual differences in newborns? Discuss whether these differences are predictive of later individual differences. Why is this problem so difficult to study?
5. The parent–child relationship is said to be reciprocal. Explain what this means, and give examples.
6. If you had to advise parents on the most appropriate practices for developing a balanced, adjusted child, what would your advice be?
7. If couples about to be married had to undertake a compulsory course in the psychological aspects of child rearing, what would you include?

Further Reading

Bruner, J., Cole, M. and Lloyd, B. (eds.) (1976) *The Developing Child*, Boston, Mass.: Harvard University Press

Chess, S. (1976) *Your Child is a Person*, Harmondsworth: Penguin

Eimers, R. and Aitchison, R. (1977) *Effective Parents: Responsible Children*, New York: McGraw-Hill

Fine, M. (1979) *Parents v Children*, Englewood Cliffs, NJ: Prentice Hall

Ginott, H. (1973) *Between Parent and Child*, New York: Avon

Ginott, H. (1973) *Between Teacher and Child*, New York: Macmillan

Gordon, I.J. (1977) *Baby to Parent, Parent to Baby*, New York: St Martin's Press

Gordon, T. (1970) *Parent Effectiveness Training*, New York: McKay

Gordon, T. (1975) *Teacher Effectiveness Training*, New York: McKay

James, M. and Jongeward, D. (1973) *Born to Win*, Reading, Mass.: Addison-Wesley

Lamb, M. (1976) *The Role of the Father in Child Development*, New York: Wiley

Lamb, M. (1978) *Social and Personality Development*, New York: Holt, Rinehart and Winston

Maccoby, E. (1980) *Social Development*, New York: Harcourt Brace

Mahler, M.S., Pine, F. and Bergman, A. (1975) *The Psychological Birth of the Human Infant*, New York: Basic Books

Mussen, P. and Eisenberg-Berg, N. (1977) *Roots of Caring, Sharing, and Helping*, San Francisco: W.H. Freeman

Perry, D. and Bussey, K. (1984) *Social Development*, Englewood-Cliffs, NJ: Prentice-Hall

Richards, M. (1974) *The Integration of a Child into a Social World*, London: Cambridge University Press

Richards, M. (1974) *Rights of Children*, Harvard Educ. Review, November 1973; February 1974

Skolnick, A. (ed.) (1976) *Rethinking Childhood*, Boston: Little, Brown

References

Baumrind, D. (1967) 'Child care practices anteceding three patterns of pre-school behaviour', *Genet. Psychol. Monogr.*, 75, 43–88

Baumrind, D. (1971) 'Current patterns of parental authority', *Dev. Psychol. Monogr.*, 4, Whole No. 2

Baumrind, D. (1973) 'The development of instrumental competence through socialisation' in A. Pick (ed.) *Minnesota Symposium on Child Psychology*, vol. 7, University of Minnesota Press

Bower, T.R.G. (1974) *Development in Infancy*, San Francisco: Freeman

Brazelton, T., Tronick, E., Adamson, L., Als, H. and Wise, S. (1975) 'Early mother–infant reciprocity', *CIBA Foundation Symposium*, 33

Coopersmith, S. (1967) *The Antecedents of Self Esteem*, San Francisco: Freeman

Emde, R. and Harmon, R. (1976) 'Emotional expression in infancy', *Psychol. Issues*, 37, Whole No.

Harlow, H. and Harlow, M. (1962) 'Social deprivation in monkeys', *Scientific Amer.*, 207, 136

Newson, J. (1974) 'Towards a theory of infant understanding', *Bull. Br. Psychol. Soc.*, 27, 251–7

Prechtl, H.F. (1963) 'Mother–child interaction in babies with minimal brain damage' in B.M. Foss (ed.) *Determinants of Infant Behaviour*, vol. 2, London: Methuen

Robson, K. and Moss, H. (1970) 'Patterns and determinants of maternal attachment', *J. Pediatrics*, 77, 976–85

Schaffer, H.R. (1971) *The Growth of Sociability*, Harmondsworth: Penguin

Sears, R., Maccoby, E. and Levine, H. (1957) *Patterns of Child Rearing*, Evanston: Row Peterson

Stern, D.N. (1977) *The First Relationship*, Cambridge, Mass.: Harvard University Press

Thomas, A., Chess, S. and Birch, H. (1963) *Behavioural Individuality in Early Childhood*, London: University of London Press

Trevarthen, C., Hubley, P. and Sheeran, L. (1975) 'Psychological actions in early infancy', *La Recherche*, 6, 51–8

Wolf, P.H. (1969) 'The natural history of crying and other vocalisations in early infancy', in B.M. Foss (ed.) *The Determinants of Infant Behaviour*, vol. 4, London: Methuen

9 MATERNAL DEPRIVATION

The sentimental assumption that mothers love their children is countered by the horrifying evidence from daily newspapers, court cases and social workers' files that brutal and rejecting mothers (and fathers) do exist. A further assumption promulgated by Freudian psychoanalysts is that no child can grow up into a normal, well adjusted person without the natural mother's love and care. The theory of maternal deprivation focuses on the role and function of the mother and on those features of the mother–child interaction that engender a healthy (or conversely an unhealthy), physical, social, emotional and mental development of the child.

Bowlby's Theory

The growth of interest in maternal deprivation stemmed initially from Bowlby's (1951) study, prepared for the WHO, of the mental health problems of homeless children in post-war shattered Europe. This report asserted that an infant and young child should experience a warm, intimate and continuous relationship with his mother (or permanent mother substitute — one person who steadily 'mothers' him) in which both find satisfaction and enjoyment, or else intellectual retardation, excessive attention-seeking and the inability to build up close and trusting relationships with others will result. He defined maternal deprivation as a state of affairs in which a child does not have this relationship. The infant needs love as much as food. If the necessary bond between child and mother has not developed during a critical period up to two and a half or three years of age, then damage is irreversible. He claimed that maternal deprivation has harmful effects, varying in seriousness with the degree of separation. Partial separation, i.e. removal for a short while from the mother's care to that of someone else, gives rise to deprivation that will be relatively mild if this someone else is someone whom he has already learned to know and trust, but may be considerable if the foster-mother, nurse or nursery attendant, even though loving, is a stranger. All these arrangements, however, give a child some satisfaction and are therefore examples of partial deprivation. The result of partial deprivation may be expressed by anxiety, excessive need for love, .

powerful feelings for revenge on mother and, arising from the last, guilt and depression. A young child, still immature in mind and body, cannot cope with all these emotions and drives. The way in which he responds to these disturbances may result in nervous disorders and instability of character.

As regards complete deprivation, where a child has no one person who cares for him in a personal way and with whom he can feel secure which, according to Bowlby, appears to be not uncommon in institutions, residential nurseries and hospitals, far-reaching effects on character development occur which may entirely cripple the capacity to make relationships with other people. He believes that complete deprivation causes a child's development to be always retarded — physically, intellectually and socially — and symptoms of physical and mental illness will appear, with some children permanently and grossly damaged, particularly those under about seven years of age, and that some of the effects are clearly discernible within the first few weeks of life. Three months of complete deprivation causes such qualitative changes that recovery is rarely if ever complete. Other research work by Goldfarb (1945) supports Bowlby's thesis.

A summary of the original studies suggests, then, that the effects of growing up without the love and security of a consistent mother figure seem to be devastating. If a mother fails through neglect or absence to satisfy the child's needs there is a likelihood the child will become maladjusted. If the infant is robbed of his mother through death or desertion he needs some permanent mother substitute. A succession of people no matter how devoted or efficient is no substitute. In residential institutions the child is handled by a succession of nurses and house mothers. No matter how kind each may be in her fragment of care, none is on duty or shift long enough to enable the child to enter into a stable relationship. The experience of transient attachments to a series of nurses, each of whom the child eventually loses, makes him act as if neither mothering nor contact with humans has much significance for him. After losing mother figures to whom he has given trust and affection he will commit himself less and less to succeeding ones. He ceases to show any feelings and becomes increasingly self centred not directing his desires and feelings to other people. A child who has been unable to form a satisfying relationship will find it hard to do so in later life. An isolation type experience can lead to an isolation type personality. Development seems most severely affected in those institutional settings markedly lacking in the experiences usually present in the complex interactions between mother and child under normal home conditions.

Influence of the Theory

Bowlby's findings had a remarkable influence on organisations concerned with child care. It led to deprivation experiments with animals; resulted in practical changes concerned with children in care and in the hospitalisation of young children; drew attention to the concepts of attachment and bonding of the child with the mother; and prompted raging controversy regarding methods of rearing children. Bowlby's writings have often been misinterpreted and wrongly used to support the notion that only twenty-four hours care, day in and day out, by the same person, is good enough. This has led to the claim that proper mothering is only possible if the mother does not go out to work and that the use of day nurseries and creches has a serious and permanent deleterious effect.

Motherhood was elevated to a position of awe-inspiring responsibility. Failure in motherhood was seen as a root cause of whatever delinquency, neurosis or psychosis developed in any child. Working mothers became guilty overnight of failing to meet the offsprings' psychological needs. The policies of social welfare agencies were revised as the improvement of mothering coupled with the provision of support for the inadequate mother were seen as ways of improving the life of the working class. However inadequate, cruel or negligent the home, it was regarded as far better to keep the child there than remove it to some institution. Many hospitals developed mother and child units so that separation is prevented when the infant has to be hospitalised, and now encourage mothers to have contact with their neonates as soon as possible after birth.

Bowlby was so convinced of the validity of his theory he gave advice to mothers urging them never to take even a week's holiday away from their children. He equally urged that incentives be provided to keep mothers at home, since the mother of young children is not free, or at least should not be free, to earn. This is a strong argument for increased family allowances for young children.

Criticisms of the Theory

Despite the very assertive and dogmatic case Bowlby made for the effects of maternal deprivation, reconsideration of the evidence and theory suggests that things are not quite as black as they have been painted.

Criticisms of Bowlby's Studies

Bowlby had based most of his assertions on two of his own studies but, when the studies are looked at in detail, the methodology and evidence leave much to be desired. His studies were unsystematic, unplanned and generally inconclusive.

Problems of Definition

The term maternal deprivation has been used very loosely to cover three different mother–child experiences:

(a) Failure to form an attachment to a mother–figure during the first three years, even when mother is normally physically present.

(b) Deprivation for a limited period — at least three months and probably more than six — during the first three or four years of life.

(c) Changes from one mother–figure to another during early childhood.

Item (a) above suggests that it is not the physical presence of the mother that counts, but the amount and quality of the interaction that takes place between mother and baby. This is an important statement, and takes into account the deprivation that can take place within an apparently normal home as well as in foster homes and institutions, when the mother is unable to bond with her infant through her own psychological inadequacies. Rutter (1972) argues this point.

So maternal deprivation becomes an omnibus term to include any adverse mother–child interaction, such as social isolation, cruelty and neglect, institutional upbringing, adverse child-rearing practices, separation practices, severe economic and cultural deprivation, and lack of or inappropriate stimulation, not just simply to the lack of a mother. Disorders of conduct, personality, language, cognition and physical growth have all been found to occur in children with serious disturbances in their early family life, and these disorders have all been included under the loose heading of 'maternal deprivation'. But it remains to be determined which type of deprivation has produced which long term consequence.

Since most of the children studied by Bowlby, Goldfarb and others who were being reared under institutional conditions lacked a father as well as a mother, Bowlby was going beyond the evidence in relating these effects to the lack of a female parent only. Parental deprivation is thus a more accurate term, though most of the literature speaks only of maternal deprivation.

Other critics have rightly called attention to the nurturing process in which a father also has a role; to the extended family with multiple mothering; to the professionalised mothering in a variety of organisations, such as the Kibbutzim in Israel; to supplementary mothering by a succession of adults in private well-to-do homes where, in addition to the natural mother, there are nurses or au-pair girls; and to the day nurseries, child minders and grandmothers for other social classes. Inferences have been drawn from all these processes to show that upbringing in the absence of the mother does not inevitably lead to pathological development or, if it does, that the results are not irreversible.

Bonding and Attachment

This concept of bonding or attachment during the critical period is crucial to Bowlby's theory. Attachment provides a secure base or to use Erikson's words 'a cradle of faith' in which needs are satisfied, emotional as well as biological, and from which the child can venture out to explore and develop self reliance. The basis for the concept of attachment lies in animal studies conducted by ethologists such as Lorenz, who described how infant ducks become imprinted on their mothers and from then on follow the mother. This bonding to the mother has obvious advantages for the vulnerable young animals, and tends to occur at a specific time after birth, the critical period; with ducklings this is the first day of life. Bonding is difficult later. The generalisation of such a process to mankind is of course not valid and is impossible to test, but many psychologists (e.g. Klaus and Kennell, 1970) believe that mother and child should be 'bonded' from birth to ensure adequate social and emotional development.

Herbert and Sluckin (1982) criticise the concept of bonding in humans and deny there is a critical period after birth when attachment occurs. They argue that animal studies are not valid indicators of human behaviour. Moreover, if bonding theory were correct, it would hardly be possible for foster or adoptive parents to form warm attachments to their charges, whom they may not have seen as babies at all. Tragic 'tug-of-love' cases have occurred because foster parents have grown so fond of the children in their care that it becomes unbearably hurtful to hand them back to their natural parents. Paternal love likewise puts a large question mark over the bonding doctrine, for it implies the father's love is of a lower order and quality than the mother's. Yet it is not always the female that cares for the baby. Most human fathers develop a fierce love for their offspring, even if they were nowhere near the delivery room when they were born. Moreover, contemporary Western society is witnessing a massive increase in the number of single-parent families, and in some it is the father who is the care-giver. May he not become emotionally attached to his children?

The mother–child bond has become invested with a particular mystique, not only in the mass media but also in learned journals, so appealing is this idea espoused by members of the medical and caring professions — pediatricians, obstetric nurses, midwives, health visitors and social workers.

To bond or not to bond that is the quandry that faces nurses in maternity hospitals. Should they encourage bonding in mothers who will shortly have their babies taken away for adoption? Should they attempt to bond other mothers to their new born infants by enforcing skin-to-skin and other forms of contact, irrespective of the circumstances and the mother's own inclinations? Herbert and Sluckin (1982) claim that there is really no need for nurses or mothers to attach any special importance to skin contact. What is right is what seems sensible and natural in the given circumstances. Everything should depend on what suits all concerned, the mother, the infant, the father and the hospital staff. And, of course, a mother's feelings on the subject of contact and separation are important to her well-being.

Herbert and Sluckin (1982) advise expectant mothers, or women who harbour secret fears that they have not been properly bonded to their infants when they were born, to stop worrying. The findings are that there is no critical period for bonding and all the indications are that maternal attachment, like child-to-adult or indeed any human relationship, develops surely, although in some cases slowly. However, Herbert and Sluckin's somewhat intuitive views, while providing a sensible warning not to assume that unsuccessful bonding is the precursor to all child development problems, are contradicted by some research findings and as we note later in this chapter, failures in bonding can in *some* (not all) cases lead to child abuse.

Kennel *et al.* (1974) performed an experiment in which a group of mothers was given normal routine contact with their newborns; a glimpse of the baby shortly after birth, a short visit at six-twelve hours, and then a visit every four hours of 20-30 min. each for feeding over the first 3 days. A second group of mothers had this routine contact plus additional contact with their infants. They were given their naked babies to hold for one hour within the first three hours after birth and five extra hours per day over the next three days. Although the mothers in each group were comparable with respect to age, socioeconomic status, colour, days spent in hospital and amount of pre-birth medication, Klaus and Kennell (1970) found some discernable differences in how the mothers in the two groups communicated with their children. After one month the extended contact mothers displayed more eye contact with their children during feeding and initiated more active play with their infants than the routine contact mothers. The extended contact mothers reported in diaries thinking about the baby more frequently and staying at home more often than the control group. They also picked up the child more frequently when it cried, soothed their children more.

Early contact may have some long-term effects as well. Kennell *et al.* (1974) report that the differences between the groups still existed one year after birth. Although about 50 per cent of the mothers in both groups had returned to work by this time, most of the control-group mothers did not mention their baby when asked how they felt about this. Most of the extended group mothers admitted that they missed their children. At two years, there appeared to be differences in the way the mothers spoke to their children. The extended contact mothers were asking more questions and issuing fewer commands and differences in IQ have been reported at 42 months.

Multiple Mothering

Rutter says that there is a lack of supportive evidence for Bowlby's (1969) claim that there is a bias for a child to attach himself especially to one figure (described as 'monotropy'). Schaffer (1971) concluded that Bowlby's views were not borne out by the facts, and that the range of the attachments was largely determined by the social setting. Schaffer also stated that it was the intensity rather than the duration of interaction that was crucial. Schaffer and Emerson (1964) showed that parental apathy and lack of response appeared to be more important as inhibitors of the child's attachment, and that the number of care-takers was not a major variable, if the other factors were held constant.

Tizard and her colleagues (1972) have looked at the effects of multiple 'mothering'. Tizard began by examining 65 two-year-olds in residential nurseries. Her nurseries were, however, much more stimulating than those studied by Bowlby. Toys, mobiles and picture books were freely available, and staff were encouraged to communicate with the children. On most measures, these children were very similar to a comparison group of working-class London children, except that their language development was slightly retarded. Tizard and Rees (1974) reported their findings on the same children at four years of age. Some of them had remained in the institution and others had been restored to their natural mothers. Both restored and institution groups had IQs similar to the working-class comparison group.

Tizard *et al.* (1972) studied 85 children of two to five years of age who were being cared for in 13 residential nurseries. The verbal abilities of the children were positively related to the frequency of informative staff talk, staff social activity and the frequency with which staff responded to children's remarks. No evidence of developmental retardation was found.

These results suggest that the quality of adult–child contact is important for cognitive and language development, but a single continuous relationship is not. The staff of these nurseries changed frequently, and close emotional contact was discouraged. The conclusions drawn for social development are, however, that frequent contact with adults is less important than continuity of care. In a follow-up to the earlier studies, Tizard reports that at eight years of age the institution-reared children seemed overly affectionate and 'clinging'. It is possible that this clinging was an attempt to obtain some sort of continuity of caregiving — a response to the frequent changing of caregivers.

Irreversibility of Effects

The extent to which the ill-effects of 'maternal deprivation' are irreversible is another point of controversy. Bowlby's views are that early deprivation was irremediable if no bonding occurred by 30 months of age is countered by numerous research examples. Bakeman and Brown (1980) found that premature infants, who provide mothers with less interesting feedback and bonding reciprocity, did not betray any signs of social and emotional disabilities at age three. Similar results have been found concerning the effects of perinatal anoxia. Although loss of oxygen at birth appears to affect the early mother–infant relationship, there is little evidence of an enduring connection between early morbidity and later psychological dysfunction (Corah, 1965).

Koluchova (1976) describes twin boys who were totally isolated from others from 18 months to seven years of age, through being locked in a cupboard for most of this time. When they were eventually released, they could barely walk, suffered from rickets and their IQs were in the forties. This long period of isolation would be expected to have severe long-term effects on their intellectual and emotional development if early experience was crucial. However after seven years of fostering in a supportive and emotionally caring home, they were found to have average IQs and average social development.

The consideration is now not whether effects are irreversible, but how readily and completely reversible are the effects with regard to each function impaired by deprivation. The evidence on these points remains limited. With cognitive effects there is some tendency to partial remission in time, but reversal becomes less likely the longer privation lasts and the older the child is when removed from the privation. With growth deficits, the compensation is rapid but often not quite complete.

A major criticism of the investigations is that one never knows for certain whether children under a given regime would not have developed similarly under any other regime. For example, studies have been cited that show orphanage children to develop poorly in intellectual skills, to be emotionally flat, and so on. But one might argue that children who are placed in orphanages tend to come from backgrounds that predispose them to these characteristics anyway. For instance, the bulk of children placed early in institutions are illegitimate, and it is said that it is the duller women who fail to take precautions against pregnancy. Control groups to answer such queries are usually impracticable.

Partial Deprivation

The hospitalisation of children is cited as the most common reason for partial deprivation, and it has formed the basis for arguments in favour of home nursing, home confinements, the admission of the mother to hospital or convalescent unit on the illness of the child and so on. Every possible attempt is made to avoid putting a child in short-term institutional care, even where the child in question is being grossly malnourished, or denied medical treatment for illness or accident, or is quite delinquent and uncontrolled. For, in the words of Bowlby himself, 'He may be ill-fed and ill-sheltered, he may be very dirty and suffering from disease, he may be ill-treated, but, unless his parents have wholly rejected him, he is secure in the knowledge that there is someone to whom he is of value and who will strive, even though inadequately, to provide for him until such time as he can fend for himself'.

A child who has not previously been parted from mother may upon hospitalisation pass through three phases according to Bowlby:

(1) Protest. Acute distress may last a week. He seeks to recapture the lost mother by crying, rages, etc. All his behaviour suggests the expectation that she will return and he is apt to reject all alternative figures who offer to do things for him.

(2) Despair. Behaviour now displays increasing hopelessness. Active physical movements diminish or end and he may sob monotonously. Withdrawn and inactive, he makes no demands on his environment. It is like a state of deep mourning.

(3) Detachment. More interest in surroundings, often mistakenly taken as sign of improvement, is apparent. He accepts care, food and toys from nurses. But when mother visits there is absence of strong attachment to her. He may hardly seem to know her. Remote, apathetic and listlessly turning away, he demonstrates his loss of all interest in her.

There are a number of modifying factors in this process. Age is important — the younger the child the more marked the effects; the older, the less severe. Systematic observations of children admitted to hospital have shown that distress is most marked in children aged between six months and four years. The sex of the child is also a factor, a male being more vulnerable to stress. Temperamental factors also have an effect; if the child is initially maladjusted, there will be a more deleterious effect. Also, children who have experienced separation once find a similar experience at a later date particularly traumatic.

Bowlby seems to have over-generalised his case, as many other studies find that some, but not all, children come through short separation without undue misery and emotional disturbance. Illingworth and Holt (1955), for example, used the stringent criteria of emotionally normal during the day and undisturbed after the departure of their visitors during the whole of the observation period (disturbance was defined as looking miserable or crying). They found that 32.4 per cent of one- to four-year-olds in hospital, 56.8 per cent of five- to-six-year-olds, and 72.4 per cent of seven- to-fourteen-year-olds were apparently quite contented.

Douglas and Blomfield (1958) found long-term ill-effects generally followed separation only when this was accompanied by a change of environment, suggesting that the distress may be due to the environment rather than the separation. This would seem particularly true in the case of hospitalisation which involves a sudden introduction into an alien environment full of strange people and intimidating equipment augmenting the normal reactions of pain and fear to any disabling illness. The Illingworth evidence above supports this view that a major reason is the amount of change in the total environment, rather than just the absence of the mother. In the Illingworth study, out of 781 visits, 28.8 per cent of the children cried for their mother when she left them, but also 27.5 per cent cried for the father and 33.7 per cent for both together. They also showed disturbance after 61.7 per cent of the 47 visits made by grandparents. This latter effect was unrelated to the age of the child.

It is very difficult to determine whether the distress and anxiety a young child exhibits is due to separation from parents, admission to hospital, the illness itself or the medical procedures suffered. Intuitively, it is likely that all these variables contribute to varying extents for different individuals. As with adults it does seem that the strange, misunderstood environment with its new routines and unfamiliar faces is a major source of upset.

In a longitudinal study of a national sample of children (Davie, Butler and Goldstein, 1972) covering a wide range of factors, two striking pieces of data relevant to our concern stand out. Firstly, by the age of seven 45 per cent of the sample had been hospitalised at least once and, secondly, the most frequent cause of this admission had been tonsillectomy, an operation the merits of which have been under critical review for some time. Hence the traumatic experience of many children might have been needlessly imposed for some doubtful medical benefit.

For children entering hospital some psychological preparation seems absolutely necessary as both long- and short-term psychological disturbances may appear as a result of hospitalisation and surgery. However, a number of psychologists (e.g. Melamed and Siegel, 1975) argue that the removal of all anxiety is disadvantageous, leading to the cushioning of the individual from reality, whereas the aim ought to be that of supporting the individual and helping him towards developing effective procedures and skills for coping with stress and the realistic conditions he has to face. Hence the major approach is to alleviate the most harmful and deleterious effects of anxiety and stress by psychologically preparing the patient for admission. The major purposes of psychological preparation for hospitalisation are threefold:

(1) to provide basic information to the child at a level he can understand about what he is going to meet and what is going to happen to him;
(2) to encourage emotional expression thereby allowing release of tension to occur within a supportive non-painful environment; and
(3) to establish a trusting relationship with the hospital professionals with whom he will come into close contact.

Melamed (1977) has reported on a series of experiments to find out the best way of preparing children for hospital. This research started from the assumption that observation of a model's behaviour towards a fear stimulus which does not result in any adverse consequences for the model will be imitated. Bandura (1977) showed how emotional behaviour can be extinguished through this modelling procedure (vide Chapter 15.)

Melamed's early studies were undertaken in a pediatric dental clinic. Thirty children who received dental treatment exhibited significantly fewer disruptive behaviours and less anxiety after viewing a film showing a fearless child model coping with the same situation. In later studies Melamed used film of a child entering hospital, undergoing surgery and eventually going home. The group seeing this film were compared with a control group who saw another film unrelated to hospitalisation, on their level of pre- and post-operative anxiety. The use of the modelling film resulted in significantly lower levels of anxiety in the experimental group as measured by palmar sweat both pre- and post-operation (tonsillectomies and hernias) though immediately after the film a higher arousal level was recorded for the experimental group. Observer rating of anxiety behaviours and self-reported hospital fears also showed significantly lower levels for the experimental group. 54 per cent of the children receiving the hospital film preparation were able to eat solid food on the day of the operation as compared to only

26 per cent of the control group. Children's attitudes to medical personnel were also more favourable after viewing the film. The results support the effectiveness of a film to prepare children for hospital experience. Fasler (1980) also reports similar success by providing information, emotional support and a modelling film using nursing and medical staff as the providers.

In a further study Melamed investigated the effects of the time lapse between receiving the film and surgery in relation to the age of the child. Younger children, as has been noted from the work on maternal deprivation, develop greater anxiety. Such youngsters may also require longer to assimilate and understand what they have seen in the film. Children who viewed the film a week in advance of hospitalisation had significantly lower palmar sweating scores at admission than those who saw the film at admission. Children below seven in both groups expressed more worry about hospitalisation than those over seven. The younger children showed that they did not benefit from preparation too far in advance of the actual stressful situation whereas older children showed more benefit from earlier exposure.

Children with previous neurotic tendencies show most disturbance on hospitalisation (Jessner, Blom and Waldfogel, 1952). These researchers also noted that the focus of anxiety changed with age. The under fives were most afraid of hospitalisation and operation; children from seven to ten feared the anaesthetic and operation while older children were mainly afraid of anaesthesia and the associated threat of loss of self control and consciousness.

Parental behaviour in handling the child's reaction in stress situations bears a relationship to how the child copes with hospitalisation. Melamed (1977) reports results showing that when children come from a home where positive reinforcement for approaching feared situations has been used consistently, they will show better coping behaviour and less anxiety during hospitalisation. But where punishment was used to threaten children for their reluctance to face threatening events such children exhibited more anxiety during hospital experience. Children who were encouraged to be dependent on their parents reported greater stress too. It would seem that reassurance from caring parents helps children to deal with stress.

In a series of studies Wolfer and Visintrainer (1975) evaluated the effect of preparing the mothers of children due for minor surgery. Their work is based on the emotional contagion hypothesis which suggests that a parent's emotional state is transmitted to a young child through imitation and modelling, and that upset emotional parents cannot help their offspring cope with stress. The preparation of the mothers involved allowing them to explore and clarify their feelings and thoughts to provide accurate information and reassurance, and showing how the mother could help care for the child. The child component of the preparation involved the provision of accurate information, rehearsals and support. All the preparation and supportive care were provided at stress points such as admission, pre-operative medication, and return from recovery room. The results showed that children and parents who received this systematic psychological preparation and continued supportive care showed significantly less upset, more cooperation in hospital and fewer post-hospital adjustment problems than the control group who had not received any preparation. The experimental group parents also had lower anxiety levels and expressed greater satisfaction with the hospital treatment than the control group parents. Thus the benefit of combining the provision of accurate information with the opportunity of developing a supportive relationship with a nurse at particularly stressful points during hospital experience is well demonstrated.

Older children can bear separation from mothers provided regular visiting is feasible. Unrestricted visiting is the best thing if mothers cannot be admitted to hospital with the child. The more often mother visits the less her departures cause upset. Young children who have not developed any great understanding of the world about them have one overriding need, the security, love and presence of a mother. Separation is hard to bear especially when strange and unpleasant things occur sometimes in a painful context. The child learns to cope with new experiences at her side. Young children have considerable difficulty in understanding the concept of time. They cannot realise how long an hour or a day is. So it is useless telling the child that mummy is coming in two hours. The concept of 'tomorrow' means something far off in the future. It is better to measure time through activities, for instance 'we will have a little lunch now, then a little sleep, and mummy will come when you wake up'.

When mother cannot be present the nurse must replace her as far as possible, one nurse if possible. It is very bewildering for a child to have a rapid succession of care-takers however devoted and caring. Emotional bonds cannot be established in that situation. This bonding of trust, security and affection can only be effected in a personal relationship with one adult. Each of us needs to know he belongs to someone. If mother has apparently deserted the child someone must take her place. When mothers are allowed into hospital with their youngsters they can relieve the nurses of a lot of duties, those which are part of the normal mother–child routine such as washing, feeding, dressing, playing, putting the child to bed, hugging him whenever he is upset. This help allows nurses to devote their time to the more specialist tasks they are trained to perform. In this way the presence of the mother can be quite useful to the functioning of the hospital. Moreover, infants respond to treatment better if mother attends to their basic needs. The child's routine should be altered as little as possible so that it resembles home routine within reason.

Small children need to take some toy or possession from home to provide a link with previous experience and provide emotional security. Personal baby language and signs should be employed by staff to increase security. Children should not be expected to give up well established habits even if they are undesirable, e.g. food fads, dummies, imaginary friends. Once the child has reached secondary school age hospitalisation, particularly the recovery stage, can be an enjoyable experience, a change from the dull routine of going to school and doing homework.

Partial deprivation can also be a result of mothers going out to work. If one followed Bowlby's advice, no mother could go out to work. While there are cases of inadequate supervision and caring while mother works, short breaks away from mother can be beneficial if the previous relationship with her was sound. A break enables a child to develop his independence and self discipline gradually, and provides a chance to relate to others provided no great stress occurs.

There is little indication in research that upset occurs if a separated child is left at home with father or grandparents yet Bowlby still warns against leaving a young child with grandparents. Similarly, whether the child is left at home or sent away, the presence of siblings is effective in preventing upset. Lewis (1954) mentions this phenomenon in her study of deprived children consigned to full-time care away from their families; and in her study of short-term placement in a residential nursery it is admitted that the presence of siblings always mitigates separation experience. If the child can stay in the environment that he is used to, even though a part of it (in the shape of the mother) goes away, or if he can take some of his environment with him (e.g. a sibling) distress is virtually absent. Harlow and Harlow's (1962) work on deprivation in monkeys also shows that the presence of siblings and peer group members can mitigate the effects of mother absence.

David, Ancellin and Appell (1961) investigated both the initial and the later reactions to short separation of children aged between three years ten months and six years six months, placed in a holiday centre for approximately one month. After an initial tearful reaction and confusion, all the children succeeded in emerging from their distress and showed an improvement in personality and broadening of social competence. The nuclear family actually imposes grave limitations even on peer-group relationships for the preschool child, let alone relationships with adults apart from the parents. The social competence of many of our young children is bound to be poor compared with those from societies that provide their young with a wide range of opportunities for social interaction. The provision now and then of a broader environment, where there is stimulation and learning from both warm accepting adults and peers, can be a maturing and stabilising force. Lewis (1954) mentions how children from problem families often ceased, for example, to wet the bed during their stay in the centre, and suggests that the new routine and the relief from disturbing home influences probably brought this about. Howells and Layng (1955) came to the conclusion that the difficulties for the disturbed children often came from being with their parents. Planned separation is seen then as a therapeutic device for some neurotic children. But Bowlby appears to allow for no healthy outcome, for even the child's observed tendency to make relationships rapidly with new care-takers, after the initial shock of a separation experience, is a bad sign for him (of repression). So whether the child succeeds in making relationships with others or not, his behaviour is maladjusted.

Child Abuse

The incidence of child abuse is difficult to ascertain. Physical abuse is visible but yet may not be reported as neighbours and relatives fear intruding on the privacy of other families. Sexual abuse and emotional abuse are far less visible. It is only recently that child abuse has been brought into the legal field.

Parents until comparatively recently have been considered to have the right to treat their children as they saw fit. Animals have been legally protected from cruelty longer than children! Once a child has been born the most extreme form of rejection is infanticide. In our legal system it is recognised that a mother's reaction to her new-born child may be affected by factors not present in other periods in her life. The verdict of infanticide is different from one of murder and applies to cases where a woman causes the death of her new-born child at a time when she has not fully recovered from the effect of giving birth to that child.

The characteristics of families associated with child abuse are many and not always consistently found in different surveys. Gil (1970) provides evidence that child abuse is associated with social conditions such as low income, poor housing and unemployment. According to this viewpoint, environmental stresses are placed on the individual, violence being one possible result. The suggestion is that anyone could become an abusive parent given the circumstances. But this prevalence in deprived conditions may also be due to the visibility issue since social and community workers more frequently visit families whose economic plight is apparent to welfare authorities, making evidence of abuse more likely to be reported. Other major factors involved are personality disturbances in the parent, and the unrewarding nature of some children who may be difficult to handle, handicapped in some way, or the result of an undesired pregnancy.

Personality disturbance in the parent may cause a failure in bonding and as a result generational replication of child abuse is produced with such children abusing their children later. We have noted already that the development of trust in parents is crucial, but this may be difficult to achieve when severe violence is experienced. Emotional as well as physical abuse may be interpreted as parental rejection with serious consequences for self-esteem and the growth of future relationships. Although abuse rarely results in death, physiological and neurological impairment is not uncommon, perhaps in up to 35 per cent of cases. The experience of violence as a child may have another important consequence: it may serve as a model for a method of resolving conflicts in later life.

Several investigators have attempted to correlate ways of coping experienced as a child with favoured methods as adults. Owens and Straus (1975) found such associations. Those who observed and received violence as children were more likely to approve of violent behaviour as adults (such as a husband slapping his wife). In this modelling procedure abused children become child abusers.

O'Connor et al. (1977) related early bonding to lower incidences of later child abuse. In their study, mothers were randomly assigned to either a control group in which the mothers had 20 min. of contact for feeding every four hours in the first two days post-partum, or they were assigned to a 'rooming-in' group, in which the child and his mother had an additional six hours together for each of these first two days. Although the children in these two groups did not differ in the frequency with which they visited the hospital for out-patient care or were ill, at least some were treated differently by their parents. Of the 277 children in the study, no rooming-in children were 'considered to have experienced abuse, neglect or non-organic failure to thrive', whereas nine control group children were considered to have suffered these conditions. Five of this group eventually died. These researchers concluded that mothers who were given close and extended physical contact with their new-born infants were less likely to abuse or neglect their children than women given more limited exposure. This lends more credence to the importance of bonding in infancy as a means of preventing emotional and social disabilities in the child and facilitating parent child interaction.

Prematurity can cause failures in early bonding. Although only 7–8 per cent of live births are premature, approximately 25 per cent of abused children are born prematurely. Perhaps these infants are more difficult to rear because they fuss and cry more than full-term infants and give fewer rewards to their parents. Prematurity is also associated with young mothers who are under stress. Perhaps these women, because of their relative social immaturity, have greater difficulty in coping with their infants' demands.

Lynch *et al.* (1976) studied the relationship between ill health and child abuse. She used the siblings of abused children as the comparison group. She found several differences, including a higher incidence of abnormal pregnancies and deliveries and, important for the attachment hypothesis, a greater likelihood of separation between mother and child for the first 48 hours after birth and over the next six months. A later study indicated that abused children were twice as likely to have been in a special care nursery after birth than a comparison group. While many parents who use violence come from deprived backgrounds, not all with such childhood experiences become abusive. Similarly, many battered children are premature, but only a minority of premature children are battered. This has two implications. First, abuse might be more appropriately considered as lying along a continuum that includes nutritional and emotional neglect as well as physical abuse, so that it is a question of degree rather than of kind. When some 95 per cent of parents report that they smack their children, 7 per cent daily, it does not seem sensible to say that physical punishment itself is a sign of serious abuse. Second, it may be more fruitful to consider violence as a result of many factors, several of which in concert can make it more probable. The cumulative effects of unwanted pregnancy, prematurity in the child, youthfulness in the parents, social and economic stresses, personality and past experience with violence may all contribute. This notion is of accumulating stress. No single negative experience is likely to have long-lasting effects on personality development, but continued deprivation and stress might.

In some hospitals all parents who may have difficulty in forming attachment bonds because of the baby's need for special care are seen by a social worker and given the opportunity to discuss practical and social problems. In another study, three groups of mothers were followed up after the birth of their child. One group consisted of mothers not considered at risk on the basis of labour-room and post-partum observations. A second group of at risk mothers was given comprehensive paediatric follow-up by a physician and a health visitor, and a third group, similar to the second, was given no such assistance. In this latter group of 50 families, five children were later hospitalised for treatment of serious injuries whereas, by contrast, none of the high-risk intervention group nor the low-risk group required such hospitalisation (Douglas, 1975).

Behaviour modification may have much to offer. By analysing the patterns of stimulus and response, the contingencies that lead to abuse and neglect can be discovered. Abuse might be triggered by loud crying in the infant, for example, so that a parent could be given systematic desensitisation treatment to increase toleration of loud noises.

Perhaps parents who abuse their children see punishment as the main means of control. They might be briefed in the basics of the operant model and encouraged to achieve control with rewards instead of punishments. This is a form of family therapy.

Helfer and Kempe (1976) have produced a scale which is useful in predicting risk of later child abuse. This method is based on observations taken in the delivery room and postnatal clinic on the mother's reactions to her neonate. It is claimed that 75 per cent of high-risk children can be identified this way. Examples of the items the doctors and nurses look for on Helfer and Kempe's scale are:

Does the family remain disappointed over sex of baby?
What was/is the husband's and/or family's reaction to the new baby?

Are they supportive?
Are they critical?
Do they attempt to take over and control the situation?
Is the husband jealous of the baby's drain on the mother's time and energy?
Concern-arousing reactions at delivery include:
Lack of interest in the baby, ambivalence, passive reaction.
Keeping the focus of attention on herself.
Unwillingness or refusal to hold the baby, even when offered.
Hostility directed toward father, who put her 'through all this'.
Inappropriate verbalisations, glances directed at the baby, with definite hostility expressed.
Disparaging remarks about the baby's sex or physical characteristics.
Disappointment over sex or other physical characteristics of the child.
Is the mother bothered by the baby's crying?
How does it make her feel? Angry? Inadequate? Like crying herself?
Are her verbalisations about the child usually negative?
When the child cries, does she, or can she, comfort him?
Does she have complaints about the child that cannot be verified?

Summary

Bowlby initiated interest in this area with an alarming picture of the maternally deprived child and dogmatic statements about future behaviour and development. His work had considerable influence on organisations concerned with child care. Current reassessments of maternal deprivation allow for more varied and benign outcomes and critically consider some of the terms and concepts involved such as 'attachment', 'deprivation', and 'critical period'. However there is little doubt that adult–child interaction in a warm, caring relationship is important for later life adjustment although if it is lacking poor adjustment does not necessarily follow.

The effect of partial deprivation in hospital has been clearly shown, and it is possible to reduce the effect by adequate preparation of the child for hospitalisation using modelling procedures. Mothers absent through going out to work do not appear to cause damage to the child's social and emotional development.

Child abuse appears to be associated with deprived social conditions and parental personality disturbance. Early bonding of mother to new born child appears to reduce the incidence of child abuse. Neonates to whom it is difficult to form an attachment, e.g. premature and handicapped babies, are likely to become victims. High risk babies can now be identified.

Activities

1. Many different kinds of day-care arrangements have been identified. The major concern about day care is that the facilities should provide more than simple custodial care for children. Visit one establishment and note how it concerns itself with these categories: (1) nutrition, (2) health and safety, (3) child-caretaker relationships, (4) peer relationships, (5) play, exploration, and problem-solving, (6) language development, (7) motor development, (8) coordination of home and day-care centre, (9) physical environment, (10) sex-role socialisation.

2. Collect some newspaper cuttings on child abuse cases, or if it is possible go and listen to a court case too. Try to identify some of the factors that are associated with child abuse in these cases.

Questions

1. What do you understand by the term 'maternal deprivation'?
2. What are the major needs of young children when they are hospitalised?
3. How might the effects of mother–child separation on young children in hospital be reduced?
4. Imagine you have been asked to talk to prospective mothers at an antenatal clinic about the effects on young children of their mothers working. What points would you include in your talk?
5. Suppose you are a member of a debating team and your opponent has argued that the father contributes very little to his child's development. Your task is to counter this argument. Present your case.

6. What factors affect the success of substitute mothering?
7. Suppose you are a social worker and child abuse is a known problem in many of the families under your jurisdiction. What aspects of the parents' social environment influence the abuse of their children? What support systems in your community could be utilised to prevent the future occurrence of child abuse?
8. What might be the psychological impact on the mother and father of the new born's unusual appearance? Consider in your answer the implications of its apparent helplessness and fragility and the impact of its lack of muscular control. Would you expect the impact to be more marked for fathers or mothers? Why?
9. Why are the effects of early experience not necessarily permanent?
10. What is known about the reasons for baby-battering, and what effect on the child could such treatment produce?
11. What psychological principles are relevant when looking after children in residential care?
12. What steps can be taken to involve fathers in both the birth and early parenting?
13. Do you think that the way in which a birth is conducted affects the parents' acceptance of the new baby?
14. Critically evaluate Bowlby's work.

Further Reading

Ainsworth, M.D. (1973) 'The development of infant–mother attachment' in B. Caldwell and H. Riccinti (eds.) *Review of Child Development Research* vol. 3, Chicago: University of Chicago Press

Bee, H. (1977) *Social Issues in Developmental Psychology*, New York: Harper

Bowlby, J. (1965) *Child Care and the Growth of Love*, Harmondsworth: Penguin

Braun, S.J. and Caldwell, B.M. (1973) 'Emotional adjustment of children in day care who enrolled prior to or after the age of three', *Early Child Development and Care*, 2, 13–21

Clarke, A.M. and Clarke, A.D. (1976) *Early Experience: Myth and Evidence*, London: Open Books

Clarke-Stewart, A. (1977) *Child Care in the Family*, New York: Academic Press

Cornelius, S.W. and Denney, N.W. (1975) 'Dependency in day-care and home-care children', *Devel. Psychology, 11*, 575–82

Doyle, A.B. (1975) 'Infant development in day care', *Develop. Psychology, 11*, 655–6

Klaus, M. and Kennell, J. (1982) *Parent–Infant Bonding*, St Louis: C.V. Mosby

Morgan, P. (1975) *Child Care: Sense and Fable*, London: Temple Smith

National Day Care Study (1979) *Final report: Children at the centre*, Massachusetts: Abt Associates

Parke, R.D. (1979) 'Perspectives on father–infant interaction' in J.D. Osofsky (ed.) *Handbook of Infant Development*, New York: Wiley-Interscience

Schwarz, J.C., Strickland, R.C. and Krolick, G. (1974) 'Infant day care: Behavioral effects at pre-school age', *Devel. Psychology, 10*, 502–6

Smith, S. (1975) *The Battered Child Syndrome*, London: Butterworth

Rutter, M. (1972) *Maternal Deprivation Reassessed*, Harmondsworth: Penguin

Tizard, J. (1976) *All Our Children*, London: Smith

Trisliotis, J. (1980) *New Developments in Foster Care and Adoption*, London: Routledge

References

Bakeman, R. and Brown, R. (1980) 'Early interaction', *Child Devel., 51*, 437–47

Bandura, A. (1977) *Social Learning Theory*, New Jersey: Prentice Hall

Bowlby, J. (1969) *Attachment and Loss* vol. 1, London: Hogarth

Corah, N. (1965) 'The effect of perinatal anoxia after seven years', *Psychol. Monogr., 79*, Whole No. 596

David, M., Ancellin, G. and Appell, G. (1961) 'A study of nursing care and nurse–infant interaction' in B.M. Foss (ed.) *Determinants of Infant Behaviour*, vol. 1, London: Methuen

Davie, R., Butler, N. and Goldstein, H. (1972) *From Birth to Seven*, London: Longman

Douglas, J. (1975) 'Early hospital admissions and later disturbances of behaviour and learning', *Devel. Med. Child Neur., 17*, 456–80

Douglas, J. and Blomfield, J. (1958) *Children Under Five*, London: Allen and Unwin

Fasler, D. (1980) 'Reducing pre-operative anxiety in children', *Patient Couns. Health Educ., 2*, 130–4

Gil, D.G. (1970) *Violence Against Children*, Cambridge, Mass.: Harvard University Press

Goldfarb, W. (1945) 'Effects of psychological deprivation in infancy', *Amer. J. Psychiat., 102*, 18

Harlow, H. and Harlow, M. (1962) 'Social deprivation in monkeys', *Scientific Amer., 207*, 136

Helfer, R. and Kempe, C. (1976) *Child Abuse and Neglect*, Cambridge: Ballinger Pub. Company

Herbert, M. and Sluckin, W. (1982) 'Mother to infant bonding', *J. Child Psychol. Psychiat., 23*, 205–21

Howells, J. and Layng, J. (1955) 'Separation experiences and mental health', *Lancet, 2*, 285

Illingworth, R.S. and Holt, K.S. (1955) 'Children in hospital', *Lancet, 2*, 1257–62

Jessner, L., Blom, G. and Waldfogel, S. (1952) 'Emotional implications of tonsillectomy and adenoidectomy in children' in R. Eissler (ed.) *The Psychoanalytic Study of the Child*, New York: International Universities Press

Kennel, J., Jerauld, R. and Wolfe, H. (1974) 'Maternal behaviour one year after early and extended post-partum contact', *Devel. Med. Child Neur., 16*, 172–9

Klaus, H. and Kennel, J. (1970) 'Human maternal behaviour at first contact with her young', *Pediatrics, 46*, 187–92

Koluchova, J. (1976) 'Further development of twins after severe and prolonged deprivation', *J. Child Psychol. Psychiat., 17*, 181–8

Lewis, H. (1954) *Deprived Children*, Oxford: Oxford University Press

Lynch, M.A., Roberts, J. and Gordon, M. (1976) 'Child abuse: early warning in the maternity hospital', *Devel. Med. Child Neur., 18*, 759–66

Melamed, B. (1977) 'Psychological preparation for hospitalisation' in S. Rachman (ed.) *Contributions to Medical Psychology*, London: Pergamon

Melamed, B. and Siegal, L. (1975) 'Reduction of anxiety in children facing surgery by modelling', *J. Consult. Clin. Psychol., 43*, 511

O'Connor, S., Vietze, P. and Hopkins, J. (1977) 'Post-partum extended maternal infant contact', *Pediatric Res., 11*, 380

Owens, D. and Straus, M. (1975) 'The social structure of violence in childhood and approval of violence as an adult', *Aggressive Behaviour, 1*, 193–211

Rutter, M. (1972) *Maternal Deprivation Reassessed*, Harmondsworth: Penguin

Schaffer, H.R. (1971) *The Growth of Sociability*, Harmondsworth: Penguin

Schaffer, H. and Emerson, P. (1964) 'The development of social attachment in infancy', *Monogr. Soc. Res. in Child Devel., 29* No. 94

Tizard, B., Cooperman, O., Joseph, A. and Tizard, J. (1972) 'Environmental effects on language development', *Child Devel., 43*, 337–58

Tizard, B. and Rees, J. (1974) 'A comparison of the effects of adoption and continued institutionalisation on the cognitive development of four-year-old children', *Child Devel., 45*, 92–9

Wolfer, J. and Visintrainer, M. (1975) 'Psychological preparation for surgical pediatric patients', *Pediatrics, 49*, 232

10 SELF-CONCEPT DEVELOPMENT

The self-concept, in contemporary psychology, is becoming a most important construct in the explanation of human behaviour. The self-concept is the set of attitudes a person holds towards himself. It is an important concept because, of all the reasons for the current surge of interest in the study of human behaviour, none is more compelling than the desire of individuals to know more about themselves, to understand what makes them tick. It influences all aspects of behaviour, because the way we feel about and evaluate aspects of ourselves influences how we will function in any situation.

The Composition of the Self-Concept

The self-concept is composed of two essential elements: (a) one's self-image or conception of oneself, the sort of person one is, and (b) one's self-esteem, or self-evaluation.

The Self-Image

The self-image is the summation of the practically limitless ways in which each person perceives himself. At this point it might be helpful to write down a list of descriptions and attributes relevant to yourself, about what you are, and how you see yourself. Your list may contain elements such as these: female, spinster, shy, atheist, car owner, student, intelligent, too tall, enjoys ballet, happy, kind, lazy.

Self-Esteem

This is the evaluation or judgement placed on each element of the self-image. Because conceptions or self-images of what one is like are so personal, they possess positive or negative connotations, which are often derived or learned from society.

It is the combination of self-image and the individual esteem or societal evaluation of those characteristics that forms the self-concept and places it within the realm of attitudes. Attitudes are evaluated beliefs predisposing one to behave in one way rather than another, and the evaluated beliefs of the self-concept direct behaviour too. In this sense we can come to regard the self-concept, not as a singular entity, for we each possess many self-concepts (evaluated self-images) relating to our roles and statuses, but as a plurality of attitudes to oneself in a variety of daily contexts and behaviours. A child, for example, may hold separate and different self-concepts (or self-attitudes) to himself as a boy, as a son, as a student, as a dare-devil, and as a member of the school football team. This evaluative loading of the self-concept is learned and, since it is learned, it can alter in direction and weighting as other learning experiences are encountered. For example, a pupil may have a concept of himself as a bright student deriving from his performance in school examinations and the feedback he receives from teacher and peers. This brings pleasure and satisfaction, since being a bright student has positive connotations within society and at home, where the achievement motive and success have been positively reinforced. However, this positive self-evaluation may fluctuate as increasingly harder work brings poorer examination results or as significant others in the peer group begin to evaluate other performances such as athletic prowess as more important. Again as time passes the bright student might find in adulthood that academic success is not the sole criterion of happiness or getting on in life, so that a lowering of the weighting occurs though it still remains positive. So self-evaluation is not fixed; it relates to each particular context. The evaluative significance of most concepts is taken from the surrounding culture in that many evaluations have become normative. Dull, fat, immature and ill all have negative evaluations for instance, while clever, muscular, dependable and healthy all possess positive overtones. Not only are the evaluative overtones learned from the culture but, by self-observation and by feedback from social interaction, such evaluative concepts come to be applied to the individual.

The Development of the Individual Self-Concept

The self-concept is learned and develops out of the mass of 'I', 'me' and 'mine' experiences which bombard the individual. At first, the infant cannot differentiate between self and not-self, and for most of the first year of his life his sense of self suffers from over-extension encompassing even his caretakers so that to be separated from them is analogous to losing a part of his own physical body.

Self-awareness is aided as the infant uses and acts on his environment. In his explorations, from which he makes eventual sense of the world, the child notices and manipulates things that are not him. At first he seems almost to proceed by accident, but later he does so by design. At first when objects are placed in his hand he is able to grasp them but not able, at will, to release them or throw or move them about. Soon, however, he is able to grasp and to release, to reach for things and place them in a certain spot. When he uses this ability he probably has a dim awareness of himself as one who can produce effects by his own actions — for instance, when he knocks a suspended mobile hanging over his cot to make it tinkle repeatedly. This discovery of self through motor activity links with the equally important means of discovering self through the sense organs. These sensations and motor activities, however simple, play an important role in defining the boundaries of the body, a vital stage in differentiating self from the rest of the environment.

Piaget (1952) emphasises that a major achievement of the sensori-motor stage is the infant's gradual distinction of himself from the external world. The self-concept, however rudimentary and diffuse, is born at the moment when the differentiation becomes a reality. As a corollary, the young child is able to view others as separate entities too, enabling him to attribute purpose and intention to them. But the process is accelerated by the advent of language — at two years old the pronouns 'mine', 'me', 'you', and 'I' come into use; such pronouns serve as conceptualisations of the self and others.

The development of the self-concept does not occur in an all-or-none fashion which permits us to say that up to one point in time the child does not possess a self-concept, but then suddenly, eureka-like, he has. Moreover, the process of self-concept development never really ends; it is actively proceeding from birth to death as the individual continually discovers new potentials in the process of 'becoming'. In summary, to have a self-concept the child must come to view himself as a distinct object and be able to see himself as both subject and object, distinguishing himself from other objects. He must then become aware of other perspectives, for only in that way can he be aware of the evaluations of others about himself.

Body Image

One of the first aspects which seriously affects the child's view of himself would appear to be his body image. Adults frequently draw the attention of children to size, other physical attributes and sex role. The body image involves an estimation and evaluation of the physical apparatus in terms of social norms and feedback from others.

The person's concept of himself as a physical person becomes difficult to separate early in childhood from his concept of himself as a total person. In early childhood and again at adolescence (Chapter 11) emphasis on the physical qualities of the individual is strongly marked and at these periods physical attributes and deficiencies (both real and imagined) can have considerable effects on the development of a person's overall self-concept. After initial sex typing by parents at birth, body size and shape is the most conspicuous physical attribute during childhood. In adolescent society greater body size offers avenues of prestige and power for the male, some socially sanctioned, e.g. sport, and some completely anti-social, e.g. gang fights. But extreme height can be detrimental as witness the 'bean-pole' girl or boy. What is apparent is that the norm is above the mean on height and strength for males, and on bust size for females, but below the mean on height and weight for females. It is quite disruptive on personality to view one's body as dimensionally too different from the desired norm. Jourard and Secord (1955) demonstrated that male students had most satisfaction with their bodies when they were big; females were more satisfied with the body if they were shorter than normal.

A person's height, weight, complexion, eyesight and body proportions become closely associated with his attitudes to himself and feelings of personal adequacy and acceptability. Like all other elements of self-conception, the body image is subjective, but no other element is more open to private and public evaluation. The body is the most visible and sensed part of a person. We see, feel and hear a lot of ourselves; the body is a central feature in much of our self-perception.

The relationship between body build and personality is at best tenuous despite the attempts of Kretschmer (1925) and Sheldon and Stevens (1942). Much of the aetiology of the relationship may lie within the realm of social learning, of stereotypes, and of expectation effects. Individuals tend to behave in line with the expectations of others. If these expectations are consistent over time and individuals, one can expect emitted behaviour consistent with the expectations. This provides a self-validating prophecy. The cultural stereotypes of the tall, thin, parsimonious Scrooge, the obese, jovial Mr Pickwick, and the active, strong, athletic Tarzan each establish specific expectations of behaviour for the possessor and for the others with whom he interacts. Research does provide quite convincing evidence that different body builds evoke different reactions from others in a consistent way. A powerful, muscular boy must experience a completely different world from his puny counterpart.

Staffieri (1957) demonstrated with boys as young as six years old that stereotypes of behaviour are associated with body types. These boys described those with endomorphic build (obese, heavy) as socially offensive and delinquent; those with mesomorphic build (athletic, muscular) as aggressive, outgoing, active and having leadership skills; and those with ectomorphic builds (tall, thin) as retiring, nervous, shy and introverted. In addition, it was also found that ectomorphs and mesomorphs were more apt to be chosen as the most popular; the endomorphic children were not only inclined to be less popular, but more often they were among those who had negative, rejecting feelings about their corpulent body image.

The mesomorphic build was regarded as most favourable by these youngsters and was regarded as the ideal male physique. The subjects also showed a clear preference to look like a mesomorph, and could with reasonable accuracy indicate their own body type at seven years of age. Since the broad shouldered, muscular boy and the well proportioned young lady are more likely to gain social approval on the basis of their body builds than others, then their self-concepts are more likely to be highly positive. It is the feedback from others plus the knowledge that one's body build is strongly culturally approved that provides the positive gain.

A child's self-concept is not caused by this or that body type, but it is possible to say that a child's physical appearance plays an important part as far as the feedback content he gets is concerned. Children employ nicknames for each other which mostly reflect bodily appearance. Consider the problems of the endomorphic child who is the target of such barbs as 'Tubby', 'Fatso' or 'Billy Bunter', and the ectomorphic child who can be tagged with 'Skinny' or 'Big Ears'. Children are past masters at picking on, rather cruelly, those physical characteristics that stand out, then exaggerating them to the level of defamatory caricatures. When these nicknames emanate from significant others, such descriptions serve not only as physical descriptions but generalise to define the total person. The primary school-age child is extremely receptive to both peer and adult input concerning his person and performance, more ready to believe and incorporate into his personality and behaviour those things he hears about himself. Even simple and superficially harmless statements can be converted in the child's mind to vital self-conceptions which are lived up to and by as if moral precepts. For instance, when John catches the table leg with his shoes Mother might say 'It's those big, clumsy feet of yours'. He may continue to regard himself as clumsy and big-footed throughout all his life, tripping up, catching furniture, showing poor coordination for jumping or climbing, etc. He behaves consistently with his conception of himself.

Do you remember your nickname at school? Do you recall the nicknames you attached to others, such as members of your peer group, your teachers etc.? How did the nickname affect your feelings about yourself? Did your friends live up to the behavioural connotations of their nicknames? It is not difficult for you to realise that carrying around a descriptive name like 'Fatty', 'Specs', 'Weed' or 'Spotty' is not conducive to the development of a positive self-concept.

'Oh, that this too, too solid flesh would melt . . .' bewails the unhappy possessor of a physical body that fails to measure up to either its owner's or others' evaluation of the ideal body image. The proud bearer of such names as 'Killer' or 'Knocker' will have little difficulty in developing a positive self-image. Names primarily employed to describe physical appearance so easily come to define the whole person. In this and other ways the body image comes to determine in considerable measure general self-esteem level.

Feedback from Significant Others

Another major source of self-conception, besides body image, is feedback from significant others. Mead (1934) elaborated on this source of self-esteem in the early days of self-concept theory. Cooley (1912) introduced the concept of the 'looking glass' self to describe the self as perceived through the reflections in the eyes of others. Parents are presumed to be the most significant others in a child's environment.

The earliest feedback to the infant about how people feel about him lies in the reduction of physiological needs. As the infant is being fed, changed, bathed, he also receives a message that he is valued and accepted. Fondling, caressing, smiles and 'baby talk' dispensed by mother (and even father!) are communications indicating that the infant is esteemed. Through this a person learns to seek out the feeling of being valued by others, since it is associated in the past with the reduction of physiological discomfort.

All humans need love, acceptance and security — most of all young children. The receipt of love and acceptance is very satisfying, but to know whether he is receiving any the child must observe the face, gestures, the verbalisations and other signs of significant others, usually parents. Each experience of love or rejection, each experience of approval or disapproval from others, causes him to view himself and his behaviour in the same way. During childhood the child anchors his perception of himself very much in his own direct experience of physical self and of the reactions of significant others to him, particularly parents.

Syngg and Combs (1949, p. 83) have also emphasised the vital effects of constructing how significant others evaluate one. They argue,

> As he is loved or rejected, praised or punished, fails or is able to compete, he comes gradually to regard himself as important or unimportant, adequate or inadequate, handsome or ugly, honest or dishonest ... He is likely therefore to be affected by the labels which are applied to him by other people.

This rather direct feedback that parents, children, adolescents and students commonly convey to each other has been shown in several studies to affect the individual's self-concept. Guthrie (1938) describes how a dull, unattractive female student was treated by some male students for a time as though she was tremendously popular and attractive. Within a year she developed an easy manner, confidence and popularity, which increased the eliciting of positive reinforcing reactions from others.

As the child grows older, extension of his environment leads to increasing social interaction and more feedback of information that is subjectively evaluated and assimilated into the self-concept. School is the major environmental extension and allows the development of new skills, providing the individual with a more evaluative context in which to compare himself with others and perceive the others' evaluation of him. In-group and out-group categories become available encouraging the labelling and categorising of others and self. School augments the processes that are involved in developing a self-picture as Staines (1958) has shown so well in his study of the subtle influences of teachers and their verbalisations to pupils. How often have teachers said such things as, 'Peter, close the window please — no, sit down, you're not tall enough. John could you close it please, you're the tallest!' Teachers' run-of-the-mill comments are fraught with evaluational, emotional and status content for pupils. During the junior school period the process of identification with parents loses some of its force as peer groups, pop idols, sport stars, etc., are substituted as models to be emulated. From this period the self-concept seems in most children to become fairly settled and stable, despite the supposed *Sturm und Drang Periode* (storm and stress period) of adolescence. Only as a result of extreme conditions does it alter drastically, for example after survival training of the Outward Bound type.

The two major empirical works on the antecedents of the self concept are Rosenberg's (1965) investigation of social conditions associated with levels of self-evaluation in adolescents, and Cooper-smith's (1967) study with younger children. They both found that broader social context may not play as important a role interpreting one's own self-concept as is often assumed. This finding was emphasised by the discovery that the amount of parental attention and concern was the significant factor. In moving away from global societal variables to the more effective interpersonal environment, Coopersmith, and Rosenberg both focused research interest on 'significant others'; day-to-day relationships rather than external standards provide the major source of self-evaluation.

Those distortions in attachment, generally studied under the aegis of maternal deprivation, which appear to create defective social relationships are learning situations which teach the unfortunate offspring to interpret himself as rejected, neglected, unloved, unacceptable or incompetent, or any combination of such debilitating attributes (see Chapter 9). So feedback from within the family circle and from school, in climates of varying degees of acceptance and warmth, seems to be the most potent source of self-conception.

Another origin of the self-concept is actual comparison with other people. These may include fairly objective measures such as height, weight, sporting ability, examination results, etc. Most people like to have information about the relative performance of those who are similar to themselves; this facilitates more accurate self-evaluation. The performance of others forms a frame of reference, and gives meaning to poor, average and good standards.

The crucial arena for arriving at a clearer and realistic picture of one's assets and liabilities does seem to be that of peer interaction. Peers approximate in size and age, whereas at home there exists an age hierarchy with even brothers and sisters being older or younger. So, at home, differences in competence are expected, but in the peer group the child need only show he is at least equal with others. At home he must be love-worthy, within the peer group he must be respect-worthy, competitive and competent. The penalties of failure are self-concept components of humiliation, rejection and derogation from self and others. These different expectations between home and peer group are due to the former placing a high premium on behaviour, while the latter places it on performance. In fact, behaviour unacceptable by parents may well be ignored in the peer group, or even acceptable!

Self-Concept and Schooling

Self-concept and educational performance are closely linked. Educational institutions are the arenas in which all young persons are compelled to compete, and in doing so are forced to reveal personal adequacies and inadequacies in public contests, frequently on unequal terms with others, in events not even of their own choosing, against externally imposed standards. Given the heavy emphasis on competition and the pressures applied by teachers and most parents on children to achieve success, it is not surprising that children employ academic attainment as an important index of self worth. The evaluations of others become self-evaluations, so that a successful student comes to feel competent and significant; a failing student comes to feel incompetent and inferior. The child's world is school, his basic tasks are school tasks; it is the most salient area of his life, and yet so public, open to inspection by significant others. It is no wonder that with the unavoidability of academic pursuits, the cultural stress on success and the ubiquity of assessment and competition, life in school is a patent influence on self esteem. There is overwhelming evidence of the positive association between self-concept and academic achievement. The numerous research studies summarised by Purkey (1970), and Burns (1982) are more than adequate testimony to the fact that low self-esteem or self-concepts that do not contain the view that the child is competent or can succeed in his school-based activities tend to produce underachievement and poor performance levels, and in some cases withdrawal from academic activities. What is equally certain is that children who possess positive self-concepts are able to make more positive and clearer appraisals of their ability to perform in the school milieu and actually produce results in their academic studies which are superior to those turned in by pupils with more uncertain and negative feelings about themselves. In surveying American research Purkey (1970, p. 15) concluded that 'overall the research evidence clearly shows a persistent and significant relationship between the self-concept and academic achievement'.

Purkey (1978) defines the teacher as an inviter, who sends invitations, through formal and non formal, verbal and non-verbal means, in writing and unwriting ways to students to see themselves as able, valuable and acceptable. Good teaching he sees as inviting students to view themselves in a positive way, enabling them to grow and realise their potential. Conversely Purkey defines a disinvitation as an interaction that tells a pupil he is incapable, worthless and not acceptable.

Rosenthal and Jacobsen (1968) attempted to explain their Pygmalion findings in terms of the probable ways teachers treated the designated 'bloomer' students. This explanation is consistent with the theory that differential expectations are communicated through differential teacher behaviours toward different students. Although this piece of research was poorly designed and analysed, other work in the area of teacher expectation does support the view that teacher expectations influence pupil academic performance through the mediation of pupil self-concept. For example Barker-Lunn (1970) in a study of streaming in Britain found that the A stream pupils had a high self-image as did children who were near the top of the B and C streams. Underachieving children in nonstreaming schools had a poor self-image and seemed ashamed of their apparent 'stupidity'. Teachers constantly compared them, much to their detriment, with the more able members of their stream or class. One teacher in the study remarked in front of the class, 'I don't like teaching dull children; I wasn't trained to teach them. Those are my bright children over there (pointing to a row by the window), the average are in the middle and the dull children are over there.' Not surprisingly, interaction with teacher and the teacher's rating of the child's ability significantly predicted self-esteem. Rist (1970) in an observational and longitudinal study of a black kindergarten teacher in America and her 30 black pupils claims that many children are 'locked in' to a particular life style, treatment and self-evaluation by early labelling such as 'retarded'.

Canfield and Wells (1976) use the term 'killer statements' to describe the means by which a student's feelings, thoughts, and creative behaviours are 'killed off' by another person's negative comments, physical gestures or other behaviour. These actions may be little more than a teacher's suddenly stiffened spine when a child of another race touches him — or as elusive as a teacher who seldom calls on certain children in the classroom. But they may be far more overt, involving a verbal barrage telling the child he is worthless, or incapable or irresponsible.

However, success cannot simply be equated with getting work correct. Attaining high scores where little effort is required to ensure full marks can be boring and frustrating, providing no positive experience. Similarly, work that is too difficult, quite beyond the knowledge and competence of the pupil, is equally frustrating and anxiety provoking. Hence, success experiences need to be perceived phenomenologically from the point of view of the pupil. This perspective suggests that success has two components: firstly, a clearly delineated goal that is potentially attainable, and secondly, progress towards that goal. Of course, the teacher guides the child to suitable goals and provides a milieu in which, by a series of progressively moving subgoals, the child is led forward academically, competing against his previous best rather than against externally imposed standards he may never be able to attain. Even the most handicapped child can obtain success experiences.

Disability, Handicap and the Self-Concept

The wearing of glasses, a freckled face or being overweight can be magnified subjectively by some as gross self defects, leading to dissatisfaction and low self-esteem. An actual physical disability must be regarded as the ultimate level leading to such self-derogation. Disability is not only a medical matter for it involves a social value judgement. A disability may be evaluated objectively, in the sense that constraints on mobility, manipulatory skills, hearing, etc., can be quantified, but the handicapping nature of the disability cannot be so accurately assessed. This will depend on the individual child's perception of his difficulties and whether the social climate either encourages or inhibits his striving to compensate for them. It is both a social value judgement and a personal one — a self value judgement which is, of course, powerfully affected by the attitudes of, and interaction with, others. Any loss of physical function is likely to be viewed negatively, and the negative values derive from three sources: the nature of the disability, negative values imposed by the self, and negative ones imposed by society.

Continued failure may mean that some disabled children reduce their expectations, and in extreme cases may so restrict themselves as to be unable to sustain a viable self-image. Cumulative failure means frustration and personal devaluation, though the limitation which the disability imposes may be less than that which the person imposes on himself. If continued over a long period, the restriction on activities and experiences will eventually restrict the kind of person he is. Such negative self-evaluation may have its roots in the temperament or personality of the disabled child or in his acceptance and application to himself of others' evaluation of his disability. Rehabilitation workers have observed this in the adventitiously handicapped who, after their injury, apply to themselves those attitudes about physical variations which formerly they shared with others. Other people's attitudes to disability form the social and psychological 'matrix' in which the disabled person lives.

A major element of the self-concept as we have seen is the body image, constructed from postural cues, tactile impressions, visual appearance, degree of functional effectiveness and from social reinforcement. The disabled child can receive negative feedback from his own body and via the responses of others during his formative years, while his body image is being constructed. The work of Richardson *et al.* (1964) suggests that disabled children share the value system of non-handicapped peers, and we may assume that perception by the handicapped of the high value placed on normal physique provides a tension between actual and ideal body images. This tension is occasionally revealed in handicapped children's self-portraits where the area of physical deviation is either exaggerated or disregarded. Generally research shows that the greater the level of disability the more negative the self-concept.

For the child handicapped from birth, the sensory and motor experiences through which a normal child learns the definition of self, are less accessible. As a baby he may have had less chance to distinguish reliably between self and non-self through moving and watching his limbs, grasping toys, and having an effect on things in general. Physical and/or sensory deficits are bound to limit learning about self, and lead to a sensing that others do not expect too much of them. Hence feedback is limited and limiting in its effect on the development of the self-concept. The handicapped child's experiences must be brought as close as possible to those of the normal child by adapting toys, tricycles etc. so that movement, experience and positive feedback can be provided. But a handicapped child must develop a self-concept that involves a realisation of handicap and a realistic appraisal of his capabilities. The self-concept of the handicapped child must include, as indeed it should for a normal child, an acceptance of limitations and a belief in developing potential to the full.

A handicap acquired later in childhood demands a more sudden readjustment. The self-concept has to be altered and a new one accepted. An important element in a person's self-concept is his perception of roles he can play towards others and his perception of the roles they might wish to play towards him. He needs to reshape what he sees as others' perception of him. If his concept of himself is too different from the way that others actually see him, he is likely to become maladjusted to his new situation.

Being sick, handicapped or disabled involves playing a particular part in relation to other people, and expecting others to perform roles appropriate to a sick person. This may involve expecting to be looked after, absolved of responsibility, and acquiesced to. Playing a sick role is necessary at times, and usual in the early stages of disability, but can cause problems within a family if it continues for too long or beyond the time when it is necessary. A series of recognisable reactions towards handicaps have been noted, all of which are normal and natural to some extent but can cause problems if they are excessive or last too long.

Denial may occur, a refusal to accept that anything is wrong: this is seen as the individual's way of unconsciously protecting himself from a too sudden shock, and has been noted particularly in cases where the handicap is acquired suddenly.

Anxiety and depression frequently occur as reactions to the loss of former self-concept and some former skills. Other reactions — generally felt to occur largely at an unconscious level without the person being fully aware of what is happening — are regression, where the child behaves like someone younger, perhaps becoming overdependent; withdrawal from contact with other people; increased use of fantasy, again, as an escape from facing the reality of the handicap; and projection, where feelings of inadequacy are deflected onto others and reversed so that he sees others as regarding him as inadequate. None of these reactions is inevitable. However, it is usual for a few of these reactions to be noticed to some degree.

Many handicapped young people often have unrealistic aspirations if they have been brought up in institutions with contact only with other handicapped young people. Competing with non-handicapped persons can be a shock. Thus training programmes for such children need to include much exposure to the world the child will have to live in. The less severely handicapped may have more stressful social situations than the severely handicapped. They are in a 'marginal' position. The mild handicap can be covered up yet they are always in a position where it might be uncovered. So some mildly handicapped persons go to great lengths to avoid some social situations or produce elaborate reasons for errors resulting from handicap.

In a major study Richardson *et al.* (1964) obtained self-descriptions from physically handicapped and normal children in order to examine the effects of severe disability on a handicapped child's conception of himself. The disabled children emphasised physical function restrictions, the psychological impact of the handicap, deprivation of social experience and limitations on involvement with others. Lack of social involvement and experience led to an impoverishment of the child's concepts of himself as one who could involve himself in interpersonal relations. The handicapped children were quite realistic, though, they shared in the peer values and culture but recognised they could not live up to the expectations that stem from the high premium placed on physical activities particularly in the case of male children. Handicapped girls more easily compensate through non-physical recreation but this is less acceptable to boys. As a result boys expressed more difficulties in their interpersonal relationships and felt that aggression was a major part of their make-up, possibly due to frustration. Handicapped boys and girls both showed greater concern than non-handicapped children with the past, possibly because of the greater uncertainty and threat in the present and future.

A current issue concerning the self-concept of children requiring special educational treatment, whether through physical or intellectual deficiencies, is how to set about that task of producing not only cognitive and academic gain, but also realistic self-esteem levels. The issue resolves itself into the question of whether educating them within normal classrooms (mainstreaming) or in special class schools is more beneficial for their educational and personal development. Administrators in the area of special education have assumed that such a child should be placed in a segregated setting where he would have a chance of success among comparable peers. The inference is that normal class placement (or mainstreaming) confronts the child with standards so out of reach that he has no substantial basis for self evaluation, and the development of positive self-attitudes becomes difficult.

Research such as that by Lawrence and Winchell (1973), Battle (1979) and Parrish and Kok (1980) brings out three themes:

(a) Generally self concepts improve when the standards of evaluation are not those of the normal child.
(b) There is a positive correlation between length of time spent in a special class/school and self concept level.
(c) Cautions are expressed that whilst the day special school provides a sympathetic, controlled environment in which self confidence and self regard are successfully nurtured, the segregated nature of the school is also providing an unrealistic yardstick of human behaviour.

However, mainstreaming or the integration of physically and intellectually handicapped children into the normal classroom is being promoted currently because (a) such children also need a realistic awareness of the normal workaday world, and (b) normal children should experience contact with, and come to accept, such handicapped persons as people with a wide range of very acceptable qualities.

Intellectual Handicap

Work by Carroll (1967) and Smith (1977) suggests that partial integration (half-day in normal classroom, with the remainder of time spent in a segregated setting) may provide better for the needs of the mentally handicapped child than

(a) a fully integrated scheme where the specialist help may be missing and evaluation is always against the normal peer group, or
(b) a fully integrated segregated system where the child builds up unrealistic self-perceptions and has only to live up to the lower expectations demanded in a special school environment.

The partial integration allows for specialist help in basic subjects for part of the day and an opportunity to mix with normal school children, come to terms with the reality of his situation and have somewhat higher expectation applied to him in subjects like art, music, handicraft, etc., where it is feasible for him to reach higher levels of performance. A very valuable offshoot of such a partial integration is that the host pupils and teachers may develop through the exposure more positive attitudes towards handicapped and retarded pupils. In addition, self-concept is maintained because some contact remains with a comparable set of significant others during the segregated setting period.

Physical Handicap

Attempts to integrate physically handicapped pupils into the normal classroom are fraught with more problems than similar integration of learning-disabled pupils. Special facilities, teaching techniques and equipment may all be required. Additionally, the perception of very noticeable disabilities by the teacher and other pupils may cause interpersonal disharmony and difficulty. Learning-disabled children do not stand out so markedly.

Work with adults suggests that in the highly evaluative school context only those disabled pupils who accept their disability and themselves will be able to deal with the negative evaluation that comes at some time or other in every child's life at school. They are more likely to be recipients of less favourable evaluations when placed in a normal school because they are likely to create more difficulties for teachers, create some disturbance to classroom routine and fit in less well with normal pupil social activities. For some non-disabled pupils, such disabled pupils might be perceived as strange and threatening, evoking quite negative non-verbal feedback. Only those disabled pupils who have integrated the disability into their self-concept and accept themselves are able to cope more adequately with this normal school environment. If handicapped pupils are to be successfully integrated into normal classrooms, it should be done primarily with those who already accept themselves as they are, not with those who feel unworthy and self-mutilated. These latter need their self-concepts strengthening through counselling procedures. Teaching strategies even with the self-accepting disabled must be aimed at providing successful experiences in a warm accepting ethos just as for any other pupil. Moreover pupil members of the 'reception' classes must have positive attitudes to others in order to provide facilitating feedback to the handicapped, for such positive acceptance of others derives from positive feelings towards self.

There appears to be no unambiguous answer to the question of whether segregated or integrated placement is superior. Zigler and Muenchow (1979) suggest that underlying the concept of mainstreaming is the issue of 'normalisation', which they feel is a denial of the child's right to be different or to have special needs. They also criticise mainstreaming on the same lines as de-institutionalisation, which often amounts to the trading of inferior care for no care at all. Moreover, without the special education received in special classes some special needs children may not function effectively in the social world as adults. For example, Zigler and Muenchow (1979) quote a deaf teacher who says that 'the paradox is that without the education I got in deaf schools I would be hopelessly lost in the hearing world now'. They suggest social competence should be the ultimate criterion monitoring the effectiveness of mainstreaming.

Some basic ground rules appear consistently through a wide variety of self-concept research. These would suggest that, to ensure the development of positive self-concepts in children, one must adopt these approaches:

(a) Provide opportunity for success and ensure that the tasks and demands placed on a child are suitable to his potential, that is, there is likely to be a successful outcome and realistic acceptance of ability.

(b) Show interest in and unconditional acceptance of the child e.g. smile, greet, talk to, etc.

(c) Don't emphasise failings and short-comings but concentrate on positive facets.

(d) Don't be too critical or cynical but provide encouragement.

(e) Make any necessary criticism specific to the context rather than let it become a criticism of the whole person so that the person fails on a particular task — he is not a failure *in toto*. Reject the bad behaviour not the whole person.

(f) Prevent a fear of trying through fear of failing.

(g) Be pleased with a worthwhile attempt and give credit for trying. Praise children realistically.

(h) Make children feel responsible beings.

(i) Make children feel they are competent.

(j) Teach children to set themselves realistic goals.

(k) Teach children to evaluate themselves realistically.

Summary

The self-concept is the set of attitudes a person holds of himself, and is composed of self-images and revaluations of those images which predispose him to behave in particular ways. The self-concept develops out of feedback about self from significant others, and from self-estimates of performance. The body image in particular influences behaviour, with the mesomorphic build being ideal. While parents are the source of much early feedback that facilitates self-concept development, they soon give way to peer groups once school life commences. Preadolescent children judge themselves in terms of objective information while adolescents consider personality, values and attitudes more central features of their self-conceptions.

Schooling has a vital impact on self-concept as a considerable amount of feedback about success, failure, friendship, acceptability and competence abounds. There is a strong relationship between academic performance and self-concept. Teachers and their expectations are important elements in school-based feedback. Ethnic minority children tend to have the same range of self-concept as majority children. Disabilities can cause negative self-concepts in the holder, particularly handicaps acquired later in childhood. Partial mainstreaming is being employed with some success in facilitating positive self-concepts in handicapped persons.

Generally to encourage positive self-esteem feedback should be positive yet realistic and indicate unconditional acceptance.

Questions

1. Why is the self-concept important in explaining human behaviour?
2. What factors influence the development of the individual's self-concept?
3. How might one try to facilitate the development of a positive self-concept in a handicapped person?
4. Write down 15 to 20 responses to the question 'Who am I' (e.g. female, physiotherapist, bossy, careless). Look at these responses and discuss the relative importance of each for you. Are your responses mainly categories or personal attributes?
5. What do you regard as the major determinant of your attitudes to yourself? Is it feedback from significant others, evaluation against objective standards, body image or what? In what way did any of these sources influence your self-concept?
6. Describe any interactions you have had with clients which you believe:

(a) Altered your self-concept,
(b) Altered the client's self-concept.
7. Describe the effects puberty and adolescence had on your self-concept.
8. What steps would you take to try and develop a positive yet realistic self-concept in a client or a friend?

Activity

This activity considers age or sex differences in self-concept. Choose *either* three or four children (all boys or all girls) at each of two ages, e.g. four ten-year-old girls and four fifteen-year-old girls *or* three or four boys *and* three or four girls all at the same age. The first alternative is looking at age differences with sex held constant while the latter alternative looks at sex differences with age held constant. Your objectives are to obtain data which will assist in enabling you to come to some tentative conclusions about some of the following hypotheses:

1. Younger children obtain (higher) (lower) (equal) scores on self-esteem compared to older children.
2. Boys obtain (higher) (lower) (equal) scores on self-esteem compared to girls.
3. Scale differences?
    Do you expect the 12 scales to differ in the positiveness of the self-esteem scores obtained by the whole group of children? Do you predict boys will be higher than girls on specific scales? Which ones?
    Do you predict girls will be higher than boys on specific scales? Which ones?

Self-Concept Scale (Figure 10.1)

Instructions to children:
Please place *one* cross on each line in a box between the two adjectives to represent how *you* feel about yourself.

Scoring

Score each cross according to the box it is in using the figures below the columns. (No value judgement is implied by the direction of scoring; it is simply a way of being able to distinguish between individuals/groups and between scales.)

You can add up total scores for each age group or sex and average this total. You can also find the average for each of the 12 scales for each age or sex group. Relate your findings back to any initial hypothesis you formulated.

Figure 10.1: Self Concept Scale

	Almost always like this	Often like this	About half and half	Often like this	Almost always like this	
Happy						Sad
Friendly						Unfriendly
Strong						Weak
Attractive						Unattractive
Obedient						Disobedient
Belligerent						Placid
Polite						Rude
Brave						Timid
Capable						Useless
Unemotional						Emotional
Successful						Unsuccessful
Rash						Cautious
	5	4	3	2	1	

Further Reading

Burns, R.B. (1979) *The Self-concept*, London: Longmans
Burns, R.B. (1982) *Self-concept Development and Education*, London: Holt Rinehart

References

Barker-Lunn, J.C. (1970) *Streaming in the Primary School*, Slough: NFER

Battle, J. (1979) 'Self-esteem of children in regular and special classes', *Psychol. Rep.*, *44*, 212–4

Burns, R.B. (1982) *Self Concept Development and Education*, London: Holt Saunders

Canfield, J. and Wells, H. (1976) *100 Ways to Enhance Self Concept in the Classroom*, New Jersey: Prentice Hall

Carroll, A.W. (1967) 'The effects of segregated and partially segregated school programmes on self concept and academic achievement of educable mental retardates', *Except. Child.*, *34*, 92–9

Cooley, C.H. (1912) *Human Nature and the Social Order*, New York: Scribners

Coopersmith, S. (1967) *The Antecedents of Self Esteem*, San Francisco: Freeman

Guthrie, E.R. (1938) *Psychology of Human Conflict*, New York: Harper

Jourard, S. and Second, P. (1955) 'Body size and body cathexis', *J. Consult. Psychol.*, *18*, 184

Kretschmer, E. (1925) *Physique and Character*, London: Routledge

Lawrence, E.A. and Winchell, J.F. (1973) 'Self concept and the retarded', *Except. Child.*, *39*, 310–19

Mead, G. (1934) *Mind, Self and Society*, Chicago: University of Chicago Press

Parrish, L. and Kok, M. (1980) 'Misinterpretation hinders mainstreaming', *Yearbook of Special Education*, 6, no. 24

Piaget, J. (1952) *The Origins of Intelligence in Children*, New York: International Universities Press

Purkey, W.W. (1970) *Self Concept and School Achievement*, New Jersey: Prentice Hall

Purkey, W.W. (1978) *Inviting School Success*, Belmont: Wadsworth

Richardson, S.A., Hastorf, A.H. and Dornbusch, S.M. (1964) 'The effect of physical disability on the child's description of himself', *Child Devel.*, *35*, 893–907

Rist, R.C. (1970) 'Student social class and teacher expectations', *Harvard Educ. Review*, *40*, 411–51

Rosenberg, M. (1965) *Society and the Adolescent Self Image*, Princetown: Princetown University Press

Rosenthal, R. and Jacobsen, L. (1968) *Pygmalion in the Classroom*, New York: Holt

Sheldon, W. and Stevens, S. (1942) *The Varieties of Temperament*, New York: Harper Row

Smith, M.D. (1977) 'School related factors influencing the self concept of children with learning problems', *Peabody J. Educ.*, *54*, 185–95

Snygg, D. and Combs, A.W. (1949) *Individual Behaviour*, New York: Harper

Staffieri, J. (1957) 'A study of social stereotypes of body image in children', *J. Pers. Soc. Psychol.*, 7, 101–4

Staines, J.W. (1958) 'The self picture as a factor in the classroom', *Br. J. Educ. Psychol.*, *28*, pt. 97–111

Zigler, E. and Muenchow, S. (1979) 'Mainstreaming', *Amer. Psychologist*, *34*, 993–6

11 ADOLESCENCE

A great deal is talked and written about adolescents and adolescence in the mass media. However, much of it is directed at a portrayal of adolescence as a period of stress with the adolescent conventionally stereotyped as erratic, emotional, unstable, searching continually for a new identity, and exploring 'way-out' styles of living (some of which commentators pejoratively term anti-social, undesirable and even immoral). This conventional stereotype is largely false and the evidence for and against will be discussed below. A further problem in any discussion of adolescence is the definition of the term, for if we cannot agree on when adolescence is or who is to be regarded as an adolescent, then any attempt to discuss the psychology of adolescence is doomed.

What is Adolescence?

In a single sense, it is the period between childhood and adulthood but this commonsense view does not get us very far.

The onset of adolescence can be defined in biological terms as the start of puberty. The ending of adolescence is often regarded as the assumption of the social, legal, economic, political and sexual rights and duties of the adult. Both these starting and end points still leave much to be desired. The beginning of puberty is not clear in most young people, and varies greatly in timing between individuals.

The termination of adolescence becomes ambiguous and is not independent of human and societal judgement. It is ambiguous because the various rights and duties vested in adults are accorded at a variety of ages. For example, legal regulations governing age 'of consent', age at which marriage is permitted, age for leaving school, for taking on hire purchase commitments, for driving a car, for joining (or being required to join) the Army, or for voting, make no logical progression in rights and duties. Adults, by altering such ages, can prolong adolescence by their decisions about what defines the termination of it. It is very difficult to envisage a definition of adolescence which has a clear-cut start and finish and which does not use two different types of criteria for the start and finish, viz., biological and sociological respectively.

219

The term 'adolescent' is so generalised that we lose sight of the fact that it stands for a heterogeneity of individuals who do not conform to an identical pattern, but display a wide range of variations. Adolescence is a form of modern day apprenticeship in advanced societies. There is a high correlation between the state of advancement of a society and prolongation of non-adult status.

Primitive societies tend not to have a crisis of adolescence. The young person, overnight, through some institutionalised rite of passage becomes accepted as an adult member of his society and does not have that psychological transition period we term adolescence. In other words adolescence is a socially created phenomenon, a product of the discontinuity in our culture between childhood and adulthood. It is a 'marginal situation' in Riessman's terms or a 'psychosocial moratorium' in Erikson's view.

Adolescence did not really exist in Western cultures until the present century, for before then formal schooling was short and entry into the world of work was early. The lengthening of education and the need for a long 'apprenticeship' in order to take a useful part in a complex technological society has created an interval between physical maturity and the granting of adult status and privileges. This transition period provides a young person with time to learn and practice social, vocational, political and economic skills for the future; but equally it provides a period of conflict and vacillation between dependence and independence, immaturity and maturity, between self-expectations/values, peer expectations/values, and adult expectations/values.

At the beginning of this century, Stanley Hall regarded adolescence as a 'new birth' in the individual; he saw the adolescent as erratic, emotional, unstable and unpredictable, the result of sexual maturing. This was the forerunner of Erikson's influential perspective. Research has disproved this point of view; no sudden, complete change takes place at adolescence. In fact, emotional and social development during adolescence will depend greatly on what has happened to the child in earlier years. If the basic needs of the child have not been met *before* adolescence, then the period of adolescence is likely to be more difficult than otherwise. Chief among these basic needs we can list security, affection, consistent and reasonable discipline, opportunities for activity and play, companionship, and harmony at home, with the father as well as the mother playing a full role in the family life. Educationally, the adolescence will have a tough time if the proper foundations have not been laid in the primary school.

Theories of Adolescence

Two major theories have been offered to account for the psychological characterisation of adolescence and they concur in viewing the period as a stressful one. Firstly, the psychoanalytic perspective claims that the upsurge of instinctual forces which occurs at puberty results in a traumatic disturbance of psychic balance which in turn leads to regression (childishness, impulsiveness, immaturity, dependence, etc), ambivalence and non-conformity. An extension of this approach by Erikson involves these factors interacting with societal factors, e.g. constraints on behaviour, expectancies, values, etc., all leading to identity crises.

One psychoanalytic writer Blos (1967) regards adolescence as the 'second individuation process' which has a parallel with the first that occurs in the preschool child. In both periods the individual has to change to a more independent organism. Blos also saw regression to earlier childhood behaviour and feelings as necessary to enable the adolescent to break close emotional family attachments. For example, emotional instability is reactivated, and the idolisation of pop stars, sports personalities and the like has a parallel in the idealised parent of the preschool child.

The second approach, by sociological proponents, claims that the stress all emanates from the adolescent's position in society as a marginal person, neither child nor adult, coping with role conflict and role transition in a world full of conflicting values and pressures.

Adolescents have become stereotyped with negative behaviour because a few involve themselves in hooliganism, vandalism, drug-taking, etc. The mass media make great play with any sensational incident and by implication all young people are indicted. This stereotyping provides an exaggerated view of adolescent turmoil. Adolescence does have its problems but no more so than any other period. Coleman (1980) has offered another theory to take account of the fact (1) that few adolescents conform to the conventional picture of maladjustment and (2) that different issues do arise at different periods during adolescence that can give rise to transient problems. He terms it the 'focal' theory, in that different concerns come into focus at different ages, e.g. for boys, fear of rejection by peer group is most important for 15-year-olds, while conflict with parents is most potent at 17 years. Hence adolescent turmoil is avoided by most as few find themselves unable to resolve more than one concern at the same time. This focal theory then explains how adolescents cope with adjusting to change yet, as empirical evidence shows, do so with relative stability. Only a minority suffer from an identity crisis and change their self-concepts. As Coleman (1980, p. 178) summarises:

> In most cases relationships with parents are positive and constructive, and young people, by and large, do not reject adult values in favour of those espoused by the peer group. In fact, in most situations peer group values appear to be consistent with those of important adults, rather than in conflict with them. Fears of promiscuity among the young are not borne out by the research findings, nor do studies support the belief that the peer group encourages antisocial behaviour, unless other factors are also present. Lastly there is no evidence to suggest that during the adolescent years there is a higher level of psychopathology than at other times. . . . although a small minority may show disturbance, the great majority of teenagers seem to cope well and to show no undue signs of turmoil or stress.

Erikson and Adolescence

One of the most influential views on the psychology of adolescence which emphasised the conventional 'storm and stress' perspective is that of Erik Erikson.

Erikson (1963) has claimed that the major task confronting the adolescent is to develop a sense of identity, to find answers to the questions 'Who am I?' and 'Where am I going?'. The search for personal identity involves deciding what is important or worth doing and formulating standards of conduct for evaluating one's own behaviour as well as the behaviour of others. It also involves feelings about one's own worth and competence. The previous identity as a child must be replaced but since society has placed the teenager in an anomalous position, Erikson argues that the creation of a new identity for future mature adulthood is difficult because of the interaction between society's requirements, pressures and value clashes, and physiological changes, and that some form of disturbance is a normal expectation in adolescence with crisis points more likely occurring towards the end of the period. He therefore lends considerable weight to the conventional view of adolescence, despite the fact that he bases his theory on clinical cases, evidence he invalidly generalised to all 'normal' teenagers.

Wall (1955) found that 80 per cent of the young men he asked about the period of adolescence had been reasonably happy between the ages of 13 and 21; 15 per cent had been unhappy, but most of these had been unhappy before adolescence. The remaining 5 per cent were 'don't knows' — they were not sure whether they had been happy or not. The women in his sample had been even happier than the men, 87 per cent stating that adolescence had been a happy period for them. However, most surveys of normal youth do not support this conception (e.g. Engel, 1959; Carlson, 1965; Offer, 1969; Douvan and Adelson, 1966; Piers and Harris, 1964; Coleman, 1980; Monge, 1973).

The largest sample used to study the presumed personality changes during adolescence is the 6000 students aged 12 to 17 in the investigation of Ellis, Gehmen and Katzenmeyer (1980). This was a cross-sectional study employing a random sample of 1000 students in each year. All the subjects took the Self-Observation Scale which includes eight scales: school affiliation, self-security, social confidence, peer affiliation, family affiliation, self-assertion, teacher affiliation and self-acceptance. The results showed a stability across the adolescent age span of seven of the scales. The only scale that revealed any change was self-acceptance.

The self-concept disturbance Simmons *et al.* (1973) discerned in adolescents was in early adolescence where the onset of puberty coincided wtih transfer from primary to secondary school. This change of school environment is a highly significant event for many a child, being a move from a protected small school context to a larger more impersonal school where he has lost his former status as biggest and oldest and where he is constantly changing rooms and teachers. This makes the self-concept more vulnerable as is particularly noticeable for the child with the high self-concept. He has most to lose on changing school environment. The low self-concept child is likely to be vulnerable too, but it would be difficult for him to sink much lower (Alban-Metcalfe, 1978). Perhaps more thought ought to be given by teachers in both types of school to providing more support and preparation for the transfer to secondary school.

Thus we are in a position where there is little evidence to support the idea of an identity crisis in older adolescence, or that changes automatically involve increasing self-derogation and identity diffusion. There are of course children of all ages who manifest negative self-concepts and identity problems. The adolescents who suffer disturbance are likely to be those who have always sustained throughout childhood such self-identity and esteem problems, for a small minority of all age levels seem to struggle with the issue. Coleman and colleagues (1977) provide a suggestion that might resolve the argument. Coleman distinguishes two forms of identity, present and future; the adolescent has two self-concepts — what he is and what he will be. Coleman *et al.* (1977) showed that with a normal sample of adolescents the concern and confusion is over the future — What shall I be? This is perhaps a response to a rapidly changing technological and computerised era in which occupational identity is hard to confirm as a permanent self-focal point, and in which occupational and marital security are no longer guaranteed.

Having said this, we must still admit that some adolescents are particularly susceptible to conflicts and emotional disturbances, though not necessarily of a lasting and severe kind. It would seem, however, that these are not so much inherent in adolescence as determined by the nature and demands of our society. In many modern cultures, including our own, the period of adolescence is fraught with difficulties, for a number of reasons. Over the past hundred years, there has been a tendency for puberty to occur earlier and earlier, yet there is, for many, a long delay between sexual maturity and sexual fulfilment. Where there is sexual fulfilment, through early marriage or otherwise, problems of finding a home or of unwanted children may present themselves. For a number of young people, particularly the most able, there is often a lengthy wait before financial independence is achieved. Those who leave school at 16 usually face an abrupt transition from the child-centred world of school to the less sympathetic arena of shop or factory. The adolescent, too, sees uncertainty and conflict in those aspects of life about which he is most concerned; he does not readily find clear-cut answers from adults to his problems about sex, religion and moral values. Public institutions and the mass media often have a dual personality. They condemn crime, aggression and the moral degeneration of the day while encouraging sensationalism and allowing an over-emphasis on sex and violence.

Surveys have shown that working adolescents are far better off financially than their fathers were a generation ago. This new affluence has created a number of problems. It is not always accompanied by a sense of responsibility; it has tempted a number of intelligent young people away from school at an early age; and it has encouraged many commercial enterprises, not all of them acting in the best interests of the adolescent, to direct their attention to the teenage market.

Parents, Peer Group and Independence

At adolescence, there is often a development of desire for social activities outside the home. The adolescent wishes to be a member of school or other societies, teams, clubs or crowds at matches. Parents need to understand how powerfully the teenager is drawn to the peer group and how strong the urge is to be 'with it', to be a member of the teenage world. Some adolescents, of course, look upon mass crazes or frenzies with amused contempt, and seek a more individual way of life; but most wish to imitate the group norms and to have a leader or idol to worship. In the absence of more positive leadership, adolescents in the past few decades have been attracted, in some countries, to the political agitator and, less harmfully, to the pop-singer in the USA and the UK.

Of course conflicts occur from time to time between most adolescents and their parents as the former try to grow up and employ their new-found competencies. Parents generally do want their adolescents to display maturity, common sense and independence, but usually within more restricted limits than the offspring would wish. Someone once wisely noted that adulthood occurs about two years earlier than any parent cares to admit, but two years later than the adolescent may claim. Most parents do not easily let go of their emerging adolescents who must work harder and cope with harder challenges to prove to their parents and themselves that they really can make it on their own and that their self-concepts are sufficiently firm to operate within the responsibilities and setbacks accompanying independence. But parents who hold on too tightly can cause a young person seeking his freedom either to feel guilty ('my parents must need me') or inadequate ('they don't trust me on my own'). As Douvan and Adelson (1966) note there is a curvilinear relation between parental involvement with a young person and the young person's developing sense of personal autonomy. This implies that both too much or too little involvement can inhibit the adolescent's achievement of independence and the feeling of security necessary for self-control is poorly developed.

Many adolescents seem to help each other through any discomforts and disturbances by mutual support in cliques with endless coffee bar chats and by stereotyping themselves as Mods, Teddy Boys, Hell's

Angels, students, etc., and likewise stereotyping their opponents, parents, teachers, police, etc. This is a period of role experimentation in which the youngster can explore different ideologies and interests, but today's academic competition and career pressures deprive many adolescents of the opportunity to explore. As a result, some 'drop out' temporarily to have time to think about what they want to do in life and to experiment with various identities. Communes, and such religious groups as the Jesus movement and the Hare Krishna sect often provide a temporary commitment to an alternative life style; they give the young person a group to identify with and time to formulate a more permanent set of beliefs. We must not assume that most adolescents go through a prolonged period of identity confusion. One suspects that the majority of adolescents accept their society's and parent's values without question and rarely suffer confusion, self doubt and insecurity. In a complex society, it is less easy for an adolescent to form a stable self image. There is a bewildering collection of inconsistent models purveyed by the mass media, peers, parents and teachers. Personal identity and feelings of competent mastery of life are not helped by the depersonalised bureaucratic computerised society that is becoming our form of society today.

Physical maturity collides with socially sanctioned social immaturity. Emotional changes consequent upon physiological changes can make the adolescent display from time to time impulsivity, emotional immaturity, anxiety and emotional outbursts. Unfavourable social reactions to these can lead to feelings of social inadequacy and inferiority. Under such tension and confusion, many adolescents do wish to retain the security of some degree of dependence on parents, despite other pressures pushing them towards independence and adult responsibilities. However, for most adolescents these emotional and social problems are transient and limited.

It is true that any problem unsolved in the past will reappear at adolescence; this means that there is a second chance to deal with the problem, before letting the adolescent go into adult life with a warped or handicapped outlook. Physical maturity is earlier now than it was in previous generations, so that the child or youth may appear to be more grown-up than his emotional development will support. Because he is in some ways mature, the adolescent's chief difficulties lie in reconciling his immaturity and his continued dependence with his wish to be independent and free of emotional childishness. Given his freedom, he cannot bear it; he still has a need for security and for the knowledge that there is in the background an ultimate source of authority on which he can depend in the last resort.

Adolescence is concerned with discovering whether or not one is independent. This can only be discovered by trying to be independent. If the opportunity to make decisions and to take responsibility is denied altogether, the adolescent has no alternative but to rebel; in this situation, rebellion is the healthy way of solving a problem that need not exist. It follows, therefore, that we should give increasing opportunities, both in and out of school, for responsibility in making decisions and carrying them out, in a reasonable step-by-step approach to adulthood. If we, as parents and teachers, refuse to allow the adolescent to become independent, in small ways at first, we cannot be surprised if his reaction is one of total rebellion. Unfortunately, rebellion all too often proves to him that he is not ready for the final assumption of independence. He is then frightened by something he cannot control, but unable to give in and become dependent again; he is 'lost' and his actions show that he is out of his own control as well as out of his parents' control.

The adolescent does not want us, either as parents or teachers, to hide behind the role of parent-figure or teacher-figure. He needs us to be real people, so that he can judge our effectiveness in the world and base his own meeting with the world on our attitude to it.

If a person feels unwanted, he loses all his self-respect and feels unworthy and unclean. If he feels unwanted at home, he may look for another group where he feels he has a value — the gang may supply his need, or perhaps a relationship with an individual of either sex will restore his self-respect and give him a new sense of having a worthwhile part to play in life. All of these demands are insistent, and the adolescent needs someone in whom to confide before things become unbearable. If he has no one who will listen, the tension may be so acute that it needs to be resolved by some other means; an outburst of aggression or a period of masturbation may be the outlet. Often, however, the adolescent does find someone to talk to, and a great deal of his time seems to be spent in just talking, talking endlessly to anyone who will listen, trying to get things into perspective and to convince others of the justice of his cause. Teachers can help, by allowing the adolescent to talk and by really listening to what he says. This is more important to any child who has an unsolved problem or a difficulty left over from earlier childhood. Adolescence can be a time of acute disturbance. At this time, any previous problems may be restated in a more acute form and the difficulties that have been in abeyance in the latency years reassert themselves. In addition, adolescents have more strength and scope for making their impact on society, so that a problem, which at the age of three would involve only a battle of wills between mother and child, may at 13 show itself as a battle with society leading to the juvenile courts and to approved school.

In our society, direct manifestations of anger and violence, or other strong emotions, shown by children and adolescents meet with strong disapproval on the part of parents, teachers and employers. It is to be expected, therefore, that these direct reactions, if frustrated, will try to find an outlet. The adolescent may find an indirect way of expressing his feelings through *fantasy*. By this means, he can fulfil his wishes, enact romances and vent anger without any ill consequences to himself. There is a good deal of day-dreaming in adolescence, which is fairly harmless as long as the adolescent keeps his feet firmly in the world of reality.

The adolescent's hostility against individuals or groups may be *displaced*. When he really wants to attack his parents, he may destroy objects or join a gang of rebels. He will also be prone, like all of us, to *project* his feelings on to others, to blame them for his own shortcomings and to cover up his insecurity with continued grievances of one kind or another. He may *compensate* for feelings of insecurity by an exaggerated urge to be on top, or pretend to be tough and not to care, when this attitude is a defence against being hurt. In our society, we all use these defence mechanisms, and others, to some extent. If they are used in an extreme way, then we are faced with cases of maladjustment or emotional disturbance.

As the adolescent gradually disengages from the family, the emotional void starts to be filled by peer group relationships. The peer group also provides support and mutual understanding as each member undergoes common experiences in the passage through adolescence. Conflicts, anxieties, new ideas, can be shared in a sympathetic audience. Girls appear to have more anxiety over peer group friendships than boys. This may be due, as we have noted, to the differing socialisation process which emphasises feminine validation through personal relationships, social intimacy and dependency (Douvan and Adelson, 1966).

Divergence of opinion between parents and adolescents is not great. The 'generation gap' is regarded by many authorities (e.g. Bandura, 1972) as a myth. Most teenagers appear to value the advice and standards of adults (Fogelman, 1976). Thus harmony rather than discord is the main theme in adolescent–parent relationships. Minor issues do arise as in any close group from time to time, but major conflict is rare. Studies of family practices and ethos considered earlier emphasised the value of democratic procedures for facilitating maturity and independence in children. Democratic procedures provide experience in decision making under parental supervision, increase the legitimacy of rules, allow experience in self reliance and the learning of adult standards of behaviour.

Contrary to expectations, adolescents do have a need for adults to exercise their authority, so long as this is kept within reasonable limits. Studies of different types of power structure within the home have shown that a permissive environment is no more preferable to young people than an authoritarian one. In general, teenagers adjust best in situations where they are able to play some part in the decision making process, but where adults are not afraid to make rules and to ensure that these are respected (Gecas, 1971, 1972).

Puberty

Puberty, which is intimately associated with adolescence, is the stage during which sexual growth and maturation occur leading to the individual becoming a sexually mature adult. The major feature is the growth of the gonads caused by the increased production of gonadotrophic hormones by the anterior pituitary gland, but the consequences of this affect the whole physical, emotional and social development of the individual. The biological changes in puberty are usually sequential but the age at which they begin and the length of time they take to complete vary markedly with individuals. Factors which influence timing aspects of development are primarily heredity, health and environment.

There is sound evidence from industrialised countries that the age of puberty has become progressively earlier — on average by about one year in every 25 — for at least the last 100 years. This phenomenon, known as the secular trend, is thought to be largely due to improved standards of nutrition. There are suggestive data that the trend has now slowed or stopped in many developed countries. For girls in the UK the mean age of menarche, the first menstrual period, is about 13 years. In boys, puberty is less precisely datable, but on average is one to two years later than in girls. In both sexes the age range of puberty is very wide; menarche may be as early as 11 years, and as late as 15 years and still be within normal range.

The rate of progression of physical changes of puberty is also very variable. Whereas some children will pass from prepuberty to the adult stage of development within a year, more commonly it is spread over two or three years or even longer. This variability among perfectly normal children, a fact not always understood by adolescents and their families, is often a source of needless concern. Youths who enter puberty later than the average range often face special concerns which will be discussed later.

Actual delay in the onset of puberty which can worry many children is often due to generalised growth delay rather than gonadal failure. Very early puberty (before nine years old) is often due to pathological causes, usually an intercranial lesion.

The changes in hormonal levels that accompany puberty are partly responsible for the mood swings. The interest in the opposite sex is stimulated by the hormone androgen which is present in both sexes during adolescence and in adult life. This interest in the opposite sex is at the core of the social and affective changes in adolescence. Early maturing boys and girls will start dating while later maturing boys and girls still congregate in the same-sex groups giggling at the opposite-sex groups or at those more mature peers who are dating.

The body image, the subjective evaluation of what one's body is like, becomes important in adolescence as puberty changes the shape and dimensions of the body. Many studies of adolescents, e.g. Lerner *et al.* (1976) show that males rate their bodies in terms of physical effectiveness whereas females rate theirs in terms of physical attractiveness. An adolescent who believes his body is not in accordance with some norm he has in mind then suffers self-devaluation of his whole being. Musa and Roach (1973) found that many adolescents wished they could change their appearance.

Puberty is a stage of heightened emotionality. The pubertal child begins to experience heightened feelings and undertakes the revision of his or her own attitudes. The increase in emotional differentiation is apparent in the various moods experienced. The pubescent becomes increasingly sensitive and reacts strongly to events and social situations. While the advanced adolescent is able to control the emotions to a considerable extent, the young adolescent is swept along by the vivid currents of feelings and sentiments. When aroused, emotions are frequently out of proportion to the initial stimulus. Attempts to control emotional expression are frequent but not always successful. The emotionally charged actions resemble the heightened negativism and temper seen during the late second and third years of life at the beginning of early childhood.

Ambivalent feelings are the rule rather than the exception at puberty. The adolescent often experiences contradictory feelings — that is, love and hate, concern and apathy — toward persons and events. Trivial disappointments often arouse his antagonism without destroying his original feeling of cordiality or enthusiasm. The capacity for keeping effective experiences in harmony seems to be lost for some time.

The effort to progress in social, emotional and sexual maturation is probably the most difficult task of the pubertal period. Transference of affection and love from parents to peers, including members of the opposite sex, represents a major change in emotional cathexis. Ambivalance and discouragement are common while this key shift of feelings is occurring. New adjustments at any age are accompanied by emotional tensions and heightened affective reactions. This transference is scarcely comparable to any earlier emotional changes. Development of new attitudes and integration of divergent peer values are parts of a painful process. Lack of preparation for the adolescent role, parental insensitivity and objections, and rising financial necessities all contribute to a state of emotional uneasiness. This leads to occasional tensions near the boiling point, the energies of which, when not sufficiently discharged physically, accumulate and interrupt the functioning of weaker or more sensitive organismic systems. Headaches, stomach aches, and raised blood pressure are examples of these disturbances. As a result, organismic balance and personal health are disturbed, especially if such states arise often. New defence tactics are needed to restore and preserve some kind of balance. Dropping carefully developed plans and reverting to daydreaming, and aggressive and hostile reactions are among the defensive reactions often used by adolescents to protect themselves from the threats of the adult or peer world. The young adolescent experiences many obstacles in finding his or her place in peer society and culture.

Emotional stability is a counterpart of the physiological and social changes occurring during puberty. Strong likes and dislikes expressed in most teenage groups press the pubertal child to change his attitudes toward parents, teachers, and other groups he comes in contact with. In group situations more than anywhere else, the young teenager feels that many of his childhood beliefs and attitudes are not tenable and feels an urgency to construct a new set. The young teenager encounters many peers who have very different attitudes toward religious practice, academic achievement, sexuality and drugs (Mussen *et al.*, 1979). Ambivalence grows, as he cannot easily discredit the position taken by others. Since the integrity of the value and belief system is central to the conceptualisation of self, it is necessary to keep it intact by defining the meaning of his existence and his role in adult and peer society and by selecting personal goals worthy of much effort. The resetting of his motivational hierarchy is often a result of peer influence that competes with and often overrules what parents have worked hard to establish. Mussen *et al.* (1979) attribute great significance to the cognitive quality of motivation and treat motives as cognitive representation of goals. Nonetheless, emotional and sexual factors rank high at this stage. They suggest that mastery and resolution of uncertainty and hostility are primary motives; if sensory pleasure is added, this comes close to the goals and strivings of the young adolescent.

Puberty: Early and Late

Physical growth can be a source of great anxiety, whether it be too slow or too fast, too little or too much. The rate of an adolescent's physical development in comparison to others in the peer group considerably affects how each youngster feels about himself.

The behavioural effects of early and late puberty on self-conception in boys seems to be different from that in girls. The results of a series of studies on males add up to a consistent picture — a large, strong stature is a central aspect of the ideal masculine model. Thus, it can be assumed that the early attainment of the physical attributes associated with maturity serves as a social stimulus which evokes from both peers and adults a reaction of respect, acceptance and the expectation that the individual concerned will have relatively mature social behaviour. Such a reaction from others serves to support and reinforce adaptive, 'grown up' actions and contributes to feelings of confidence and security in the early maturing boys. On the other hand, the late developer must cope with the developmental demands of the secondary school period with the liability of a relatively small, immature-appearing physical stature. His appearance is likely to evoke from others at least mildly derogatory reactions, and the expectation that he is capable of only ineffectual, immature behaviour. Such reactions create a kind of social environment which is conducive to feelings of inadequacy, insecurity and defensive, 'small-boy' behaviour; once initiated such behaviour may well be self-perpetuating, since it is likely only to produce the negative environmental reactions of others which gave rise to it in the first place. This interpretation implies that the late developer is likely to be involved in a circular psychosocial process in which reactions of others and his own reactions interact, with unhappy consequences for his personal and social adjustment (Mussen and Jones, 1957).

In contrast to the dramatic effects bodily change has on the male adjustment in adolescence, physical change, whether early or late, is a much less potent influence on the personality of adolescent girls. This difference in effect may be due to the male cultural norm of tall, brawny masculinity, whereas early maturing for girls contains no prestigious advantage; it can in fact be a calamity; the girl will stoop to hide her tallness, or wear sloppy jumpers to disguise her developing breasts. Early maturing girls are perceived as listless, submissive and lacking poise (Tryon, 1939), and are judged to have little popularity or prestige among their peers (Jones, 1958). This picture contrasts very much with that painted of early maturing boys. The early maturing girl is of course, developmentally three to four years ahead of the average boy, and has to seek social outlets with much older males. Thus the slower maturing girl is likely to enjoy more social advantages. In a similar study to the one conducted on males, Jones and Mussen (1958) compared early and late maturing girls in terms of their self-conceptions, motivation and interpersonal attitudes. They found that early maturing girls had more favourable self-concepts and less dependency needs, but the relationships were far less clear-cut than for males, for whom physical strength and athleticism are so important. The feminine sex role stereotype does not place such a high premium on total physical make-up, though specific physical elements are important, such as an attractive face, well-endowed bosom etc. A girl need only possess one of these qualities to elicit favourable responses; a deficit in one aspect can be more than compensated for in another. Girls are expected to make themselves attractive and are judged on how they look, whereas boys are expected to perform feats with their bodies, and the response of others is to their total physical make-up, not to specific aspects of it. On the existing evidence it is possible to make a tentative speculation that physical maturation in adolescence has a less dramatic effect on girls than boys because the former have flexibility for altering or changing their looks through a sensible use of cosmetics, padding, etc., whereas the latter can do little to alter their performance.

Health and Energy

Late childhood is usually a healthy age, marked by good adjustment to home, school, and peers, but the situation changes rather drastically after major pubertal changes erupt. Often the young adolescent feels ill and suffers headaches, bodily discomforts and stomach pains. At times he or she has little energy for work or even play, feels tired if not exhausted, or is annoyed by other minor disturbances of a psychosomatic nature. The adolescent may experience a generally run-down condition or be bothered frequently by influenza, sore throat, or tonsillitis; but sometimes 'feeling ill' is used as an escape from disagreeable duties and responsibilities. There are no severe illnesses specific to this stage and, excluding accidents and narcotics, very few adolescents die from illnesses or their complications.

There are some physiological explanations for the young adolescent's lack of energy and frequent colds and aches. First of all, the slower growth of blood vessels in relation to the heart raises the blood pressure and creates both strain on the heart and feelings of tension and tiredness. At this phase of accelerated growth, a young person should not be pressed into robust activities or excessive competition in athletics. Usually, though, the pubertal child feels inclined to expend a great amount of energy, even beyond his or her capacity. By overexpending energy in sports and late hours and endless unnecessary activity, often with an irregular intake of food, the adolescent occasionally develops an enlarged heart or respiratory disturbances.

At puberty the oil-producing glands increase their activity, resulting in skin eruptions and acne. Rapid growth, emotional turmoil, and unpredictable eating and activity patterns also contribute to skin disturbances. Difficulties in social relationships and the resulting conflicts and frustrations are additional contributing causes. But following the completion of major pubertal changes, physical health usually reaches its highest level in late adolescence and early adulthood.

Sexual Maturation and Behaviour

Sexual maturation is the background to many of the emotional and social changes of the teenage years. There have been considerable changes in sexual attitudes during the last 20 years in Western society and this has affected the behaviour of teenagers, the way that behaviour is viewed by teenagers and others. Extra-marital relation-ships and divorce have become more common, a variety of sexual practices are viewed more tolerantly, the mass media portray and discuss the new morality frequently, openly and (as it seems to many) supportingly. No one can insulate themselves against these changes which are now part of society.

As a result, young people are themselves more open about sexual matters and regard sexual behaviour as a matter of personal rather than public morality. Almost paradoxically they also have come to regard adequate sex adjustment between marriage partners as a necessary basis for a stable long-term relationship. So rather than regarding sex as a 'fun' thing to do and becoming promiscuous, there is a general feeling among today's teenagers that while it is a good thing for sexual behaviour to be openly discussed, sexual behaviour is only valid within a framework of a permanent relationship to give it meaning. This for some adolescents does not imply marriage but does imply a negative view of casual liaisons.

So attitudes have changed but is this reflected in actual behaviour? Responses of young people in interviews or to questionnaires on sexual behaviour are not likely to be accurate (or reliable) since sexual behaviour is an emotional and intensely personal element of life. Boasting of conquests, often exaggerated, is a typical male teenager's tendency. Female sexual behaviour is on the other hand likely to be under-reported. Generalising from a range of research in the USA, Britain and Europe around three-quarters of male 17-year-olds report having had intercourse but girls of a similar age report a considerably lower percentage, with middle-class members having far less 'experience' than working-class teenagers. The two main sources of evidence in Britain are the surveys of Schofield (1965) and Farrell (1978). The fact that promiscuity does not seem to be rampant among contemporary teenagers, nor even acceptable to many of them is of great significance in view of the pressures impinging on them.

Finally it is vital to note the current legal position (which could change, of course) with respect to aspects of sexual behaviour. While the general age of majority is 18, a person of 16 can give consent for dental, medical and surgical treatment, i.e. no parental consent is required. Hence a 16-year-old is 'medically' an adult with the right to professional secrecy and able to prevent information being passed on, even to parents. Thus contraceptive advice, abortion, etc. do not require parental consent or even knowledge. As far as sex education is concerned, it is essential that it extends beyond biological facts and medical matters to encompass social implications in which teenagers are seriously interested today. Teenagers also prefer to have sex education outside the home, in school programmes, though obviously parents have a role to play.

Summary

Adolescence is impossible to define and tends to be a creation of Western industrial societies. The psychoanalytic approach to adolescence suggests that instinctual forces upsurging at puberty cause traumatic personal crises. The sociological approach argues that adolescent stress emanates from the adolescent's position in society as a marginal person, neither child nor adult. Erikson attempts to integrate these two approaches and produces the conventional stereotype of every adolescent having to pass through a period of storm and stress, with the major task being that of achieving a sense of identity. Research evidence suggests that adolescence is not a period of change in psychological terms. Most adolescents pass through the period with equanimity, though change of school and vocational choice can provoke insecurity. The development of formal operational thought produces insecurity, too, as awareness develops of possibilities other than the existing state of affairs.

There is a general demand for more independence and a greater commitment to the security and friendship of the peer group as home and parents become less important. The peer group provides for the needs of self-acceptance and partial independence. The 'generation gap' does not appear to be as wide as once thought. Most teenagers value the advice and standards of adults. Adolescents have less conflict with parents when democratic procedures are employed within the household so that they can play a part in the decision-making. Adolescents feel most authentic in peer contexts and least authentic in school contexts.

Puberty is occurring earlier in industrialised countries. It is the changes in hormonal levels that are mainly responsible for adolescent mood swings. The body image becomes an important element of self-evaluation as puberty changes body shape and dimensions. Early and late entry into puberty affects the self-concept and personality of adolescents. Health and energy levels can run down as adolescents pass through puberty, and suicide and depression rates increase.

Contrary to public opinion, adolescents generally tend to frown on casual sexual liaisons and regard sexual behaviour as valid only within a permanent relationship, though this may not imply marriage. Adults can help adolescents generally by adopting a phenomenological perspective, by providing consistent guidelines within which to operate and by helping them to understand that decision-making is usually never a choice between absolute right and wrong.

Activity

Interview several young adolescents (say 12- to 13-year olds) and several older adolescents (say 16- to 18-year olds). Write down a list of topics on which you wish to interview them e.g. attitude to school, attitude to adults, feelings about themselves, hobbies, school performance, peer group relationships, relations with parents, vocational aspirations, etc. Note their responses. (It might be a good idea to tape the interviews with the subjects' permission.)

Write a brief account of each of the interviews to bring out the salient features of the child's attitudes to himself, peer groups, parents, school, future, etc. Then discuss the main trends emerging from the younger subjects and compare them with the older subjects. Can you relate any of the trends or interview responses to theory/ research you have met with on the course?

Questions

1. What do you consider to be the problems of the position of the adolescent in our society?
2. What do you consider to be the major difficulties facing those going through the stage of adolescence? Can such difficulties be avoided?
3. What advice would you give to adolescents, to their parents, or to anyone in charge of adolescent people which might help to facilitate the adolescents' passage through the period?
4. Try to remember your own adolescence. What difficulties and problems did you meet? How were they solved? What benefits and pleasure did adolescence bring you? Does Erikson's account match your experience?
5. How would you define adolescence?
6. Give some reasons for early sexual maturation. Explain the social

effects of early sexual maturation for boys and girls.
7. Describe some health disturbances that frequently occur during the adolescent period.

Further Reading

Atwater, E. (1983) *Adolescence*, Englewood-Cliffs, NJ: Prentice-Hall
Lindsay, G. (ed.) (1983) *Problems of Adolescence in the Secondary School*, London: Croom Helm
Rogers, D. (1985) *Adolescents and Youth*, Englewood-Cliffs, NJ: Prentice-Hall

References

Alban-Metcalfe, B. (1978) 'Changes in self concept on transfer to secondary school', unpub. MSc thesis, Bradford University
Bandura, A. (1972) 'The stormy decade', in D. Rogers (ed.) *Issues in Adolescent Psychology*, New York: Appleton
Blos, P. (1967) 'The second individuation process of adolescence', *Psychoanalytic Study of the Child*, 22, 162–86
Carlson, R. (1965) 'Stability and change in the adolescent's self image', *Child Devel.*, 36, 659–66
Coleman, J. (1980) *The Nature of Adolescence*, London: Macmillan
Coleman, J., Herzberg, J. and Morris, M. (1977) 'Identity in adolescence', *J. Youth and Adolescence*, 6, 63–75
Douvan, E. and Adelson, J. (1966) *The Adolescent Experience*, New York: Wiley
Ellis, D., Gehmen, W. and Katzenmeyer, W.G. (1980) 'The boundary organisation of self concept across 13–18 year age span', *Psychol. Meas.*, 40, 9–18
Engel, M. (1959) 'The stability of self concept in adolescence', *J. Adn. Soc. Psychol.*, 58, 211–15
Erikson, E. (1963) *Childhood and Society*, New York: Norton
Farrell, C. (1978) *My Mother Said*, London: Routledge
Fogelman, K. (1976) *Britain's 16-year-olds*, London: National Children's Bureau
Gecas, V. (1971) 'Parental behaviour and dimensions of adolescent self evaluation', *Sociometry*, 34, 466–82
Gecas, V. (1972) 'Parental behaviour and contextual variations in adolescent self esteem', *Sociometry*, 35, 332–45
Jones, M. (1958) 'The study of socialisation patterns at high school level', *J. Genet. Psychol.*, 93, 87–111
Jones, M. and Mussen, P. (1958) 'Self conceptions, motivations and interpersonal attitudes of early and late maturing girls', *Child Devel.*, 29, 491
Lerner, R., Orlos, J. and Knapp, J. (1976) 'Physical attractiveness and self concept in adolescents', *Adolescence*, 11, 317–26
Monge, R.H. (1973) 'Developmental trends in factors of the adolescent self concept', *Dev. Psychol.*, 8, 382–93
Musa, K. and Roach, M. (1973) 'Adolescent appearance and self concept', *Adolescence*, 8, 387–94
Mussen, P. Conger, J. and Kagan, J. (1979) *Child Development and Personality*, 5th edn., New York: Harper
Mussen, P. and Jones, M. (1957) 'Self conceptions, motivations, and interpersonal

attitudes of late and early maturing boys', *Child Devel.*, *28*, 243–56

Offer, D. (1969) *The Psychological World of the Teenager*, New York: Basic Books

Piers, E. and Harris, D.B. (1964) 'Age and other correlates of self concept in children', *J. Educ. Psychol.*, 55, 91–5

Schofield, M. (1965) *The Sexual Behaviour of Young People*, London: Longman

Simmons, R., Rosenberg, F. and Rosenberg, M. (1973) 'Disturbance in the self image of adolescents', *Amer. Soc. Rev.*, *38*, 553–68

Tryon, C.M. (1939) 'Evaluation of adolescent personality by adolescents', *Monogr. Soc. Res. Child Dev.*, *4*, no. 4

Wall, W.D. (1955) *Education and Mental Health*, London: Harrap

12 SEX ROLE DEVELOPMENT

In virtually every culture the individual's gender is one of the most powerful determinants of how he is treated by others and how he views and treats himself throughout his life. Established unalterably at birth, the person's physical sex soon directs and pervasively moderates psychological and social development, identity, and roles and values during the entire span of life. Perhaps no other categorisation is as important psychologically as the one that sorts people into male and female and dichotomises their characteristics as masculine and feminine.

In humans, distinctively male and female development begins soon after conception. From birth, cultural and social pressures act upon an organism which already has certain predispositions and propensities resulting from early hormonal influences; these influeces have been operative from the first few weeks of foetal life.

Some writers have gone so far as to deny strongly that any factors other than cultural ones enter into the question of sex differences, e.g. Mead (1935, 1947) concluded that the characteristics of males and females in any society are solely the product of the expectations of that society and are not dependent on any biological basis.

In 1975 Maccoby and Jacklin published an analysis of over 1,400 studies of differences between the sexes published since 1965. Comparing the results of these studies and looking for consistently reported sex-differences they found that many commonly held beliefs were unfounded (for example that girls are better at late learning and simple repetitive tasks and that boys are more proficient on high level learning tasks and are more analytic). The only consistently reported differences they found were that:

(1) Males are more aggressive than females.
(2) After age ten or eleven girls begin to excel in verbal tasks.
(3) At about the same age boys begin to excel in visual spatial tasks and in general quantitative tasks. Even these conservative findings have subsequently been questioned. Whether such differences are innate or are the result of socialisation is almost impossible to determine as the effects of the environment have impinged on the individual before birth.

However, even these findings must be treated with some degree of caution, since:

(1) When behavioural sex differences are found, they are only averages. A great deal of variation exists within each sex, and the characteristics of the two sexes overlap greatly.

(2) A sex difference has new value. A finding of no sex difference has not. Thus, there is a bias in reporting. This bias makes it difficult to balance what is known about differences against what is known about similarities.

(3) When a sex difference is found consistently in a number of studies, it is assumed that the difference must be 'natural' — that is, primarily biological. In fact, establishing a difference usually says nothing about its origin. Moreover such origins are difficult to determine for, as we noted in Chapter 2, the interaction of heredity and environment commences even before birth.

Physiological Sex Differences

Males and females differ in every cell of their bodies, in that the nucleus of every cell in normal individuals contains either the XX or XY chromosome pair, according to whether the individual is female or male. In mammals the active process of sexual differentiation is that of the male. In the presence of the Y chromosome the embryo differentiates into a testis (in the seventh week of pregnancy in humans). The hormone secreted by the foetal testis then organises internal tracts and genitals into the male form and finally acts upon the brain to organise it according to a male pattern. Female differentiation is not a similarly active process — it simply occurs in the absence of the male hormone. The growth of a female-type CNS is apparently dependent only on the absence of the male hormone and not on the presence of female hormones, because the female-type CNS develops if testosterone is absent whether estrogens are present or not.

In this sense, the female-type nervous system may be said to be more basic, and it is in this sense that Ford and Beach (1951) have described the male as more highly evolved. There could be anatomical differences consistent with this. For instance, Morel and Weissfeiler (1931) have called the grey commissure a regressing feature of the brain, pointing out that as one ascends the phylogenetic scale this structure becomes less complex and prominent, though it is present in all mammals below man. Only in human brains is it sometimes absent altogether, and presumably it is in the course of evolutionary disappearance. However, it is markedly more often absent from male brains than from female ones.

There are three related characteristics which seem to be inherent in masculine development. First, the male is more vulnerable and more at risk for a variety of disorders: more male than female foetuses are aborted, the male infant is more susceptible to a variety of perinatal and postnatal complications and throughout life men remain more at risk for many diseases and accidents. This difference is apparent from the moment of conception. There are more than 120 male conceptions to every 100 female ones, but prenatal mortality is higher among male foetuses so that by the end of term the ratio is reduced to about 105 male live births to every 100 female ones. The greater mortality of males continues beyond this time, and during the first year of life there are about 25 per cent more deaths among male babies; this seems to be independent of culture. The higher male mortality continues, and at present in the United States the life expectancy for a female is about 78 years, and that for a male, 67. (Studies of life spans of nuns and monks sheltered in cloisters from the usual rush of life show approximately the same figures, and this suggests that the stresses and strains of modern life are not the critical factor in the higher male mortality.)

Nor is this vulnerability confined to the physical aspects of development: mental retardation is more common in males and so are a number of disorders like autism, speech defects, reading disabilities, visual and hearing defects and behaviour disturbances. Truancy, delinquency and referrals to child guidance clinics are also far more common among boys than among girls. Bentzen (1963) suggests that the high incidence of behaviour disorders among boys is due to slower male maturation. If development is protracted, it follows that periods of risk or sensitive periods in boys are extended, thus both benign and malign influences are allowed more time to operate. This fact would also contribute to the greater variance and inconsistency observed in males. As part of a longitudinal study of over 1,000 children in a Swedish town, Bergmann of the University of Stockholm analysed the intellectual performance of boys and girls who, between the ages of 10 and 13 years, had missed long periods of school due to illness or who had experienced some domestic upheaval. These adverse circumstances were found to depress the performance of boys, particularly in non-verbal skills, whereas the performance of girls remained relatively unimpaired.

Despite their developmental retardation, males have many physical advantages. In all human societies, as far as is known, men are bigger and stronger than women. On the average the male is about 6 per cent taller and 20 per cent heavier, with larger bones and with greater bulk and strength of muscle. Men have a higher metabolic rate, produce more physical energy, and hence require more food. Correlatively, the male heart beats more strongly and male blood is richer in red corpuscles to the extent of some 300,000 more per cubic millimetre. These differences have an obvious relationship to the higher oxygen supply necessitated by the activity of the male.

Williams (1956) reports that the basic musculatures of men and of women are different, which is the reason the average woman cannot throw a ball as a man can or run as fast as he. The muscular difference is apparent even at birth, despite the more advanced maturation of the female. Bell and Darling (1965) found in the prone head reaction that male neonates raise the head higher and for longer periods than females do. The differences in the musculature and CNS of males and females are reflected in the typical manners of throwing seen in young boys and girls. No doubt with training these patterns can be modified but, left to perform these actions spontaneously, girls throw a ball overhand by holding the ball at the back of the shoulder and throwing with a forward and downward movement, the weight of the body being mainly on the right foot. Boys on the other hand, spontaneously tend to throw with a horizontal motion at shoulder level; they draw the hand up at the side and rotate and twist the body to place the weight on the left foot, and the whole body, especially the shoulders, enters into the actual throwing movement. Such differences are perhaps also basic to the characteristics of gesture in males and females.

Hormones and Aggression

Boys are more aggressive than girls, both physically and verbally. There are other attributes like assertiveness, competitiveness and ambition which have some affinity to aggression but are less disruptive. Evidence to date suggests that all these features are to some extent influenced by the action of the male hormone. Many of the other sex-typical patterns of behaviour, too, are shared by several primate species and clearly have their origins in the hormonally controlled masculinisation or feminisation of the foetal brain. There are three quite distinct sources of evidence which substantiate this case. The first source consists of the results obtained by Harlow and Harlow (1962) in Wisconsin. Male rhesus monkeys show a relatively high incidence of rough and tumble play, chasing and threat, while females show a correspondingly high incidence of grooming. From shortly after birth, Harlow reared infant monkeys with dummy surrogates. Nevertheless, from about three months of age these animals exhibited the sex-typical patterns of threat, rough and tumble play, grooming, etc., with near-normal frequency.

The second source comes from the hormonal manipulation of the sexual differentiation of the brain. When androgens (male sex hormones) are administered to a pregnant monkey, any genetic female foetus is masculinised and subsequently shows levels of threat, chasing and rough and tumble play comparable with those of normal genetic males. Conversely, the administration of anti-androgens which inhibit the action of the male hormone, has a feminising effect both upon morphology and upon behaviour, reducing both aggression and physical activity. The third source concerns the human analogues of these animal experiments, namely the sexual anomalies that result from 'natural' accidents, which have been closely studied by the staff of the Johns Hopkins University School of Medicine, in Baltimore. Genetic females exposed *in utero* to excess androgens secreted from the adrenals due to a metabolic disorder subsequently manifest 'boyish' interests; they show a preference for physical activities and boys' toys, are generally described as tomboys, have little interest in marriage and child-care but are keen on pursuing a career. Boys who were similarly exposed to excess androgen *in utero* are found to be more aggressive and inclined to fight than are their brothers.

Conversely, cases of testicular feminisation (genetic males who are phenotypic females due to the ineffectiveness of their sex hormones) show predominantly feminine interests. Very recent evidence from a group of boys whose diabetic mothers had been treated with female hormones during pregnancy suggests that subsequent levels of aggression are reduced as a result of this exposure.

Sensory Differences

Boys and girls also differ in certain sensory and perceptual capacities, the differences often being evident soon after birth. Girls have lower touch and pain thresholds, a keener sense of smell and are better at sound discrimination and localisation. For example McGuinness (1975), using pure tones, found that females had lower thresholds to high frequency sounds, and had a far greater sensitivity to volume. Women were found to set a comfortable loudness level significantly below that of men across the entire frequency range. In practice this finding means that when a hi-fi or television is set to fairly loud levels (80–85 db) women will hear the sound as phenomenally twice as loud as the men. Women were also found to be less tolerant of repeating auditory signals, such as a ticking clock. Boys on the other hand have superior visual and spatial abilities. The early reliance on particular sensory modalities has special implications for learning and education. Women are also superior to men in tactile stimulation. According to a study by Bell and Costello (1964), who found evidence of greater tactile sensitivity in female neonates, this sex difference is present at birth. This greater tactile sensitivity is incorporated into the ability to exhibit a high control over discreet digital coordination. This ability is exemplified in tasks of handwork, writing, typing, musical performance and so forth (Hutt, 1978).

Sex differences in sensory perception are caused by differences in the basic neurophysiology, specifically those that influence the rate of conductivity of nerve tissue. Because longer refractory periods are characteristic of males, statistically more of rapidly repeated stimuli fall into the refractory period of previous ones, and the adaptations of men are therefore slower. Women, on the other hand, have a shorter refractory period and a greater number of nerve impulses per unit time and therefore are able to respond quickly to more details and to adapt more quickly.

Environment and Socialisation

Terminology

The clarification of a few terms would be useful at this juncture before discussing sex role socialisation.

(1) Sex is the ascription to an individual of maleness or femaleness on the basis of biological features such as gonads and hormones and external genitalia.
(2) Gender refers to masculinity or femininity, *not* to male and female which are biological descriptions. Masculinity and feminity

are the collection of behaviours and attributes deemed appropriate and relevant in a specific culture at a particular time to males and females respectively. There is no biological law, no God-given imperative that males are undoubtedly going to manifest masculine behaviour, or females feminine behaviour. These behaviours are learned as part of the socialisation processes. Being a feminine female or masculine male and emitting the correct sex-typed behaviour elicits from others' confirmatory responses that indicate the acceptable congruences between biological and psycho-social attributes. To be male or female, and to behave appropriately facilitates effective personal and social functioning.

3.   Sex role identity, or sex typing is the internalisation of the behaviour that the culture labels masculine or feminine. Thus sex role identity may also be considered as the sex role self-concept, i.e. the evaluated self-image fits the demands of the masculine or feminine stereotype. So the individual's perception of his/her own degree of masculinity/femininity is based on how far the individual fits the publicly shared beliefs about appropriate characteristics for males and females.

4.   Sex role stereotypes are conventional images of gender, i.e. which behaviours and attributes are regarded as masculine and which feminine. Such sex role stereotypes control our expectations of other men and women, with particular respect to their behaviour, their interests, their occupations and their psycho-social characteristics. At the same time, each person attempts to 'fit in' to these cultural expectations themselves, in the way they behave. Stereotypes form a straitjacket from which it is difficult to escape. Stereotypes often have no rational basis on which they can be justified and are learned as part of socialisation. Thus there are subtle and sometimes not so subtle social pressures to conform to sex role stereotypes. Using these stereotypes, then, society allocates abilities and characteristics to individuals on the basis of sex with a degree of arbitrariness which can amount to a denial of individual ability and autonomy.

5.   Identification is a necessary process involved in achieving sex role identity or sex role self-concept. Psychoanalytic theory was the source of the concept of identification. Identification is essentially an unconscious process that enables a child to think, feel and behave along similar lines to significant others in his environment. More specifically the child starts to behave as though he were that other person. Earliest and most potent identifications

are with parents, though of course peer group members, teachers, pop stars etc., will later take on identification properties. Some of the young child's developing self-concept, especially sex-role-appropriate behaviour, derives from identification with people significant to him.

Theories of Identification

Freud's Theory

Freud attempts to explain identification in male children through the resolution of the Oedipus complex, whereby the boy identifies with the father, the potential aggressor, out of fear of castration, should the father ever find out about the boy's desire for the mother as a sexual object. By identifying with the father, the male child can vicariously enjoy the mother's love, and at the same time acquire masculine values and traits. To explain the identification of the female child with the mother, Freud has to manipulate the male case into an even more contorted explanation. He suggests that the girl feels she has suffered castration already and wants the father as he has the prized organ. However the girl fears the loss of mother's love and takes her as an identification model. Sex role identity and sex-appropriate behaviour emerge for Freud out of a maelstrom of unconscious fears and conflicts, not out of social reality and learning.

The nature of Freud's theory does not lend itself to experimental verification, and acceptance of his view implies an acceptance of other major hypothetical Freudian constructs such as the role of the unconscious, the primacy of sexuality etc. All this strains the credibility of the theory. In an extension of this Freudian drama, identification has been seen as being based on the power held by the model. This use of the parent as a model leads into another approach to identification.

Social Learning Theory (Bandura, 1977; Mischel, 1966)

The learning of appropriate sex roles, according to the social learning approach, involves reinforcement, punishment, imitation and modelling. The model is chosen accordingly for its reinforcing properties, particularly those of power and nurturance. The child imitates models with these qualities and of course parents, teachers, and other caretakers possess these qualities as well as being accessible to children for considerable periods of time. Differential reinforcement, the shaping of behaviour plus the attachment of verbal tags ('good girl'; 'you are a baby!') as secondary reinforcement ensure each child becomes well aware of what is expected of him, and that behaviours are differentially appropriate to the sexes. Social learning theory has been considered in more depth in Chapter 4.

The process of learning appropriate sex behaviour is usually facilitated or retarded by the parents who act as models. This factor has been primarily studied with children who have a father absent rather than in families where the mother is absent. Most of the research has been done on the influence of father absence from the home, and little is known about the effects of mother absence. In general, it has been found that father absence from the home has a disadvantageous effect on boys. The disadvantageous effect of father absence is moderated by the time of absence. If the father is present until the boy is five years old, the effect of later absence appears to be minimal (Hetherington, 1966). The fact that father absence influences the development of male children indicates that the effects of modelling are crucial in sex-typing. If the father is not present in the home, both male and female personality development are likely to be characterised by increased femininity. In general, the findings support the role of modelling in the development of sex-appropriate behaviour.

Kohlberg's Cognitive Developmental Theory

Kohlberg argues in his approach to sex role attainment that each child makes a cognitive judgement early in his life that leads to identification and the performance of sex-appropriate behaviours. Kohlberg views gender as the only fixed category by which a child can discriminate itself from others. The onset of this cognitive judgement is believed to be around four years of age but the child is six or seven before the process is complete. In other words the understanding of sex roles depends on the development of cognitive ability. In the early stages Kohlberg argues that children comprehend sex roles in physical terms e.g. size, and shape. A full understanding of the constancy of gender can only come with the development of conservation (cf. Piaget, Chapter 5). The child's difficulties in establishing clear and stable gender definition closely parallel his difficulties in establishing stable definitions of other physical concepts and the former are resolved around the same time as the latter are.

This self-categorisation of gender identity is the anchorage point for future sex role behaviour and sex role self-concepts. It is relatively immutable once formed. The Kohlberg sequence is, 'I am a girl; I want therefore to do girlish things, and derive therefrom approval and reward'. In social learning theory it was the reward that encouraged the child to behave in appropriate ways.

Evaluation

Three different models of sex role identification have been considered in outline but none seems sufficient on its own to explain the development of sex role identification. Imitation, reinforcement, cognitive development and appropriate models are all required in varying degrees depending on context and behaviour. However, there is general agreement that the major sources of sex role identity for the young child are the identifications with the same-sexed parent and the degree to which this identification is congruent with wider cultures' definition of sex roles. So while parents are the original prototypes the gradual extension of the child's environment to include peer group and school provides direct confrontation with the stereotypes of the broader community which force the child to bring his original definitions into line.

Research evidence tends not to provide much support for any theory of identification. Freud's theory in any case is untestable.

Sex Role Socalisation

It is generally accepted that boys and girls are socialised differently in our culture. Differences in toys, in the furnishing of bedrooms, in clothing and in expectancies of behaviour, subtly and sometimes not so subtly cued via verbal and non-verbal communications, are all part of the traditional social conspiracy to ensure that boys and girls function according to their prescriptive stereotypes. Perhaps few teachers and parents are consciously aware of their moulding of the child to meet specific sex role standards and much of the differential treatment handed out is a reflection of the adults' own life history, their firm sex role socialisation dimming awareness of its generational replication.

The learning of the differences between male and female behaviour begins early. By age two years, children can identify male activities as being 'male' with a high degree of accuracy. At age two and a half years, children can identify items by appearance and task according to sex linkage at 75 per cent accuracy for both male and female items (Vener and Snyder, 1966), and by age three they can judge a wide range of activities according to sex appropriateness. Sex differences in preferred play activities and in actual play also are noted by age three (Fagot and Patterson, 1969).

But when the adult experimenter goes out of the room, boys will experiment with the feminine objects, while for the girls the presence or absence of the experimenter makes little difference (Hartup and Moore, 1963). It is as though boys are interested in these things but know that they must not play with them when anybody is watching — a clear sign that they have learned to expect negative feedback for showing such interests. The consistency of individual children's sex typing may not be strong, particularly in play behaviour and a number of writers have argued that masculinity and femininity are not opposites — that there is a considerable overlapping in the qualities regarded as characteristic of a given sex (Bem, 1974). When these researchers assessed feminine and masculine sex typing independently, they found that some individuals rated high and some low on both sex's characteristics, although the majority of people had more same-sex than cross-sex characteristics. Bem has used the term androgynous for people who achieve high scores on both masculinity and femininity scales. Why some children are more sex-typed than others and why a young boy fears being thought of as an effeminate weakling far more than a young girl fears being labelled a tomboy seem to reside in social pressures when applied in child rearing practices.

A very young boy who tries on his mother's high-heeled shoes or puts on lipstick may be regarded with amused tolerance or gently ridiculed, but such behaviour in an older child is regarded as outrageous rather than funny. Fathers react especially strongly to any such signs of feminine tendencies in their sons. A possible interpretation of such reactions is that many men experience emotional revulsion over signs of homosexuality in other males. Little girls are allowed more latitude for cross-sex interests and play, but they too are pressured to behave in sex-appropriate ways — again primarily by their fathers. Many fathers react warmly to signs of femininity in their daughters. Fathers then appear to play a crucial role in exerting pressure for sex-appropriate behaviour, compared to mothers.

The importance of fathers in the development of children's sex-typed behaviour is further emphasised by Hetherington's (1967) studies of the relationship between parents' attitudes and attributes and children's characteristics. She found that preschool and kindergarten girls who were most stereotypically feminine had fathers who were warm and assertive, and liked and approved of feminine behaviour in their daughters. Boys who were most highly sex-typed had fathers who were dominant (in the sense that they tended to win when there were differences of opinion with their wives). Thus, the fathers' attitudes and behaviour had an effect on the degree of sex-typing in both girls and boys, although each sex was influenced differently. The mothers' attitudes and behaviour, by contrast, showed little relationship to sex-typing in children of either sex.

Sex Role Stereotypes

In most Western societies, the following are identified as appropriate to the male role: self-confidence, responsibility, maturity, independence, decisiveness, powerfulness, leadership, achievement motivation, aggressiveness and protectiveness toward women and children. Women, on the other hand, are frequently described as the bipolar opposites of men. As such, they are described as warm, passive, nurturing, selfless, emotional, obedient and as having a developed intuition. Additionally, female roles continue to be stereotyped primarily in terms of domestic responsibilities and female competency is portrayed in terms of fulfilling supportive, expressive roles to assist husband and children rather than self (Broverman *et al.*, 1972; Burns 1977; Prescott 1978).

Sears (1970) in a study of eleven-year-olds found that for both boys and girls femininity characteristics were associated with low self-concepts. The femininity characteristics were those of occupational and recreational choice, timidity and social conformity. It would seem that by the age of eleven, children feel that female work/activities and qualities are not valuable possessions compared to male ones. Thus high self-concept males are very masculine in outlook, while for women to have high self-concepts means denying some basic elements of femininity since to be feminine is to be inferior.

Characteristics relating to traditional sex roles show great resistance to change with feminine ones (e.g. passivity and dependency) showing a high degree of stability from childhood to adulthood in females but not in males. Boys and girls who are equally dependent in childhood diverge at adolescence in response to different social pressures. The boy perceives sexual pressure to become independent and manly; the girl, on the other hand, can continue to be passive and dependent because of traditional concepts of femininity. The sex role stereotyped characteristics are usually uncritically accepted and incorporated into the self-concepts of male and females (Chapter 10).

For the early adolescent at least, the male role is more rewarding than the female, regardless of whether it is adopted by a male or female (Connell and Johnson, 1970). Society's definitions of the male role emphasise mastery and competence, whereas society defines the female role negatively as dependent and submissive. Consequently the female may be positively reinforced for adopting certain male characteristics (e.g. competence), or she may be positively reinforced for fitting into the stereotype that society has structured for her. The male has a much less ambiguous choice; the male role is the only sex role for which he can receive consistent positive reinforcement.

Stereotypes influence adult perceptions of newborn infants. When seen for the first time through the viewing window of a hospital nursery infants known to be boys are seen as strong and robust while girls are perceived as soft and delicate even when there is no basis in fact for such attributions (Rubin, Provenzano and Luria, 1974). In another study on infants, Condrey and Condrey (1976) showed to a college audience a videotape of a nine-month-old's reactions to a variety of situations. Some students were informed it was a girl, others led to believe that it was a boy. When the infant showed a strong reaction to a Jack-in-a-box, the reaction was labelled fear if the infant was thought to be a girl and anger if it was thought to be a boy. So expectations and cultural stereotyping impinge on the child as soon as it is born.

Schools and Sex Role Development

The effect of the school environment on sex role development can be immense. Firstly each teacher, like the parents, will transmit their own specific sex role expectancies, and reinforce appropriate behaviours, punishing inappropriate ones. This may occur as part of controlling behaviour, or as part of the teaching curriculum, in which early reading material, text books and careers advice provide very definite stereotypes about sex roles.

The assignment of tasks in the classroom reflects the opportunity for sex typing as does the range of subjects provided for each sex. Expectations of performance in maths, science, art, reading, etc. all transmit a message about sex role standards. The norms of the classroom — quietness, literacy and conformity — are female rather than male. An analysis of children's books reveals conventional sexual stereotypes being taught, alongside reading.

Concern has been expressed for the sex role development of boys. As child rearing and teaching are primarily in the hands of females, it has been suggested that young boys are deprived of male models necessary for learning the male role. The school environment is considered as 'feminine' — requiring conforming, submissive and passive behaviours associated with the traditional female role rather than the male. Clearly these pupil role behaviours criticised as 'feminine' in school (conformity, silence, obedience) are those imposed by the armed services in order to make a man out of you during training!

Levitin and Chananie (1972), for example, found that student teachers and infant teachers had well-defined sex role expectations of their students and defined their preferred pupils as orderly, conforming and dependent. Fagot and Patterson (1969) found that nursery school teachers reinforced almost exclusively 'female' behaviours in both boys and girls (86 and 97 per cent respectively).

Stanworth (1981) found that a majority of the teachers interviewed believed boys to be brighter, and interpreted their work accordingly. And Stanworth found that this had repercussions for the self-evaluation of pupils. In her sample, all of the girls underestimated their ability (as stated by the teacher) in relation to the boys and, with the exception of one boy, the boys overestimated their ability in relation to the girls. The boys were very confident, the girls were not, and both sexes have good reason for developing these qualities, for the school (and the society) persistently encourages the development of these attitudes.

We know that confidence and self-esteem play a role in learning; those who have high levels of confidence and self-esteem are likely to achieve more than those who do not. In many mixed sex classrooms students are divided on the basis of sex and the growth of confidence and self-esteem is fostered in boys, and undermined in girls; one would expect that this treatment would have implications for the academic performance of the sexes, subject choice and future career.

Curricula and Vocations

By the time they are nine years old, girls' visions of occupations open to them tend to be limited to four: teacher, nurse, secretary or mother. Boys of the same age do not view their occupational potential through such restricting glasses.

There is an inconsistent relationship between girls' actual intellectual abilities and performance before leaving school and their subsequent employment. This means that while girls of poorer intelligence go on to achieve accordingly, this is not necessarily the case for girls of higher intelligence. At some point during their adolescence, girls begin to *underachieve* in relation to their real capacities (Sharpe, 1976). Very few skilled jobs in industry can be obtained without some kind of apprenticeship or training, and entry to these almost always requires maths and science qualifications. Arts subjects are of limited value for direct entry to jobs and usually lead to different routes in higher and further education, so that after leaving school girls are likely to follow different paths to those taken by boys of comparable ability level and social class background.

Thus although boys and girls go to the same schools, sit the same exams and are taught by the same teachers they have very different school experiences, particularly in relation to curricula options, lesson content and vocational aspirations. For example, girls tend to avoid maths and science because of a conventional view that girls are poorer at these subjects than boys, and a stereotype of the scientist is essentially male (Weinreich-Haste 1979; Walford 1980; Pedio *et al.*, 1981).

Failure of girls to select and succeed in mathematics and physical science subjects at secondary school leaves them unqualified for most courses leading to professional qualifications for which there is a high demand in the labour market and which lead to the more remunerative and powerful positions in the community. A choice of English literature, French and History might appear to offer promise of personal fulfilment, but even this is doubtful in the predominantly scientific and technological age in which we live (Byrne, 1978).

Mass Media and Sex-role Identity

The books children read and the television programmes they watch portray highly steretypic views of males and females. Studies by Saario, Jacklin and Tittle (1973) of children's reading books, and by Gerbner (1972) of TV content have shown this to be the case. In the Saario study, the reading-book series used in public schools (and published by several different companies) were analysed for their content. The researchers found that there were far fewer female than male characters, particularly among the central characters. Women were portrayed as less effective, less physically active and more conforming. What they did do in the stories was talk and give directions. When children are the characters in the stories, the boys take an active role (good things happen from others' efforts). Boys solve problems but girls get rescued. (Children's books have become significantly less biased in their presentations of men and women in the past few years, partly because of pressure brought to bear on publishers by women's groups.) The sex-role expectations purveyed by these are that boys and men are more highly valued than girls and women; that boys are active and achieving while girls and passive and emotional. As Weitzman *et al.* (1972, p. 1126) point out children's books reflect cultural values and are important instruments for persuading children to accept those values. They also contain role prescriptions which encourage the child to conform to acceptable standards of behaviour.

An American survey in 1972 by Women on Words and Images reported in Tavris and Offir (1977) looked at 2,750 stories from 134 children's books and found that the traits Americans value were mostly portrayed by men and boys. Boys make things; they rely on their wits to solve problems. They are curious, clever and adventurous. They achieve, they make money. Girls and women are incompetent and fearful. They ask other people to solve their problems for them . . . . In story after story, girls are the onlookers, the cheer leaders . . . even accepting humiliation and ridicule. In 67 stories, one sex demeans the other — and 65 of these involve hostility of males against females (Tavris and Offir 1977, p. 177).

Television offers a diet of stereotyped sex roles for children to devour too. Cowboys, gangsters and other adventure shows most often feature males while females are relegated to ancillary and domestic positions. Women are sometimes specifically presented as sexual objects with no other function than adornment and enhancement of the male image. Men are often portrayed in aggressive roles, e.g. in detective and western shows, where the moral of the story usually is that the more aggressive man wins in the end. Situation comedy again reveals conventional roles. The highly exaggerated picture presented by television is alarming since many children are glued to the television set out of school hours (Gerbner, 1972).

Clearly these portrayals of males and females are highly stereotyped, and repeated exposure to them may help to account for the strength and persistence of sex role stereotypes. Such a link is shown directly in one study by Frueh and McGhee (1975), who found that elementary school children who watched more than 25 hours of TV a week had more traditional sex role development than did children who watched less than 10 hours a week. It is possible, of course, that children who watch less TV come from families that differ in other respects as well; perhaps they have parents who display less stereotypic behaviour themselves. But TV viewing alone probably has some impact.

Summary

Sex differences are another aspect of the heredity–environment issue. There are a number of physiological differences between males and females which underlie behavioural differences. Males tend to be weaker in most respects and slower in maturing.

Differential identification with parents and teachers, acquisition of sex-typed skills and proper sex-role experiences all determine the degree to which an individual labels himself as masculine or feminine. Appropriate sex-role identity demands a same-sexed parent whose behaviour is relevant, who is nurturant and rewarding, and an opposite-sexed parent who also supports and rewards the correct identification.

Three major theorists have described sex-role development. Bandura emphasises the role of reinforcement and modelling, and argues that children are reinforced for imitating same-sex models. Kohlberg suggest that such same-sex model imitation occurs only after the child has achieved gender constancy, and that reinforcement plays little role in the process. Freud emphasised the process of identification as the resolution of the Oedipal crisis at about age four. None of these theories does a very good job of explaining the current data on sex-role development.

Evidence across different researches is largely consistent, revealing a common core of stereotyped characteristics. Females are described as warm and sensitive, socially skilled and inclined toward interpersonal and artistic interests. Males are described as competent and logical, possessing self-confidence, direct in manner and dominant. These expressive and instrumental traits are incorporated into the self-concepts of females and males respectively.

Such stereotypes are slow to change in our culture. Girls generally show lower self-esteem than boys by adolescence. This may be due to the tests being biased towards boys or because traits associated with femininity are less valued generally by society. Boys establish their esteem through achievement in many areas; girls derive their self-esteem mainly through social competence.

Television and books strongly reflect sex-role stereotypes and thereby help to perpetuate them. Within school, teachers transmit sex-role expectancies and the curriculum tends to reinforce them.

Activities

1. Watch at least eight hours of TV, spread over several time periods, and record the number of male and female characters shown, and whether they are the central character or a minor character. Note, too, the activities of each male and female character in the following categories: aggression, nurturance, problem-solving, conformity, constructive/productive behaviour, physically exertive behaviour.
2. Watch and analyse the commercials on at least ten programmes, making sure that the programmes cover the full range of types, from sports to soap operas. You might count the number of male and female participants in the commercials, and the nature of their activity in each case, using some of the same categories as listed in (1) above.

For both activities you must define your terms carefully, and record your data in a manner that makes them understandable. In writing up your report, include the following: an introductory section, in which some of the background literature is described and your hypotheses are given; a procedure section, which must include details of the programmes you observed, how you selected them, what specific behaviours you recorded, how you defined your behavioural categories, and any other details that a reader would need to understand what you actually did; a results section, in which the findings are reported, using graphs or tables as needed; and a discussion section, in which your results are compared to those of other researchers (as cited in the book or elsewhere), and any puzzling or unexpected findings are discussed and explained if possible.

Questions

1. Outline the various theories of identification and discuss whether research evidence supports any of them.

2. Are women the weaker sex? Discuss.
3. In what ways do schooling and the mass media affect sex-role learning in children?
4. Parents rear their children to conform to sex-role stereotypes. Do you agree with the statement?
5. Why is sex-role development regarded as part of the heredity–environment issue?

Further Reading

Archer, J. and Lloyd, B. (1982) *Sex and Gender*, Harmondsworth: Penguin

Bandura, A. (1977) *Social Learning Theory*, Englewood Cliffs, NJ: Prentice-Hall

Bem, S.L. (1974) 'The measurement of psychological androgyny', *J. Consult. Clin. Psychol.*, *42*, 155–62

Bronfenbrenner, U. (1960) 'Freudian theories of identification and their derivatives', *Child Devel.*, *31*, 15–40

Brooks-Gunn, J. and Matthews, W.S. (1979) *He and She: How children develop their sex-role identity*, Englewood Cliffs, NJ: Prentice-Hall

Broverman, I.K., Vogel, S.R., Broverman, D.M., Clarkson, F.F. and Rosenkrantz, P.S. (1972) 'Sex-role stereotypes: A current appraisal', *J. Social Issues, 28*, 59–79

Hutt, C. (1972) *Males and Females*, Harmondsworth: Penguin

Hutt, C. (1978) 'Sex role differentiation in social development' in H. McGurk (ed.) *Issues in Childhood Social Development*, London: Methuen

Kohlberg, L.A. (1966) 'Cognitive–developmental analysis of children's sex-role concepts and attitudes', in E.D. Maccoby (ed.) *The Development of Sex Differences*, Stanford, Conn.: Stanford University Press

Maccoby, E.E. and Jacklin, C.N. (1974) *The Psychology of Sex Differences*, Stanford, Conn.: Stanford University Press

Mischel, W. (1970) 'Sex typing and socialism' in P. Mussen (ed.) *Carmichael's Manual of Child Psychology*, vol. 2, New York: Wiley

Montemayor, R. (1974) 'Children's performance in a game and their attraction to it as a function of sex-typed labels', *Child Devel.*, *45*, 152–6

Rosenberg, B.G. and Sutton-Smith, B. (1960) 'A revised conception of masculine-feminine differences in play activities', *J. Genetic Psychol.*, *96*, 165–70

Rosenberg, B.G. and Sutton-Smith, B. (1972) *Sex and Identity*, New York: Holt, Rinehart and Winston

Saario, T., Jacklin, C. and Tittle, C. (1973) 'Sex role stereotyping in the public schools', *Harvard Educ. Review, 43*, 386–416

Sutton-Smith, B., Rosenberg, B.G. and Morgan, E.F., Jr. (1963) 'Development of sex differences in play choices during preadolescence', *Child Devel.*, *34*, 119–26

Wesley, F. and Wesley, C. (1977) *Sex-role Psychology*, New York: Human Sciences Press

References

Bandura, A. (1977) *Social Learning Theory*, New York: Prentice-Hall

Bell, R. and Costello, N. (1964) 'Three tests for sex differences in newborn tactile sensitivity', *Biol. Neonate*, *7*, 335–47

Bell, R. and Darling, J. (1965) 'The prone head reaction in the human neonate', *Child Devel.*, *36*, 943–9

Bem, S.L. (1974) 'The measurement of psychological androgeny', *J. Consult. Clin. Psychol.*, *42*, 155–62

Bentzen, F. (1963) 'Sex ratios in learning and behaviour disorders', *Amer. J. Orthopsychiatry*, *33*, 92–8

Broverman, E., Vogel, S., Broverman, D. and Clarkson, F. (1972) 'Sex role stereotypes: a current reappraisal', *J. Social Issues*, *28*, 29–78

Burns, R.B. (1977) 'Male and female perceptions of their own and the other sex', *Br. J. Soc. Clin. Psychol.*, *16*, 213–20

Byrne, E. (1978) *Women and Education*, London: Tavistock

Condrey, J. and Condrey, S. (1976) 'Sex differences', *Child Devel.*, *47*, 812–19

Connell, D. and Johnson, J. (1970) 'Relationships between sex role identification and self esteem in early adolescents', *Devel. Psychol.*, *3*, 268

Fagot, B. and Patterson, G. (1969) 'An *in vivo* analysis of reinforcing contingencies for sex role behaviours', *Devel. Psychol.*, *1*, 563–8

Ford, C. and Beach, F. (1951) *Patterns of Sexual Behaviour*, New York: Hoeber

Frueh, T. and McGhee, P. (1975) 'Traditional sex role development and amount of time spent watching TV', *Devel. Psychol.*, *11*, 109

Gerbner, G. (1972) 'Cultural indicators: the social reality of TV drama', Unpub. paper, Annenburg School of Communication, University of Pennsylvania

Hartup, W. and Moore, S. (1963) 'Avoidance of inappropriate sex typing by young children', *J. Couns. Clin. Psychol.*, *27*, 467–75

Hetherington, E. (1967) 'The effects of family variables on sex typing' in J. Hill (ed.) *Minnesota Symposium on Child Psychology*, vol. 1, Minneapolis: University of Minnesota Press

Hetherington, M. (1966) 'Effects of parental absence', *J. Pers. Soc. Psychol.*, *4*, 87–91

Hutt, C. (1978) 'Biological bases of psychological sex differences', *Amer. J. Diseases of Children*, *132*, 170–7

Levitin, T. and Chananie, J. (1972) 'Responses of female primary teachers to sex typed behaviour in male and female children', *Child. Devel.*, *43*, 1309–16

McGuinness, D. (1975) 'The impact of innate perceptual differences between the sexes on the socialising process', *Educ. Rev.*, *27*, 229–47

Maccoby, E. and Jacklin, C. (1975) *The Psychology of Sex Differences*, Stanford, Conn.: Stanford University Press

Mead, M. (1935) 'Age patterning in personality development', *Amer. J. Orthopsychiatry*, *17*, 231–40

Mischel, W. (1966) 'A social learning view of sex differences', in E. Maccoby (ed.) *The Development of Sex Differences*, Stanford, Conn.: Stanford University Press

Morel, F. and Weissfeiler, J. (1931) 'The grey commissure', *L'Encephale*, *26*, 659–70

Pedio, J., Fennema, E. and Becker, A. (1981) 'Election of high school mathematics by females and males: attributions and attitudes', *Amer. J. Educ. Res.*, *18*, 207–18

Prescott, P.A. (1978) 'Sex differences on a measure of self esteem', *J. Genet. Psychol.*, *132*, 67–86

Saario, T., Jacklin, C. and Tittle, C. (1973) 'Sex role stereotyping in the public schools', *Harvard Educ. Review*, *43*, 386–416

Sears, R.R. (1970) 'Relation of early socialisation experiences to self concept and gender role in middle childhood', *Child Devel.*, *41*, 267–89

Sharpe, S. (1976) *Just Like a Girl: How Girls Learn to be Women*, Harmondsworth: Penguin

Stanworth, M. (1981) *Schooling and Gender*, London: Women's Research and Resources Publications Centre

Tavris, C. and Offir, C. (1977) *The Longest War*, New York: Harcourt Brace

Vener, A. and Snyder, C. (1966) 'The pre-school child's awareness of adult sex roles', *Sociometry*, *29*, 159–68

Walford, G. (1980) 'Sex bias in physics textbooks', *School Science Rev.*, *62*, *December*, 200–27

Weinreich-Haste, H. (1979) 'What sex is science?' in O. Hartnett (ed.) *Sex Role Stereotyping*, London: Tavistock

Weitzman, L., Eifler, D. and Ross, C. (1972) 'Sex role socialisation in picture books for preschool children', *Amer. J. Sociol.*, *77*, 1125–50

Williams, R. (1956) *Biochemical Individuality*, New York: Wiley

13 PLAY

Play is a simple, commonly used word that is hard to define; it has little scientific value and tends to be a layman's label for the non-constructive and unrealistic antics of the child. When a mother tells a child to go out and play, she means 'Do anything, but don't bother me'! Schiller, the German poet, described play as 'the aimless expenditure of exuberant energy'. But what is play to one person is work to another. The difference does not depend on the activity but on the attitude of the person involved and the meaning it has for him. Work that is pleasurable and creative takes on the aspect of play. A brief, acceptable definition of play is: 'an activity engaged upon from choice for its own sake.' In this sense play can be seen to include leisure hobbies and recreational interests, anything that is pleasurable and voluntary.

Psychologists consider play or activity to be of the utmost relevance to the all-round development of the child. Play is a relationship between the child and other children, between the child and adults, and between the child and its needs and problems. 'Just playing' is a crucial ingredient in human development. Froebel put it very succinctly that play is children's work and work is children's play.

The Value of Play Activity

Value for Physical Development

This value is especially predominant in infancy when children spend most of their time in physical activity. Repetition in physical play is important as it develops coordination and skill e.g. walking, holding, climbing etc. The child learns to control his body and, at the same time, gain physical health and self-confidence. When a child is playing, there is general body movement, exercise, activity and repetition; through this comes neurophysical coordination. There is the stimulation of the actual growth and increase of strength of muscles, an increasing demand for oxygen creating greater respiratory activity; digestion improves and the blood carries more oxygen and removes more waste. Play, therefore, improves child health and physical development.

Value of Play for Learning

A child learns naturally and willingly through play. Opportunity and materials provide experience of things and this builds up functional intelligence so strongly emphasised by Piaget (Chapter 5) and by Hebb (Chapter 7). By the manipulation of material, the child begins to learn about shape, hardness, texture and weight. By making things, he learns relationships, sizes, shapes, makes judgements, decisions, compares and contrasts. He learns to attend and concentrate. Play is highly motivated behaviour as it is done for enjoyment and the implications for the home and classroom are self-evident. It means that parents and teachers have a strong educative force working on their side. The borderline of what is work and what is play is blurred and, through play, children are highly motivated to learn. As the dichotomy between work and play vanishes, children are less inclined to develop undesirable attitudes to work. If we regard education as something more than the learning of facts, then we will try to give the child experiences which will develop his whole person and enrich his future life.

The tendency to exploit children's activities for educational ends began long ago when Rousseau's fictitious program for the education of Emile was published. Since then the rate and extent of imposition of goal-oriented adult intervention has increased rapidly. At this time we see an intense interest displayed by educators in utilising the earlier, more plastic years of the child to achieve their ends. The proliferation of preschools, nursery schools, day-care centres, head start programs, educational toys, and television programs like 'Sesame Street' attests to the growing concern for children outside the traditional boundaries of the formal educational system. The boundary between play and education is rapidly becoming blurred and many disparate groups of professionals are concerned with the management of play. There is an increasing concern for the management of play to achieve goals judged worthy by the professionals concerned, particularly intellectual goals.

Value of Play for Social Development

Play involves the child in learning to share and take part. By playing with others, the child voluntarily submits to law and order, obeying rules and subordinating himself to a leader which prepares him for the social roles and hierarchies of adult life. Qualities required for citizenship are fostered and developed. The child learns to adapt his wishes to the wishes of others, to cooperate, to lead and be led. All this helps a child to build up a picture of himself, his self-concept, and even a child limited in ability can obtain some prestige, a sense of achievement in play with others. Moral learning can be derived from social play with qualities of unselfishness, reliability, loyalty, obedience, self-control, courage and promptness developing, as there are others as well as oneself to think about.

Value of Play for Emotional and Personality Development

This is interlocked with play as a learning and social process. Feelings of success, failure, happiness, uneasiness in the learning and social situations, influence a child's emotional and social development. Moreover play from a psychoanalytic view is a safety valve for inner tensions, anxieties, fears and frustrations. Children will project such tensions into their imaginative social and physical and intellectual play. Thus play can be considered to have a therapeutic value. The mother instinctively seems to understand what her child is feeling and wanting; she is the instigator of baby games and provides contemporary companions, toys and play materials.

In this way, the child at home is free to live his fantasy life and work out his problems in it. But what can be done for his emotional needs in other contexts such as school, hospital or where children may be required to behave in ways inappropriate to their other establishment, present development, background and life situation outside, and where there are too many children to ensure that each obtains individual attention in their own particular problems? These difficulties are somewhat alleviated by activity methods and projects. The success of these methods depends on the facilities they provide for the child to follow his interests and to develop free relationships between himself and those around him. A child identifies himself with an activity chosen by himself rather than with one imposed on him from outside. Approval and understanding of the product of the child's activity, e.g. his paintings or his writings, means approval of him as a person. According to the type of play, this may mean acceptance of him by adults in all his goodness and his ambitions to grow up, or acceptance of him as vulnerable and chaotic in the present or, perhaps, an acceptance of him in all his badness of the past. For example, the child breaking up the teddy-bear may be telling us implicitly of all his evil thoughts towards his baby brother and, in asking us to accept him as a teddy-bear beater, he is asking us in fantasy to accept him as the destroyer of the baby. This may not be conscious between the child and the teacher/mother but it is implicit in our genuine acceptance of him. With this sharing, the guilt is alleviated. We need to be sensitive to the child's play and what it means. Play therapy is a technique used deliberately by child psychologists to enable children to express themselves and give vent to their fears, angers and guilts in a natural situation. By playing out these feelings the child brings them to the surface, gets them out in the open, faces them, learns to control them, or abandons them (Axline, 1947, p. 16).

Gilmore (1966) found that when anxious a child will prefer to play with items which are salient to that anxiety. This action allows the child mastery over the anxiety-invoking experiences and a reduction in the psychic tension they create. For example, Gilmore found that hospitalised children preferred to play with toys related to hospitals (toy stethoscopes and the like). Any children who have had experience of hospitals, even if it is only for a day or two, carry with them very strong memories of being left by their mothers in a strange place where unpleasant things are done to them. However good the hospital may be, it is still a terrifying situation for a child; the size of the building alone can be frightening. In the same way he may relate feeling pain to a visit to doctor and dentist. However much the adult may explain, they cannot wholly accept the explanation. In order to get this understanding they play it out in fantasy. Many nursery schools realise the need to promote this play and provide, for the children's use, nurses' aprons and caps, a doctor's bag, a miniature stethoscope made from rubber tubing, and a bed where a patient may lie. Any given child may be in turn patient, doctor or nurse and so come to a greater understanding, at their own level, of the frightening situation. Again, as they are in command of the play they can stop it if it becomes too frightening for them to take. Other frightening experiences can be helped in the same way by the provision of dressing-up clothes.

Adults often wonder why children join in games where they are chased shrieking across the garden or room, but if they are playing out their fears in a fantasy role, from which they can escape at any time, it will help them to realise that their fears are not all-powerful and that they can come to terms with them. Even very young children will play at ghosts or burglars without having any idea what either are. By playing out a ghost or a burglar a child can demonstrate to himself his powers over these frightening entities and so come to terms with these fears of the unknown. There are so many 'unknowns' at this stage of life and all of them may contain aspects which to the child are frightening.

We can learn from children's play and obtain insight into their emotional conditions. Children whose parents want them to mature quickly adopt infantile roles in their play i.e. they regress. Other children who lack warmth and affection from their parents seek these in their play. Others identify themselves with a dominating parent and it seems as though imitating the parent helps the child to tolerate being dominated. Play becomes a safety valve, having intense personal meaning. Anger, frustration, fear, are directed at, and soaked up by, neutral, non-punitive, non-criticising symbols e.g. dolls, toys. Aggression has to be restricted in society and fighting is a natural response to obstruction but children face social standards which do not allow them to express anger and the emotions remain bottled up. One of the claimed functions of fighting and chasing games is to rid the child of such emotions. During air raids in the second world war, children got rid of their fear by playing at air raids in a very vigorous fashion and, as a result, very few ever developed neuroses. A similar playing-out of anxiety-provoking events has been noted in young children in contemporary Northern Ireland.

Value of Play for Future Adulthood

All the aspects of play already dealt with are directed at producing a balanced, integrated person. The production of such an adult is the end product of play. Preparation for actual adult activity is apparent in primitive societies where children run, hunt, fish, climb etc. In civilised society, activities take their place in developing basic skills, both physical and mental, in understanding the roles of adults, learning skills and introducing necessary social and moral attitudes. The child's imitation of adult activities means they are not so novel to him when he is an adult.

Socialising aspects of play are necessary for citizenship and the therapeutic aspects help to remove tensions and fears, creating better adjustment. In a nutshell, play enables a child to release all kinds of behaviour under conditions where success or failure has little importance.

Types of Play

Pre-Social Play. The first type of play that infants engage in is pre-social. That is, the six-month-old infant plays with a mobile dangling over its crib; it plays with bells, rattles, balls and teddy-bears — and it plays with itself. Only later does it learn the value and capacity for play that animate objects (such as its mother and siblings) offer. Indeed, at this age, the infant seemingly treats its mother as little more than a willing and cooperative toy. Three types of pre-social play — exploration play, parallel play and instigative play — are generally found, all of which Piaget would define as belonging to the pre-operational stage.

Exploratory play involves the child exploring its environment by crawling around and by inspecting anything that exists in its restricted life space. Given a spoon to eat with the child may bang the utensil on the table again and again, until it annoys its mother with the noise. Given green peas to eat, it may studiously drop them on the floor one by one, as if trying to discover its own version of the law of gravity. It may discover its own nose, or fingers, or toes, or sex organs, and explore them by the hour until it grows tired, or its parents express their disapproval. Later, it may build castles out of blocks, push toy trucks around, or exercise its artistic talent with crayons and colouring books.

Put briefly, during pre-social play the child goes about the necessary task of building up expectations about the behaviour of objects in its physical environment. The more that it explores, the better the child can become at predicting what it must do to get what it wants.

Parallel play is often the child's first step toward social contact with its age-mates. Even before an infant is ready to interact wtih other children, it may choose to play beside them, but not with them. A child may bring a favourite toy to another child's side, then sit and play with the toy (but not the other child) for minutes on end.

In instigative play, the child may indulge in follow-the-leader, mimicking 'Peek-a-boo', in which the actions of another person (perhaps even watched on television) directly instigate or lead the child's activities. Yet the young person does not really interact socially with the 'leader'. Instigative play is the final step, possibly, toward true social interaction.

Social Play. As the child passes from the pre-operational to the operational stage of intellectual development, its play becomes more complex and other people begin to become animate partners in its life rather than mere objects to be manipulated. Social play seems to be of three major types, formal play, creative play and free play. Of the three, physical free play with other children is, perhaps, the easiest for the child and, hence, often the first to appear. It is also the most disturbing to the middle-class parent who is often afraid the child will either hurt itself or be hurt by others. Yet free play is of critical importance in the socialisation process. As the child becomes more and more verbal (during the operational stage of its development, rough and tumble play drops off sharply and formalised play begins. The mock-fights of five-year-old boys develop rapidly into games of tag, cops and robbers and other activities in which rules must be obeyed.

In Piaget's terms physical free play is almost always a matter of accommodation to the responses of other children and of imitation. Creative play, on the other hand, is primarily a matter of assimilation, of 'pretending' that things might happen that have not yet happened. The child is thus trying to anticipate what kind of reactions (feedback) might occur if things were different than they at present are. Creative play is often a matter of using an object for other than its original intended (adult) use. A stick becomes a doll, a doll becomes a human, a human becomes a horse to be ridden — all in the mind's eye of the child as it tries out certain possibilities that do not at present exist. Piaget believes that creative play is the child's way of learning to manipulate symbols rather than objects and regards it the high point of all types of play.

Formal play involves cooperation with others in games and activities that are rule bound. Such formal play often fills the Physical Education and games lessons in schools. Such formal play is often structured around competition. The contemporary scene imposes competition and competitiveness to such an extent that there is cause for concern that behaving for the rewards attendant on the processes themselves (trophies, money, power) rather than for the enjoyment, is dominant. In this sense competition and play are antithetical. There is a tendency for those organising recreation programs, inside and outside school, to lose sight of the playful ingredient and substitute competition for cooperation. Competition is easier to manage. The process of striving for excellence relative to others is the logical extension of an activity for those who are relatively able in an activity.

Children's and school leagues in sport substitute concern for the end rather than the process. The young children who participate should be cooperating to milk the sport-like setting of the interactions and uncertainties that are inherent in their activities. The application of athletic models to the play of young children is inappropriate.

When unfettered by league requirements the children gradually escalate the complexity of their interactions with a sport from playing with its techniques and constraints, through informal continuous and unresolved cooperative games, to low grade competitions informally organised among themselves. Only at twelve years old according to Eifermann (1971) would the need to escalate the complexity of these informal games make sense of leagues and formal competitions.

Play Engagement in the Home, School and Neighbourhood

The importance of early experiences for the development of the very young child is clear. From sense data resulting from his experiences the very young child constructs the basic cognitive or symbolic connections between events that provide the foundations for later development. The influences on the very young child stem largely from the mother in our society, and there are growing attempts to provide the mothering one with guidance as to provision of a 'kitchen sink' full of early experiences. It boils down to a concern for what the mother or parent actually does with the child.

Parents should actively seek to create situations where the child is given opportunities to explore, investigate, and manipulate the items in its world. Further, the items furnished for the child should present 'pacer' stimuli. The items should allow the child to experience novelty, and/or increasing complexity and dissonance. In other words, they should possess arousal potential or impact by requiring the processing of information. After the child has explored, there follows the investigation of the properties of an object with the child identifying the cause-effect relationships embedded in the object. At this stage the child needs to test the reliability of its hypotheses about what will happen given a response. The establishment of reliable effect predictions depends upon repetition. In the life of the very young child this repetition is especially apparent. The limiting constraints of the physical environment are tested. The child who drops items from the highchair can be thought of as making repeated tests of what happens when things are left unsupported in the air. They then disappear. Alter the circumstances, do they always fall? This kind of experimentation takes many replications.

A child needs myriad interactions to maintain optimal arousal. Some homes and schools provide these. These homes contain much varied material, kept there for use by both adults and children, and they are populated by adults who are willing to interact with the children, despite their other tasks. When to this is added a willingness to reduce constraints to the minimum consistent with the preservation of life and material and the enculturation of the child, then the home will foster the growth of the child's complexity and development. In homes where there is a paucity of material or cooperative adult-child interactions, where there are massive and rigid constraints on what responses are permissible, or where the behaviour of the child is preempted by other prepotent needs then play cannot develop (Bishop and Chance, 1971). Soon the complexity of the child exceeds that of the environment, the available interactions are redundant and boring, and further development is slowed.

In situations requiring quiescence for long periods, the smaller capacity of young children to generate arousal from cognitive events faces them eventually with serious sensory deprivation. Their behaviour while waiting or travelling exemplifies the strength of the arousal-seeking drive. They brave the punishments of adults repeatedly in order to drive up the level of stimulation in their environment.

'High-Rise' Constraints

High-rise apartments, the places that many young families are now forced to call home, also necessarily constrain the opportunities of the child to indulge in the stimulation seeking of play. They are usually small, with little space available to contain the material chaos that results from the free play of children. They are designed for adults, with space for what adults do. Apartments require high density living and from this there follows a pressure not to disturb others.

Further, the space in which an apartment-dwelling child may explore during his play time is sadly curtailed. The interposition of stairways, elevators and access-ways makes mothers reluctant to allow even their older children to wander far from the territory they control. These limitations on the access to play of children of apartment dwellers are causing increasing concern, particularly in Europe.

Deliberate Provision: Toys

Toys and playgrounds are external provisions made by adults solely for the purpose of facilitating play in the child. As an outcome of having made these special provisions, many adults fall prey to the idea that children should only play with toys or playgrounds and feel justified in stopping children playing with real objects. Deliberate provision implies to some extent that the object is selected with the ultimate use of the toy or playground in mind, when then raises the issue, 'What are good playthings?'

It is possible to derive some guidelines for the selection of a plaything from the three principles that form the core of the arousal-seeking model. The principles are that:

(1) children play for the stimulation they receive;
(2) that stimulation must contain elements of uncertainty (it is to some extent novel, complex, or dissonant); and
(3) the interactions producing the stimulation must rise in complexity with the accumulation of knowledge about or experience with the object (the extent to which the uncertainty concerning the object is reduced).

Some playthings provided are better than others in that they sustain play longer, which means that they elicit a greater variety or complexity of responses. Better playthings provide novelty from the point of view of a particular child. The plaything has attributes that are to some extent outside the previous experience of the child, thereby engendering exploration prior to actual engagement with it.

Better playthings possess sufficient complexity to require investigation of their physical properties. A plaything should puzzle the child sufficiently so that it has to be handled, poked, pulled and tested. If the purpose of each element in the plaything is immediately apparent to the child so that its physical properties are predictable prior to the child's engagement with it, then it is less of a plaything.

Better playthings are responsive. They must produce some effect that is under the control of the child. They are manipulable. The more effects produced by the child's manipulations of the plaything's physical nature discovered during the investigatory phase, the better.

Deliberate Provision: Playgrounds

Playgrounds are no more than a combination of large playthings placed together in one location. There is no reason that playgrounds have to be outside but the tradition that has imposed this unnecessary constraint is strong, and few playgrounds are built indoors. Tradition has also decreed that a playground be designed to provide opportunities for gross motor activity by simulating, in galvanized steel, some primitive jungle setting. But the average traditional playground is not stimulating.

The children agree. Playgrounds are often deserted. Wade (1968), for example, studied playgrounds in Philadelphia and noted that the average visit time to a playground was 15 minutes, and that during times identified for peak use the non-manipulable items stood idle the large majority (89 per cent) of the time. Attendance at a playground was inversely related to the existence of other activities provided by a neighbourhood, among other factors. The arousal-seeking explanation for play suggests the answers. Playgrounds are not used because they do not provide pacer stimuli, or interactions with an environment that spiral upwards in complexity as the child revisits a playground. The principles and statements laid out above can be applied just as easily to playgrounds as to playthings.

Despite the fact that toys are largely purchased by adults, children have had some influence on their selection and toys have slowly improved. Not so with playgrounds. There has been little evolution in the standard playground; this year's playgrounds look very similar to those of 50 years ago.

Finally, it has only rarely been considered necessary to staff a playground with a leader who has the responsibility to guarantee the provision of appropriate raw materials, and to catalyse changes in the playground and its activities. While playground leadership is sometimes provided during the summer, the leaders are often drawn, temporarily and untrained, from the ranks of the summer unemployed, frequently students, and asked to administer programs on the conventional playgrounds. Since the only elements that can be manipulated by the leader in the playground are the children, the program has to rely almost exclusively on games and competitions rather than cooperations, with the danger that individuals and their play rarely surface.

The neighbourhood playground should represent a conscious attempt to make the children's neighbourhood environment more complex so that there are opportunities to explore, investigate and manipulate.

The adventure playground that has evolved in Europe since World War II has proved successful. These are interesting areas filled with bricks, lumber, dirt and scrap metal. Here are provided the tools, the materials, and the discreet leadership and supervision such that children can dig, build, change their environment and undertake cooperative projects that can last a whole summer. Such playgrounds are consumable. Each child can manipulate the playthings and produce effects on them. The setting is dynamic, changing as the various children add their own modifications. Cooperation in the management of material and the development of plans is necessary and projects can be progressively elaborated. In junk playgrounds, children use real materials to construct their own playthings and the play occurs during the process of their building as well as in their use.

The Handicapped and Play

Handicaps inflict a cruel blow on the development of an individual. They limit the potential of the individual, and they handicap the process whereby the person achieves his potential. The constraints of a handicap must be recognised, but because certain responses are denied the ill or handicapped individual, it does not mean that their need for arousal is lessened. With the exception of those whose arousal mechanisms are damaged, the need for play must be considered together with other needs.

Confinement of the ill or handicapped individual to bed for treatment or rest closely approximates to sensory deprivation. If the individual does not need sleep and is not sedated, then confinement rapidly leads to sensory deprivation which faces the individual with an additional problem. The provision of arousing events to the sick and handicapped is a responsibility of the hospital. It is a service made necessary by the inherent nature of the patient.

Nowhere are recreation services to the ill and handicapped needed more than in institutions delivering medical services to children and the developmentally retarded. Again, the lesser capacity of the children to engage in play behaviour, and the critical importance of play to their cognitive development, makes these services more critical. While short-term confinement may be tolerable by virtue of the novelty of the new setting, eventually as this becomes redundant the need for delivery of opportunities to continuously enter into arousing activity appears. This drive may not be strong if children are acutely ill, since their energies are preempted by the demands of their disease, but when they begin to recover, their engagements with hospital environments soon become boring. Thus long-term confinement while ameliorating one condition may generate another. Opportunities for arousal-seeking behaviour are usually provided by occupational or recreational therapists. These workers are professionals, involved in the patient as a whole, who provide things for the patients to do within the constraints of their medical condition. It has been necessary for these professionals to justify their presence as members of the patient care team on the grounds that they intervene directly and influence the treatment of the patient's condition. While this may be the case on occasion when an activity is selected by the therapist on the grounds that its side effects beneficially influence the illness or handicap, in the majority of cases their provision of services does not have, nor does it need, a medical justification. Their job has only been questioned because of a puritanical attitude that considers play or arousal-seeking as trivial. If optimising arousal is recognised as a basic human need, a need that maintains the engagement of the patients with their environments, then the provision of recreation services will become important in its own right as a human, not medical service.

The ill and handicapped humans have greater need for recreation or play services because their limited circumstances to some extent prevent their exploring for opportunities themselves. The principles for intervention to facilitate play in the ill and the handicapped are identical to those for delivering such services to the healthy. They require only an additional insight into the constraints imposed by the medical conditions so that, where possible, the activities contribute to its cure and, where they are not therapeutic, they do not hinder the effects of the treatment.

Summary

Play is a voluntary activity. Most theories which attempt to explain why children play are inadequate. The most promising approach is to explain play as a means of generating optimum arousal levels. All humans have a need for stimulation and will seek an optimum amount. Satisfaction leads to repetition of the behaviour in terms of Behaviourism's law of effect, with the rewards often being intrinsic. Cognitive level will influence the actual activities indulged in.

Parental provision of play items, parental attitudes to play, and environmental conditions all affect a child's playfulness and creativity. Parents who dislike untidiness, high-rise apartments, inadequate playgrounds can all impede children's learning and social development from play. Handicapped children need to play and arousal-seeking opportunities can be provided for them using sensitive insight.

Play has value for physical, intellectual, social, and emotional development. Play behaviour shows a developmental trend with pre-social play preceding parallel and social play. Children should not lose the enjoyment and self-fulfilment derived from play through the organisation and competition of recreational activity.

Activity

The activity that follows is an attempt to index masculinity and femininity by preference for recreational activities. It thus combines an analysis of play, discussed above, and sex-role development, discussed in Chapter 12.

Several studies (Sutton-Smith *et al.*, 1967) have shown that with increasing age boys show an increased preference for such boy-type games as wrestling and football, while girls exhibit less clear-cut sex typing in their game preferences as they get older. In fact, there are some masculine-type games for which girls show increased preference with age. Thus, although there are clear sex differences in game preferences at age eleven they are less marked than at age seven. With respect to sex differences in game performance, it appears that children perform best when they believe that a particular game is appropriate or suitable for their sex. The purpose of this observation is to examine children's play preferences over two age levels and the reasons given by children for their preferences.

Choose approximately three girls and three boys at each of two age levels, separated by two or three years. Administer individually the list of games in Table 13.1. Ask the child to check those games that he likes to play best. If he experiences any difficulty in reading some of the words, provide assistance. Following the child's completion of the list, select five to ten of the games checked and ask him why he likes those games. Record his responses. Compare the preferences by age level and by sex. Attempt to identify some patterns emerging from the reasons given by the children for their choices.

Did your results support the finding that there are greater sex differences at the younger age level than at the higher age level? Did the reasons given by the children confirm the notion that game choices are an index of masculinity-femininity? That is, was mention made of the sex-appropriateness of the games?

Did particular games stand out as 'masculine' or 'feminine' ones?

Table 13.1: Children's Games

____ Basketball	____ Dolls
____ Bingo	____ King of the castle
____ Blind Man's buff	____ Leapfrog
____ Boating	____ Make model planes
____ Bows and arrows	____ Make scrapbooks
____ Boxing	____ Musical chairs
____ Build forts or huts	____ Paint
____ Build snowmen	____ Pillow fights
____ Camping	____ Play records
____ Cartwheels	____ Read books
____ Chess	____ Ride horses
____ Clay modelling	____ Ring around the roses
____ Climb trees	____ Roller-skate
____ Computer games	____ School
____ Cooking	____ Draw
____ Cops and robbers	____ Dressing up
____ Cowboys	____ Fishing
____ Cricket	____ Football
____ Dancing	____ Gardening
____ Darts	____ Give plays
____ Hide and seek	____ Spacemen
____ Hiking	____ Spin the bottle
____ Hockey	____ Statues
____ Hopscotch	____ Swings
____ Horses	____ Tag or Tick
____ Jacks	____ Tail on the donkey
____ Scrabble	____ Throw snowballs
____ See-saw	____ Noughts and crosses
____ Sewing	____ Tiddley-winks
____ Playing with toy guns	____ Electric train set
____ Simon says	____ Use tools
____ Sledging	____ Volley ball
____ Soccer	____ Work with machines
____ Soldiers	____ Wrestling

Questions

1. What is the function of play for the child?
2. There are many theories which attempt to explain why children play. Which theory do you feel is the most reasonable explanation? Why?
3. What problems face the urban child in his play activities?
4. Play is 'the aimless expenditure of exuberant energy'. Do you agree?
5. Why and how is play activity used as a therapeutic technique?

Further Reading

Bretherton, I. (ed.) (1984) *Symbolic Play*, New York: Academic Press
Bruner, J., Jolly, A. and Sylva, K. (1976) *Play: Its Role in Development and Evolution*, Harmondsworth: Penguin
Garvey, C. (1977) *Play*, Cambridge, Mass.: Harvard University Press
Millar, S. (1971) *The Psychology of Play*, Harmondsworth: Penguin
Pepler, D. and Rubin, K. (1982) *The Play of Children*, London: Karger
Riddick, B. (1982) *Toys and Play for the Handicapped Child*, London: Croom Helm
Weller, B.F. (1980) *Helping Sick Children Play*, London: Bailliere Tindall

References

Axline, V. (1947) *Play Therapy*, Boston: Houghton Miffin
Bishop, D. and Chance, C. (1971) 'Parental conceptual systems, home play environmental and potential creativity in children', *J. Exp. Child Psychol.*, *12*, 318–38
Eifermann, R.R. (1971) *Determinants of Children's Games Style*, Jerusalem: Israel Academy of Sciences and Humanities
Gilmore, J.B. (1966) 'The role of anxiety and cognitive factors in children's play' *Child Devel.*, *37*, 397–416
Sutton-Smith, B. (1971) 'Children at play', *Natural History Magazine*, Dec., 54–9
Sutton-Smith, B., Rosenberg, B.G. and Morgan, E.P. (1967) 'The role of play in cognitive development', *Young Children*, *22*, 361–70
Wade, G.R. (1968) 'A study of free play patterns of children in playground equipment areas', unpubl. MA thesis, Pennsylvania State University

14 CHILDREN'S DEVELOPMENTAL AND BEHAVIOUR PROBLEMS

Problems in Psychological Development

Categories of Problems

It is not intended to provide a comprehensive account of all of these; the present section will briefly focus on three particular areas, viz:

(1) Conduct disorders;
(2) Emotional disorders; and
(3) Developmental disorders.

The so-called conduct disorders are characterised by aggressive and socially disapproved behaviour. They form the single commonest group of psychological problems found in older children and in adolescents. The causes are not well defined but most of the evidence points to the importance of certain adverse environmental factors. The vast majority of these children do not show evidence of brain damage or mental handicap.

The emotional disorders found in children are not dissimilar to those found in adults. Thus they are characterised by such feelings and behaviours as anxiety, fearfulness, unhappiness and social withdrawal. There is inevitably a range of fears and worries found in all children, particularly in response to strange or stressful situations. Many behaviours such as bed-wetting and nail-biting, which are found in children with emotional problems, are also found in children without psychological difficulties. The diagnosis of emotional disorder is therefore made when a pattern of 'neurotic' symptoms is found consistently and causes problems for the child. A rate of such problems in the region of 2.5 per cent is found in ten- and eleven-year-old children, about half the rate for conduct disorders. Although some emotional disorders persist into adulthood, most emotionally disturbed children go on to become 'normal' adults without obvious neuroses.

Developmental disorders are behaviours that result from the stresses and crises of growing up. The disorders may present themselves as conduct disorders, emotional disorders or physical disorders. Frequently, the developmental disorder can involve the child manifesting forms of behaviour more appropriate to a younger child, i.e. there is a regression in behaviour.

In the most general terms development implies meeting new experiences with the possibility of stress or strain. To counter this, any individual calls upon his inner resources or those skills, abilities and attitudes which are the product of both inheritance and experience. With increase in stress, people may either suffer breakdown or surmount it, according to the strength of these resources. Human nature and relationships are so complex that it is unlikely than an individual is ever, throughout his lifetime, completely adjusted, but maladjustment can be said to result from inadequately resolved conflicts that tend to persist and recur. Children must inevitably meet some degree of conflict throughout their developmental stages and every child is faced, at some time, with choosing between two or more responses in relation to some object or activity. The making of successful choices leads to favourable adjustment, while indecision, or poor choices, may lead to developmental disorders and maladjustment. Good adjustment is therefore a matter of degree, and the child who is able to meet environmental situations and personal relationships satisfactorily gives evidence of being well adjusted. One can understand in simple terms how a child 'breaks down'. Difficulties arise if, in terms of experience or resources, he is limited and the situation of stress or strain is more than he can meet. The capacity to withstand strain will obviously be increased or diminished according to the early emotional conditioning the child has received. If security and confidence have been promoted in the child by early successful relationships, particularly with parent-figures, such a child will tend to build up enduring 'ego-strength'. This will enable the individual to surmount stress more easily. The converse is also true. Negative and disturbing experiences at an early age will result in the child being more vulnerable to breakdown in some form or another. The two categories of conduct and emotional disorders are consistently found in most writings on children's behaviour problems though the category names may differ.

For example, Lunzer (1960) produces two groups, viz. of aggressive and of withdrawing children. An alternative grouping is into antisocial and neurotic, the former being those referred to as aggressive or possessing conduct disorders. Children in both groups tend to do more poorly in school than better adjusted children, have difficulty in developing social relationships, and are often in trouble with the law.

Stott (1969) views maladjustment and behaviour problems as manifestations of deficits in appraisal function, i.e. the ability to interpret the environment in a realistic way. Three deficits are identified by Stott:

Effectiveness Deficit. According to Stott, one important motivation of human behaviour — one which starts right from the earliest days of life — is the desire to achieve and practise control over the environment. The young baby may discover that, if he moves his arm, the rattle in front of him shakes. He repeats his action many times, enjoying his ability to demonstrate his effectiveness. Progressively, we attempt to achieve greater mastery over our environment and we enjoy practising our skills. But such practice and enjoyment depend on a measure of success. For a variety of reasons, e.g. given excessively difficult tasks or severe criticism, this effectiveness motivation may be impaired. The child then sees new situations as threatening, he expects to fail, and he may become established in the habit of avoiding new demands made of him. He may not even be willing to practise those skills he has already achieved, although here his impairment may be less severe.

Failure in Temporal Integration. The young child seems to live largely in the present. Most, if not all, of his actions are concerned with the satisfaction of immediate goals, or with the avoidance of immediate dangers or unpleasant experiences. He does not plan for the future and he finds it impossible to inhibit present actions for long-term benefits. As we grow older, we develop the ability and the willingness to defer action, to plan for the achievement of more distant goals as opposed to taking immediate, short-term, short-sighted action on an impulsive basis. Obviously, there are considerable variations in the extent to which, whenever we act, we take into account both the 'history' of the present situation and the future consequences of our projected actions. But in the case of some children, temporal integration, as Stott calls it, is badly lacking; it may even break down.

Failure to take the consequences of behaviour into account will, of course, often land a child in trouble. His seeking for effectiveness may be normal, but he gratifies it by whatever opportunity presents itself. If his ball goes over a spiked railing he may injure himself or tear his clothing by trying to climb over it. He is easily dared by other boys into foolish acts. In school he may play the clown and be a bane to his teacher. When failure of temporal integration results in such forms of behaviour-disturbance, it may be termed inconsequence (Stott, 1969, p. 145).

Social Attachment Deficit. Normally adjusted children expect help from adults and are prepared to trust them. Poorly adjusted children may expect adults to show hostility and rejection or excessive weakness. They may show unwillingness to trust teacher and parent figures and expect inconsistent treatment from them. Many of these children are the victims of maternal deprivation (Chapter 9).

There are differential effects of child-rearing practices even in what we would consider to be relatively normal homes with normal children. The severity of the child's behaviour problems will, of course, depend on how extreme the parental characteristics are and on the child's own constitution, as well as on his experiences with teachers, other adults and his peers. Rutter (1965) quotes Hewitt and Jenkins (1946) and other studies which contribute to a sorting out of types of disorder. These distinguish between:

(a) Over-inhibited withdrawn behaviour, which Rutter classifies as a neurotic-type disorder;
(b) socialised delinquency, where the child may steal and play truant but can be on good terms with his peers;
(c) unsocialised aggressive behaviour, where the child is openly 'at odds' with others.

Neurotic behaviour was found to be associated with parental repression and constraint, socialised delinquency with neglect and bad company, and unsocialised aggression with parental rejection (Table 14.1). Items (b) and (c) above are conduct disorders. While we may seem able to categorise several major types of behaviour disorder problems into neurotic and conduct categories, there exist a number of problems in identifying children with such problems.

Identifying Disordered Behaviour

There is a great deal of disagreement both among the general public and professional workers as to what kind of behaviour is maladjusted. Some behaviour which is nowadays considered perfectly acceptable would have been regarded as maladjusted some years ago. For example, Wickman (1928) found that teachers rated masturbation as

Table 14.1: Parental Behaviours and Personality Characteristics of Children

	Restrictiveness	Permissiveness
Warmth	Submissive, dependent, polite, neat, obedient Minimal aggression Maximum rule enforcement (boys) Dependent, not friendly, not creative Maximal compliance	Active, socially outgoing, creative, successfully aggressive Minimal rule enforcement (boys) Facilitates adult role taking Minimal self-aggression (boys) Independent, friendly, creative, low projectile hostility
Hostility	'Neurotic' problems. More quarrelling and shyness with peers. Socially withdrawn. Low in adult role taking. Maximal self-aggression (boys)	Delinquency Non compliance Maximal aggression

Source: Based on Rutter, 1965.

the third most serious behaviour problem in children out of their list of 50 behaviours. Replications of the Wickman study in America by Sack and Sack (1974), and in this country by Whitehead and Williams (1976), show that teachers no longer regard masturbation as a serious problem, ranking it 39th and 46th respectively.

Mitchell and Shepherd (1966) found how difficult it is to pin a label such as maladjusted to an individual child. Many children can be identified at home as maladjusted, as anxious or acting-out children, whose behaviour at school is considered perfectly normal. The reverse is also often true. The reason for this is that adjustment is always adjustment to something, to another person or to a particular situation. Children who have difficulties with their parents may carry these over into school and into their relations with teachers who occupy parent roles, or they may not. Furthermore, a child's problems may be transient. The maladjusted child of today can be perfectly happy and settled at home and in school a few weeks later. Even more deep-seated and long-lasting adjustment difficulties can sometimes clear up in a way in which physical disabilities or serious intellectual difficulties just cannot.

But perhaps the most important point is that decisions as to what constitutes problem behaviour are, to quite an extent, value judgements. What is a problem in one context or to one person may not be regarded as such in other contexts or by another person.

Some Behaviour Problems

Many 'disturbed' children demonstrate *developmental* problems in that their behaviour is a problem only in so far as it does not accord with the chronological age of the child. Thus, enuresis (bed wetting), grossly uneven sleep rhythm, and egocentrically impulsive behaviour are all acceptably normal behaviours in infants and very young children. Such behaviours may only be regarded as maladjusted if they persist into or reappear in later childhood.

Enuresis

Perhaps the most frequently met psychological upset during childhood is that of enuresis. It is the most important single factor accounting for the attendance of children at child guidance clinics, and a large number of untreated children continue bed-wetting well into late childhood or even into adulthood. Estimates vary but there would appear to be a proportion of around 10 per cent of enuretic children whose problem is primarily a physical abnormality directly inhibiting normal bladder control. Much bed wetting reflects underlying emotional problems. For example, a child may react to the trauma of being displaced by the arrival of a new baby by reverting to an earlier phase of development. In wetting the bed, the child demonstrates his own need for attention and affection. Enuresis may again occur as a result of the anxiety aroused by separation, and many children react in this way when first coming into hospital. Children, in face, react in many forms to emotionally disturbing situations and bed-wetting is undoubtedly one such reaction. If the underlying cause is of this type, one would expect the enuresis to clear up with the removal of the situation producing it and bed-wetting of this type is most often of a temporary nature. The habit may, however, be strengthened and the underlying emotional disturbance intensified by lack of understanding on the part of the adults responsible for handling the child. Direct punishment or the practice of attempting to shame the child out of his enuresis is seldom successful and usually only serves to worsen the situation. A simple appraisal of the possible situation to which the enuresis may be a reaction is more often likely to produce the most direct results. However, in the majority of cases, the cause appears to be somewhere between the two extremes of being purely physical or purely emotional. Studies indicate that most enuretic children fall into two discrete categories that are more directly related to the training regime *per se* than any other underlying causes. These categories consist of children who were trained too early and too rigidly and children who have received virtually no training. Treatment of the latter group presents few difficulties, merely taking the form of introducing the child to the toilet training which has hitherto been absent. Treatment of the other category is somewhat more difficult and prolonged. Most children spontaneously adapt themselves to toilet training at around the age of 15 months through imitation of parents and siblings. Although this represents the most desirable sequence, it involves a great deal of patience and work on the part of the mother and one can readily sympathise with mothers who prefer to establish some degree of toilet training at a much earlier age, although, as we have already commented, there can be no conscious control by the child during his first year. The real difficulty is that many adults who advocate early training do so out of an unhealthy attitude towards hygiene, or more specifically, an abnormally strong abhorrence of the child's excretory functions. The child's control over these functions is of such emotional importance to the mother that training is severely rigid and any lapse on the part of the child is treated as a major catastrophe. Apart from the anxiety this may raise in the child, the parental attitude may have the effect of emotionally over-weighting the whole toilet situation in the child's mind. In such a case, there is obviously more chance that the child will later react to emotional disturbance by a breakdown in his previously stable toilet habits.

As the majority of cases of enuresis are the product of faulty training, it is perhaps not surprising that the most effective forms of intervention involve a retraining approach. The most commonly used method employs pads inserted between the bed-sheets. As soon as the sleeping child begins to micturate, the dampness completes an electrical circuit, setting off a buzzer which wakes the child. The child is initially trained to rise and pass urine when wakened by the buzzer. Through a process of conditioning, the child eventually wakens to the stimulus of a full bladder and the apparatus can be dispensed with. This simple approach is so effective in the majority of cases that the manufacturers of the 'pad-buzzer' equipment often offer an unconditional return of the cost if results are not forthcoming after a fairly short period of use.

Although enuresis is a common symptom of maladjustment in childhood, it is obviously by no means the only one. Many of the psychological disorders at this time are in fact an exaggeration of normal emotional responses. Temper tantrums, aggressiveness, and anxiety associated with various childhood fears are, for example, some of the most frequently found forms of emotional disturbances in children. The underlying disturbance may also be manifested in the form of antisocial behaviour such as habitual lying, stealing, and the whole gamut of delinquent behaviour.

Aggression and Withdrawal

In the classroom, many problems arise in connection with a child's aggressiveness or withdrawing attitudes. Such exaggerations in conduct tend to appear when the child cannot cope with his frustrations or when he is deprived. At times, both reactions may be present, in that concealed or repressed aggression may be present in the withdrawn personality. Teachers find aggression more disturbing than withdrawal and note it more frequently. Aggression may be expressed in bullying, kicking or fighting with other children. Temper tantrums may be present, or, with older children, hostility with antisocial conduct: failure to obey rules, defiance of authority and generally insubordinate behaviour. These children may be reacting to failure, deprivation or rejection. Emotional deprivation is a strong factor in aggression and lack of parental affection or security appears to be among the most important of these experiences. Parental disappointment and lack of overt expressions of affection are frequently regarded by children as rejection. While the loss of a parent or parental affection can create great insecurity in a child, other experiences of rejection by peers can also shake confidence. If a child feels out of his group, or different from it, whether on economic, social or cultural grounds, this can badly undermine self-assurance. Aggressive reactions can also spring from failure. Where an individual is inadequate, or where the demands of the environment are too high, reaction to this failure can show itself in aggression in the form of destructive behaviour, restlessness, lack of concentration and application to work.

At times, the overdisciplined child may burst out into open hostility. Recurring outbursts of hostility may alternate with withdrawn resentment. The pressure of excessive demands nearly always produces hostility which may, however, be open or concealed. Overdisciplined children may not always show open rebellion but may displace their hostility, and vent their aggressiveness against someone other than the person to whom they feel hostile.

A tendency to day-dream may also be found in the withdrawn child, who, in contrast to the aggressive, is extremely timid, shy and retreats from group contact. Withdrawal is related to anxiety. Where the demands of a child's environment are too great, as in cases of parental perfectionism, then a child may retreat and show the withdrawing mechanism with severe self-criticism and self-doubts. If anxiety becomes excessive, fantasies begin to replace reality and to transform the world for this child. These children are frequently solitary. They tend to stand alone in the playground or find difficulty in making friends. They are the 'lone wolves' of the pack. On the whole, teachers disregard and underestimate the problems of the child who does not disturb the class. A child's tendency to be timid and fearful can be strongly reinforced by a nervous and fearful mother.

'Nervous' Disorders

The withdrawn child is often a nervous child too. Such children are easily frightened and disturbed by situations which, in reality, do not justify anxiety. The birth of a brother or sister may, for example, induce in such a child anxiety symptoms which have their origin in jealousy. This jealousy may not be anticipated by the parent, or, if recognised, its strength may not be realised. These children are also excessively timid, afraid of facing strangers, often sick at parties and frequently are afraid of school, because of the open competition which they must face. Often an elaborate fantasy life is found, as reality appears to hold so much danger for them. They, therefore, devote more and more attention to their make-believe worlds. In school, they appear withdrawn, quiet and shy and are often unable to make friends with their classmates. Such symptoms may be paralleled at home by food faddiness, or inability to sleep well, and thus a vicious circle can be set up whereby their parent tends to overprotect them. With this type of nervous child, it does not matter whether the cause is justified; what does matter is the reaction which is as intense as though the situation in reality were bad. At school, work is often poor and on the report card are frequently found comments such as, 'he could make far greater effort', 'better progress if he tried harder'. The inability to make the effort appears to be more an expression of lack of confidence than unwillingness to try. One commonly finds that such children feel that the people who scold them, particularly their parents and teachers, do not like them. With some nervous children, whose fears are less generalised, anxiety becomes attached to certain objects or rituals such that an element of compulsion becomes involved in the situation. Such children may perhaps fold their clothes in certain ways before getting into bed at night; some children require to run up and down stairs several times per day, perhaps feel a compulsion to kneel, or touch a certain door at regular intervals. The child cannot usually explain why he must perform such obsessive acts. It appears as if the ritual serves to deflect anxiety from the real source of the strain. These are some of the more extreme instances of nervous reactions.

Habit Disorders

Nervous disorders are also linked with other developmental disorders, such as excessive nail-biting, thumbsucking, soiling, stammering, excessive shyness and masturbation. As the name suggests, many children require help with these types of problems, because they have failed to develop some habit regarded as normal and appropriate for their age. On the other hand, such children with habit disorders may be those who have continued a habit which could be regarded as abnormal at their age, perhaps thumbsucking or stammering. Thumbsucking may be acceptable during babyhood but older children are expected to outgrow the habit. Where a child fails to establish a normal habit, this is due to the degree of his maturity or immaturity, and a clue to the root cause may often be found in the relationship with the mother. Her demands of the child in relation to fundamental habits are manifold, and frequently difficulties are created by her handling of transition steps from dependence to independence. This can be seen in regressions to baby ways after some period of stress, such as separation from the mother.

Exhibitionist

Some children are exhibitionists. They show off. The exhibitionist is often a nuisance, perhaps by clowning and drawing attention to himself. His behaviour may perhaps be an expression of, and compensation for, a basic feeling of inferiority. Frequently, older children who wish to remain the leader of a circle show off to gain the approbation of their friends. Positive reinforcement and extinction techniques can be used to eliminate such behaviour.

Truant and School Phobic

The truant may stay away from school for many reasons. With well-balanced children, isolated instances of truancy may simply be a normal manifestation of growing up. Truancy in a young child is frequently indicative of an inability to be separated from the mother or the home, particularly where there is a rival sibling. Older children who are easily led may play truant at the suggestion of others. A frequent cause is to be found in poor progress in school work. Where school offers little satisfaction to the child, he seeks more pleasant and interesting ways of employing his time. The older child who stays off school is usually found to be the anxious child. There is a significant difference between what is known as school phobia and truancy. In the former situation, a real element of panic and anxiety is usually present. The child wishes to go to school, but for various reasons is unable to get there. Usually the child cannot explain why he is afraid to go to school. Frequently this fear starts suddenly without an obvious precipitating cause. Coercive measures on the part of the parents usually end in the child becoming physically ill. The child remains at home, tense and upset, worrying very often because he has no idea what is frightening him. Such children appear to be in a state of acute panic, embarrassed at not being in school and unable to explain their absence to friends if they call. Anxiety and shame, therefore, become a feature of their condition. School phobia can be helped by behaviour-modification procedures as indicated later.

A child may be physically sick each morning before going to school and reach a state where the physical condition precludes attendance. The important factor may, however, be psychological and this aspect may be conditioning the sickness. Such a situation may arise where a child is unable to read or count, and is aware of his failure. Consequently, such a child may develop anxiety symptoms, and as a result he retreats from what to him is an intolerable situation. Subconsciously, to enable him to retreat or avoid school, he develops physical symptoms. When the psychological difficulty is removed the child is no longer sick and is able to attend. In other words, when his educational failure is dealt with constructively, then he has no 'need' to be sick.

Character Disorders

A further group of children who are a problem appear to show character disorders. These children are erratic in behaviour, impulsive and appear unable to sustain efforts or persevere with a task. One finds with them a lack of responsibility and obligation. They show shallow feelings and are unpreoccupied by worries, anxiety or guilt. Sometimes they show high intelligence and can be creative and artistic, but they are emotionally volatile, making friendships quickly and just as quickly forgetting. They are frequently referred to clinics because of their inability to reach their potential in work or behaviour. They are also met in the delinquent group and are difficult to help as they have little depth of feeling or integrity. In their severest forms, they are psychopathic personalities.

Hyperactivity

Hyperactivity is an adult complaint about children. Children are presented by teachers as being excessively active in the confines of a classroom or day room. They fail to sit still and attend. They talk, turn, wriggle and are easily distracted. They disrupt their peers. Parents complain that the child is too active at home and behaves badly in structured elements of the family life. They are a nuisance at the meal table, will not concentrate and are restless at bedtime. Hyperactive children become management problems for adults when the required or expected activity is not produced by a child.

The word hyperactive has become fashionable and large numbers of children are 'hyperactive'. In the United States it is estimated that from 3 to 5 per cent of elementary school age children are hyperactive. A large proportion of these children are treated medically by the prescription of amphetamine drugs that para-doxically often reduce the problem, albeit at the cost of some side effects like anorexia. Despite the success in treating hyperactivity pharmacologically there is clear dissatisfaction with a method of treatment that only erases symptoms.

The causes of hyperactivity are ill understood and among numerous offerings are minimal brain damage, chromosomal disorders and food sensitivity. But the most obvious explanation for hyperactivity among those free of organic deficits is that it is normal. In every sphere of human behaviour there is variability among people. It is to be expected that the propensity to emit activity despite constraints will vary. So it is normal for some children to be more active than others. This would imply that, while inconvenient, it should be expected and planned for. The constraints on being active should be altered to accommodate a normal range of activity rather than altering the internal environment of an otherwise healthy child by means of drugs.

A related explanation postulates that hyperactive children have higher than normal needs for stimulation. Their hyperactive behaviour may be generated by a continuous search for information within themselves and their immediate environment. These children emit relatively large quantities of information seeking behaviour. When this cannot be tolerated by adults they produce the complaints that lead to the labelling of these children as hyperactive. In a sense, this explanation characterises hyperactivity as an incapacity to inhibit activity when necessary. It coincides well with the notions that hyperactivity is often merely 'inappropriate activity'. It is in agreement with reports that hyperactive children have low tolerance of frustration and are impulsive with unreliable self-control, and that they exhibit an activity level that is relatively continuous; it is not turned off in appropriate situations. This explanation suggests that the structure of the setting must be altered to allow children with differing capacities to inhibit their activity to function independently.

Another explanation is that the behaviour of the child labelled hyperactive is learned behaviour. The child, for one reason or another, thrives on the increased attention generated by inappropriate behaviour. Such a child's behaviour is adaptive and is maintained by the social reinforcement inherent in the setting. Here of course management would require the analysis of the contingencies sustaining the behaviour (see Chapter 15). In one study comparing the play activity of normal and hyperactive children it was found that hyperactivity is situationally determined. In the play context there was no generalised excess of activity. In the classroom the problem most likely stems from the failure to comply with external constraints. Thus, on all the measures, the normal children and hyperactive children behaved alike in the absence of constraint. In constrained situations the hyperactive children do not or cannot inhibit their behaviour and so emit the behaviour of which adults complain. Such children would seem to need the delivery of more information per unit time than normal to meet their optimum stimulation level. So it seems more accurate to define hyperactivity as resulting from a child's conflict with the demands for compliance to a social setting that results in the emission of socially inappropriate responses.

Autism

Autism is a marked disorder of development which usually begins in the second or third year of childhood and has profound effects on social and cognitive adaption. Rutter (1976) describes three broad groups of symptoms which are found in autistic children:

(a) A profound and general failure in developing social relationships.
(b) Language retardation involving impaired understanding and production, as well as the tendency to echo the speech of others.
(c) Various ritualistic or compulsive behaviours, which are mainly manifested in stereotyped behaviours or routines.

The impaired social development found in autistic children has a number of characteristic features. There tends to be a lack of attachment or emotional bonding to specific individuals. The quality of social interaction also appears to be quite different since autistic children do not show an appropriate use of eye contact. Play with other children is absent. The language disorders in autism are sometimes confused with deafness.

There is a wide range of explanations for autism, from the environmental to the biological. The earliest explanations of autism tended to be environmental and based on an abnormal pattern of parent-child interaction. It was claimed that autistic children were more commonly found in emotionally cold, obsessive families but the evidence for these assertions is inconsistent. More recent explanations have focused on the cognitive deficits. One consistent finding that overrides some of the earlier ideas is that about three-quarters of all autistic children are found to have an IQ in the mentally handicapped range. Unlike the mentally handicapped they often show a marked variability in their cognitive abilities with a particular deficit in linguistic and coding skills. Because of this association with specific and general cognitive disabilities, there has been an increasing tendency to impute a biological cause. Organic brain dysfunction has been suggested since there is an association with later epilepsy and some evidence of EEG abnormalities.

Psychological approaches to treatment have undergone a change along with the change of thinking concerning aetiology. Earlier treatments tended to be based on psychotherapy but it is now acknowledged that these were fairly ineffective since autism does not appear to be a withdrawal into a psychotic-like state. There is now more emphasis on the language deficit. Specific behaviour modification programmes are often used to bring improvements in linguistic and social functioning. These have been found to be of help although it is always necessary to provide supportive help for the parents since the presence of an autistic child can cause a great deal of stress within the family.

Developmental Disorders in Adolescence

The main difficulty is in differentiating between the true psychological disorder or neurosis and the reactions to adolescence itself. In essence every neurotic reaction represents a faulty adjustment to the social environment. The failure of the individual to make a satisfactory adjustment may occur when the environment makes impossible demands on the individual. The failure may also have an 'internal' cause in that the individual lacks the maturity and stability to face his social environment. In most cases the cause of neurotic disorder lies somewhere between these two extremes involving both the individual's approach to his environment and the effects of the environment upon him.

The adolescent is often a rather insecure, anxious person bewildered by the many changes that are taking place over the adolescent period. Certainly, the behaviour of many young people, judged in the context of our more stable and secure adult existence, would appear to deviate from normal standards. When this behaviour is understood, however, in the background of the period of adolescent development, we can see that much of the young person's apparently odd behaviour is an only too normal reaction to an abnormal situation. The sources of disturbance in adolescence may be manifold. Conflict with parents, vocational difficulties, over-concern with religious and philosophical issues, sexual problems, and in fact any of the trials and tribulations of growing up, may result in subjective feelings of anxiety and insecurity.

Psychiatric Disorder

The prevalence of psychiatric disorder in adolescents is approximately the same as that in child and adult populations (Rutter *et al.*, 1976). However, the type of problem reported in adolescents is different. Depression, anxiety and emotional disorder, suicide and psychotism become more common in adolescence than in younger ages (Graham and Rutter, 1977), though more similar to adult disorders. About 13 per cent of adolescents have such problems.

Suicide

Shaffer (1974) showed that there were no deaths from suicide in children under twelve years but the rate increases from 12–14 years. The most common precipitating cause was that the parents were to be told of the adolescent's antisocial behaviour or failure on some task. Actual parent-child disputes rarely caused suicide. Many adolescents modelled their suicide on others, read in the mass media, or actually known. Suicide rates increase rapidly after 15 years old; boys are more successful while girls make more unsuccessful attempts! Jacobs (1971) provides a four-step sequence in the emergence of suicidal behaviour:

(a) Presence of depressed mood, eating and sleeping disturbances which continue.
(b) Social withdrawal and isolation.
(c) Breakdown in communication with significant others in adolescent's life.
(d) History of previous suicide attempts.

Depression

Depression can be a transient normal mood swing, shortlived and self-righting, usually a reaction to some minor misfortune in daily life. However, depression can also be a secondary symptom of disturbance, for example it can accompany anxiety and anger. If depression becomes long-lasting affecting the total functioning of the body — feelings, thinking, energy level, sleep pattern — it has become an illness and needs psychiatric treatment.

Depressed adolescents may present with straightforward complaints of feeling depressed but more often than not depression appears in the guise of fatigue and a falling off in ability to work or study, or as a physical symptom. This unexplained fatigue and malaise is often attributed to diet or climate and the possibility of psychogenic cause is often rejected by the teenager. Often there is considerable resistance to the idea of any psychological disturbance because of the adolescent's fear of mental illness.

Headaches and indigestion are common presenting symptoms of depression and, more rarely, multiple bodily aches or dizziness. In fact, it seems that almost any symptom can occasionally be depression in disguise.

A falling off in work or study efficiency is another common herald of depression. This is particularly marked in students as compared with, say, adolescents who are working in industry, where, though the adolescent may be mildly depressed and under-functioning, the specific job, with its relatively clear-cut function and hours, can carry the depressed person in a passive way for a while until the depression becomes so severe that he cannot even function from day to day. The student, whose work, through its very nature, requires constant intense concentration, is immediately adversely affected by depression or any other emotional upset. He quickly falls behind, starts to worry desperately about this under-functioning, and this worry itself increases his original upset. A vicious circle is therefore set up which quickly leads to academic disaster unless there is therapeutic intervention.

Other psychological disorders are often combined with depression, particularly anxiety. Anxiety reactions are usually triggered off by a stressful situation which brings underlying personality problems into painful focus. These underlying problems are the unresolved conflicts of early adolescence and the remains of childhood outlook and behaviour which have been lying in a state of uneasy moratorium while the late adolescent got on with his day-to-day life.

Physical symptoms of psychogenic origin are legion in this age-group too. Headaches, fatigue, menstrual difficulties, vague abdominal pains, fainting, weakness, multiple aches — the list is formidable. Thse psychophysiological reactions are difficult problems, because each case has to be carefully evaluated to exclude serious physical illness. It is also worth mentioning here that adolescents, in common with older patients, often use a minor ailment, such as a sore throat or a verruca, as a strategem to see what the doctor is like, and if he appears not to be too frightening they will then mention the psychological worry that is the main purpose of the visit.

Eating Problems

Many adolescents become overly concerned with weight, body size and shape. The body image and self-concept are closely bound up with pubertal physical changes. Of course, a person's weight and shape is a function of many factors while hormonal changes can cause weight fluctuations. Obesity and excessive overeating may have several origins. For some it is a failure of the physiological feedback of hunger cues. Others lack self-control and a sense of personal autonomy. It is only in their eating habits that they are able to express their own wishes and needs. Overeating can be a reaction to trauma so that the adolescent reduces depression and emotional loss by eating as a compensation. Since fatness is negatively evaluated in our culture, overeating can be used as a defence against sexual attractiveness and popularity. It ensures rejection and the confirmation of a negative self-image.

Some adolescent girls who are abnormally concerned about their weight make repeated attempts to control it by dieting and engage in occasional eating binges, secretly stuffing themselves. They usually plan their binges and choose food sweet in taste, high in calories and of a texture that can be gobbled down without much chewing. Once they start on their binge of eating, they feel that they cannot stop and must sometimes search out more food. They keep eating until they fall asleep or have abdominal distension and pain, which they relieve by self-induced vomiting. This pattern of abnormal behaviour is called bulimia. Usually after indulging in a binge, bulimics eat normally for a while or alternate between normal eating and fasting. Their weight remains within a normal range but has frequent fluctuations of ten pounds or more.

Weight loss or anorexia nervosa is typically an adolescent girl's condition. Society does portray an ideal female figure as a slim one and some girls will deliberately reduce their food intake. But it goes further than that, for an anorexic person also shows erroneous perceptions of her body image, and excessive interest in bodily activities. Those suffering from this syndrome lose 25 per cent or more of their weight within a few months by denying the body its physiological needs for nutrition and rest. Their dieting knows no bounds. Moreover, they expend great amounts of energy on physical exercise as long as they are able. Almost half of them are bulimics.

Amenorrhea is a common accompanying symptom. Many workers believe that anorexia is a function of psycho-sexual development, an important element of which is an irrational fear of sexuality. To be thin is a denial of femininity, attractiveness and heterosexual needs. Anorexics have often been model children (Bruch, 1974), fitting in with parental expectations and demands.

At adolescence the demands of maturing and becoming independent from parents cause the facade of health to crumble. Fear of growing up, combined with a yearning for parents' attention, causes them to reduce their bodies to an emaciated, childlike form. In a fictionalised case study, written by psychotherapist, Sven Levenkron (1978), who has treated many anorexic girls, Kessa expresses her fears of growing up as she attempts to deny the signs of puberty:

> Somehow it seems very important that her mother not know. If she did, if she knew that Kessa had stopped being a dependent little girl who needed her desperately, her mother would stop loving her. Kessa was sure of that. It had been the same when her breasts had begun to develop. Kessa had not let her mother see her without clothes for almost a year after that. If she had seen her body, had seen her become a woman, her mother would not have wanted to take care of her anymore. So she'd been delighted when her breasts had begun to shrink and her periods had ceased to appear. (p. 26)

Anorexics spend much time before mirrors, scrutinising their bone-knobby, broomstick figures, which they see as either too fat or finally at an attractive weight. They also develop a preoccupation with food, even while they limit themselves to miniscule, low-calorie amounts. They become interested in its preparation, collect recipes, plan and cook elaborate meals for others. Anorexics may eventually realise that they are starving, but this realisation is not enough to make them eat. Marlene Boskind-Lodahl (1976), who has treated a number of anorexic young women, found them to have no confidence in their own ability to control their own behaviour. They had never gained a sense of self-mastery. The high academic achievement of all these young women was not an effort at self-fulfilment but, in every case, an attempt to please parents. One in 300 adolescent girls succumbs to anorexia and most require hospitalisation in order to cure the problem medically and psychologically. Without proper treatment, up to 20 per cent of anorexics die of their self-inflicted, chronic starvation (Brody, 1982).

Psychological Treatment

Treatment is more difficult with adolescents than with children or adults since they have often been forced to attend the clinic and this adds to their general resentfulness and lack of cooperation. The wide-ranging mood swings, a common feature of a disturbed adolescent, hampers treatment and the building up of a constructive relationship with the therapist. Those working with adolescents also have to face the problem of acting out behaviour, i.e. the threat to take an overdose or leave home. Does the professional take each threat seriously or ignore it; this is a terrible dilemma since the threat might be put into operation. Another dilemma is whether to treat the adolescent as a child or as an adult. This is a 'no win' situation for whatever the professional worker does the young client can deliberately manipulate the argument the other way.

We must always be wary of assuming that if an adolescent gets drunk, tries drugs, etc., that such behaviours are indices of serious maladjustment. They may simply be transient experiences indulged in for fun, for experiment or because others do it.

Summary

Major groups of childhood behaviour problems are conduct disorders, emotional disorders and developmental disorders. Environmental influences, particularly parental practices, are seen as major factors in the development of children's maladjustments, though disagreements exist over what behaviours are problem behaviours and the role of context. Most behaviour problems appear to be a reaction to the environment as perceived from the point of view of the child who may respond with aggressive, withdrawal or phobic behaviours.

Common problems with younger children involve enuresis, school phobia, hyperactivity and autism. With adolescents, depression and eating problems are noticeable as major problems.

Activity

Hold an open-ended interview (i.e. free response) with several adolescents on adolescent problems. Enquire into what they see as their main social, emotional and physical problems, and what they perceive as the sources of these problems.

Further Reading

Erickson, M.T. (1982) *Child Psychopathology, Behaviour Disorders and Developmental Disabilities*, Englewood-Cliffs, NJ: Prentice-Hall
Hallahan, D.P., Kaufman, J. and Lloyd, J.W. (1985) *Introduction to Learning Difficulties*, Englewood-Cliffs, NJ: Prentice-Hall
Wicks, R. and Israel, A. (1984) *Behavior Disorders of Childhood*, Englewood-Cliffs, NJ: Prentice-Hall

References

Boskind-Lodahl, M. (1976) 'Cinderella's stepsisters: a feminist perspective on anorexia and bulimia', *Signs*, *2*, 315–20
Brody, J. (1982) 'Therapy helps teenage girls with anorexia nervosa', *New York Times*, July 14th, Section 4, p. 20
Bruch, H. (1974) *Eating Disorders*, London: Routledge
Graham, P. and Rutter, M. (1977) 'Adolescent disorders' in M. Rutter and L. Hersov, (eds.) *Child Psychiatry*, Oxford: Blackwell
Hewitt, L. and Jenkins, R. (1946) *Fundamental Patterns of Maladjustment*, Michigan: Child Guidance Institute
Jacobs, J. (1971) *Adolescent Suicide*, New York: Wiley
Levenkron, S. (1978) *Treating and Overcoming Anorexia Nervosa*, New York: Scribner
Lunzer, E. (1960) 'Aggressive and withdrawing children in the normal school', *Br. J. Educ. Psychol.*, *30*, 1–10
Mitchell, S. and Shepherd, M. (1966) 'A comparative study of children's behaviour at

home and school', *Br. J. Educ. Psychol.*, *36*, 248–54

Rutter, M. (1965) 'Classification and categorisation in child psychiatry', *J. Child Psychol. Psychiat.*, *6*, 71–83

Rutter, M. (1976) 'Infantile autism' in M. Rutter and L. Hersov (eds.) *Child Psychiatry*, Oxford: Blackwell

Rutter, M., Graham, P., Chadwick, O. and Yule, W. (1976) 'Adolescent turmoil', *J. Child Psychol. Psychiat.*, *17*, 35–56

Sack, R. and Sack, K. (1974) 'Attitudes of teachers and mental hygienists about behaviour problems of children', *Psychol. in the Schools*, *11*, 445–8

Shaffer, D. (1974) 'Suicide in childhood and early adolescence', *J. Child Psychol. Psychiat.*, *15*, 275–92

Stott, D.H. (1969) 'Personality and adjustment' in E. Lunzer and J. Morris (eds.) *Contexts of Education*, London: Staples

Whitehead and Williams (1976) 'Teachers' Perceptions of Behaviour Problems', reported in Block 9, Open University Course E201, Open University

Wickman, J. (1928) *Children's Behaviour and Teachers' Attitudes*, New York: Commonwealth Fund

15 TREATMENT OF DEVELOPMENTAL AND BEHAVIOUR PROBLEMS

There are a number of possible approaches to 'treatment', many of which overlap with each other. However, for the purposes of discussion it may be helpful to provide a rough categorisation. In the first place, we can say that there are two types of approach; in one, situational adjustment, the main emphasis is on changing the environment so as to reduce the stresses or conflicts the child is experiencing; in the second, treatment, or some kind of help is offered to the child directly.

Situational Adjustment

A variety of people come into contact with children who are having difficulties, and find themselves having to help. These may include doctors, head teachers, social workers and psychologists. They may decide, after reviewing the knowledge they have of the situation, to change the child's class or school, to have him taken away from his present home, foster home or children's home and placed elsewhere, or to make some other radical change to his daily or permanent environment. Sometimes this is all that is needed and a previously troublesome and unhappy child soon settles down happily. At others, however, this is not enough and either additionally, or in any case, some form of direct treatment is offered.

Child Psychotherapy

Child psychotherapy has a number of forms. It can include full-scale psychoanalysis, adapted for children to varying extents, but essentially following the classical Freudian pattern in which the patient talks about his dreams, and uses dream material and free association to help recall and work through earlier conflicts, so arriving at insight into his or her main problems. But very few psychiatrists or psychologists consider that even bright, highly verbal children can best work through their problems in this direct way; accordingly, they practise a number of indirect techniques. These include play-therapy approaches in which the child can express his conflicts symbolically and indirectly through painting, sand and water play and the use of other materials. Some therapists work entirely with the patient; at the other extreme, parents or others close to the child may be seen frequently in counselling sessions either by the therapist or a social worker. The outcome of this type of treatment is surrounded by the controversy over the validity of Freud's theories. At an intuitive level, there seems no doubt that many children are helped by the child guidance psychotherapeutic experience; but it really is impossible to say how much progress the same children would have made without this kind of help. Certainly, it cannot be claimed that there is conclusive evidence in its favour as, in any case, this type of treatment is frequently accompanied by other forms of help.

Counselling

Child psychotherapeutic techniques are essentially highly expert procedures but behaviour modification approaches, still usually under the guidance of a psychologist, are beginning to be used in ordinary classrooms. Counselling is a less specialised technique in the sense that almost all adults practise it with each other and, in particular, nearly all teachers, at varying levels of sophistication, give counselling to their pupils.

The most powerful model in counselling is the non-directive one which stems from the client-centred therapy of Carl Rogers (1951). The central assumptions are that the pupils will provide the lead in the counselling process, while the task of the counsellor is to provide a climate of unconditional acceptance for the child. The counsellor will take a stance which avoids overt evaluation or judgements; his aim is to understand the pupil's feelings and to accept him without laying down conditions for the acceptance.

The objectives in this non-directive model seem to be:

(1) The child's self-discovery of his aspirations, goals, and needs.
(2) The strengthening of the pupil's ability to make his own decisions and set his own direction in life.
(3) The pupil's building up of a positive picture of himself as a person of worth, meriting the respect of others.

Although this model fits the aims of modern education and our ideas of the value of individuality, we must ask if it is suitable to the type of interaction existing within the secondary school and to the needs of pupils. It seems to stress self-definition and self-setting of objectives, but we must question its utility for all sections of the secondary school. Do all pupils possess the skills and experiences necessary to reach self-awareness of aims? Even if they reach this level, can we be sure they have sufficient resources to achieve their targets? If they do not, then the counsellor would seem to have a responsibility for providing such skills or ensuring that they are provided. We must ask, therefore, if the non-directive model is meaningful to a large section of the school-age population. While we may accept the aims of the non-directive model of counselling, we have to mount a search for new and more effective methods to achieve those aims.

Behaviour Modification

Behaviour modification is the application of knowledge from experimental psychology with animals to humans and mixed with a lot of scientifically stated common sense (Poteet, 1970).

Behaviour modification is the management of behaviour through the manipulation of the environment. Gelfand and Hartmann (1968, p. 205), define it as 'treatment techniques derived from theories of learning and aimed at the direct modification of one or more problem behaviours rather than at effecting more general and less observable personality or adjustment changes'.

Behaviour modification has as its goal the change or removal of a client's symptoms, usually concentrating upon the directly observable manifestations of behaviour. Exponents of behaviour modification regard neurotic behaviour purely as a learned pattern of behaviour which is inappropriate and maladaptive. It has to be unlearned, with more adaptive behaviour learned in its place.

With humans one of the earliest studies which pointed to the relevance of conditioning to the acquisition of a phobia is the celebrated case of Little Albert (Watson, 1920). In short, Watson's study demonstrated that a simple conditioning procedure could bring about a generalised fear response of a lasting kind. In the same way a burnt child not only dreads the gas cooker, it also fears pots and pans, ovens, salt and pepper shakers (if they were on the stove when it got burnt), pictures of flames, fireplaces, bonfires and even stories about the Great Fire of London.

The behaviourist psychologists working in the clinical area take the position that it is profitless to spend time trying to find out the inner causes of the disturbed person's behaviour (e.g. Freud) and that effort should be concentrated on manipulating conditions in the environment that will produce behavioural change. One does not try to find out why Jimmy misbehaves, but one does try to arrange conditions so that Jimmy's behaviour will be shaped into a form more acceptable to the teacher. The position implies that thoughts, feelings, inner attitudes and personal goals have nothing to do with how a person behaves and that the behaviour of the individual is controlled by conditions in the environment that surround the person.

Derived partially, but not totally, from the behaviourist learning principles, a variety of techniques such as systematic desensitisation, flooding, modelling, aversion therapy and operant conditioning have been found to be extremely effective in producing more adaptive behaviour in particular areas. Fear (phobic) and anxiety states can be effectively reduced by the first three techniques while undesired antisocial or immoral behaviour can be removed by aversion therapy, with a wide range of possible applications evident for operant conditioning. In all these situations the general approach of behaviour modification is to enable the subject to learn adaptive behaviour patterns he never learned originally or to unlearn maladaptive behaviours.

Positive Reinforcement

Positive reinforcement (often using tokens) combined with extinction procedures has been mainly employed in schools and hospitals.

In Schools. Behaviour modification in school tends to be aimed at keeping children from doing the kind of things that irritate teachers. The assumption is that if pupils 'behave' they will learn more. This is a doubtful assumption, but one that is accepted generally without question. Table 15.1 lists some of the behaviours teachers can either maintain or modify by the use of appropriate techniques.

A number of successful outcomes using operant conditioning in the classroom have been reported. In a study by Becker, Madsen, Arnold and Thomas (1967), the effects of behaviour modification techniques used by the teacher on ten such disruptive children were examined. A typical child was Alice who sulked a lot and sat in her chair moving her hands and legs or sucking her thumb. Before the experiment observers had rated the incidence of her disruptive behaviour, defining 'disruptive' behaviours as those which interfered with classroom learning, violated rules for permissible behaviour established by the teacher and/or reflected particular behaviour a teacher

Table 15.1: Stimulus Events and Examples of Positive and Negative Reinforces Commonly Used

Behaviour	Increase behaviour by Positive Reinforcer	Decrease behaviour by Negative Reinforcer	Eliminate by Extinction
Talking without permission	Answering, or threatening without following through	Punishing as promised (e.g. removing privileges or having student leave group)	Not answering or taking any notice
Correctly answering question	Saying immediately 'That is right'	Not praising student	Ignoring responses
Failing to have required equipment (pens, ruler etc.)	Allowing student to borrow	Not allowing borrowing and/or giving failing daily marks	
Disrespectful acts towards teacher	Entering into verbal argument with student OR giving lecture on bad manners	Ignoring student OR rapidly punishing without verbal interchange	Ignoring behaviour
Inappropriate verbal behaviour towards another student	Ignoring it or merely disapproving verbally	Immediate social isolation without verbal interchange	
Turning in extra relevant work	Approval and public acknowledgement	Accusing student of trying to curry favour etc.	Failing to give any approval
Consistently not paying attention to directions and asking that they be repeated	Repeating directions OR mildly scolding the child	Continuing with instructions	Ignoring child

wanted to change. In Alice's case, disruptive behaviour had been noticed in about 50 per cent of the observations made over periods of twenty minutes a day for five weeks.

For the experimental procedure Alice's teacher was given specific instructions, together with necessary training and support, concerning her reactions to Alice's disruptive behaviour. Some of the instructions were common to all the children in the study. For example, the teacher was told to ignore behaviours that interfered with learning or teaching, unless a child was being hurt by another and to give praise and attention to behaviours that facilitated learning, at the same time telling the child why he was being praised by using such phrases as 'I like the way you're working quietly', 'That's the way I like to see you work' and 'Good job! You're doing fine'. There were special rules for Alice, for example, the teacher was told to praise her for sitting in her chair and concentrating on her work, for using her hands for things other than sucking and for attending to directions given by the teacher or to communications from other students. Alice's behaviour was observed for a period of eight weeks during which the teacher carried out these instructions. During this period the incidence of deviant behaviour in the observation periods, as rated by observers, dropped from 50 per cent to around 20 per cent and stayed at this reduced level. Alice's disruptive behaviour had been very considerably reduced.

All but one of the ten children studied in this experiment made similar improvements and it is unlikely that all these changes were due to chance. Originally, disruptive behaviour occurred in the ten elementary school children on 62 per cent of the occasions on which they were observed. When a teacher followed the instructions specified by experimenters, the figure dropped to 29 per cent. A particular technique found effective when a child was disruptive, was to ignore the misbehaviour but, at the same time, praise a child who was behaving in a manner compatible with learning, i.e. combine extinction with positive reinforcement.

Harris *et al.* (1964) provide another practical application of behaviour-modification techniques. A little girl, aged three years and five months, who had just been admitted to a nursery school, served as the subject in the investigation. The nursery group consisted of six boys and six girls, all around three years of age, who attended five mornings per week and were supervised by two teachers. On her first day in the nursery group the little girl showed unusually strong withdrawal tendencies. She crouched on the floor and when she was approached either by an adult or by another child she would turn away her face or hide it in her arms. She did not speak to anyone, staying silent and unresponsive, while the other children laughed and behaved in a noisy and active manner. By the end of her third week at school the child still avoided all contact with children and adults, and her behaviour prevented her from playing with the toys and educational equipment provided by the nursery. She crawled everywhere and never walked.

It was decided to apply reinforcement principles in an effort to help this child acquire habits permitting her to benefit more fully from the nursery situation. The investigators concentrated on trying to modify the child's tendency to remain off her feet, since this was the aspect of her behaviour that most clearly prevented her from participating in the range of available nursery activities. The chosen procedure was for the teacher to attempt to weaken off-feet behaviour by not providing any reinforcement except at times when the child was on her feet. This was done in a relaxed way, the teachers carefully avoiding any actions that might suggest anger or dislike. No punitive measure was used at any time.

At first, since the little girl stood on her feet very infrequently, the teachers attended to any actions that approximated standing. To reinforce desirable behaviours the teachers would immediately approach the child and talk to her in a friendly and encouraging manner. To make immediate reinforcement possible one of the teachers stayed close to the child at all times.

Within a week of the teachers' starting to reinforce the child's being on her feet, and ignoring her off-feet activities, the original proportions of her time spent on and off the feet were reversed. After two weeks her behaviour was indistinguishable from that of the other children at the nursery.

A further illustration (Williams, 1959) demonstrates the maintenance of socially disruptive behaviour by reinforcement, and its subsequent modification by alterations to the reinforcement schedule. The child observed was a boy aged 21 months who had been ill for much of the first 18 months of his life and had consequently received very close care from adults. Understandably, he continued to demand almost continuous attention, although his physical health was now perfect. The child was especially demanding at bedtime, when he unleashed violent and lengthy tantrums. These were successful in closely controlling the activities of the parents, since if a parent left the child's room at bedtime the child would scream loudly and fuss until the parent returned. As a result, the parents were unable to leave the room until the child was asleep, and this often necessitated their staying in the room for periods of over an hour. If a parent merely picked up a book while he was waiting for the child to go to sleep, the child would scream and scream until the book was replaced.

The parents considered that the child was exerting too much control over them! To alter this state of affairs an experimental change was introduced, by which the child's crying and tantrum behaviour was no longer to be reinforced. Quite simply, the chosen procedure was that after ensuring that the child was comfortable and safe, the parent would bid him goodnight, leave the room and not return. A record was made of the duration of crying each night, and on the first occasion the child cried for about 45 minutes. However, on the subsequent four nights he only cried for an average of about five minutes, the duration never exceeding ten minutes. By the seventh night there was no crying at all. Clearly, in this case, once the effective reinforcement was removed, crying behaviour quickly disappeared.

Schools have long used systems whereby students accumulated points for good behaviour. These points could then be turned in for some material reward. Psychologists have taken over this idea but have preferred to award tokens rather than points. However, criticism has been voiced at the use of tokens. Levine and Fasnacht (1974) have summarised some fascinating research showing that the use of tokens reduces interest in the academic task. Levine and Fasnacht conclude with the warning, 'Tokens do lead to powerful learning, but the learning may, in fact, be token' (p. 820).

A further problem is that what is positively reinforcing for one pupil may not be an acceptable one for another child. Some children respond well to public praise, others would fight shy of it and respond far better to extra play time and so on. Thus the teacher has to employ his choice of reinforcement sensitively to each individual. With a token economy, of course, the child can exchange the tokens for his chosen reinforcement, e.g. sweets, a book, a trip out.

In Hospitals. In many institutions and wards for children who are mentally ill, or severely intellectually impaired, there is a tendency for the work to be somewhat custodial rather than aimed at training the client to learn new skills and to participate in more of the normal everyday life. Despite the best intentions of staff many of these kinds of clients do create for themselves a squalid and degrading habit with sights, vocal sounds and smells which ought to be eradicated. If we regard most of such behaviour as behavioural deficits then behavioural modification techniques can provide methods of teaching the child more adaptive behaviour.

Operant conditioning techniques provide a means of moving from custodial care to active education and training, enabling those in care to cope with everday personal tasks, such as feeding and washing; to acquire social competence, for example, willingness to intereact with others and not withdraw; and to eliminate disruptive behaviour. All these behavioural deficits can be removed through extinction (that is paying no attention), while simultaneously new and more appropriate patterns of behaviour are learned by shaping through positive reinforcement. The much-sought-after reward of nursing attention is typically provided, in the generally under-staffed institutions, only when the patient claims to be unable to feed himself, talks in a disturbed fashion, engages in disruptive behaviour, and so on. In contrast, when he is sitting quietly reading, or conversing with other patients, then he is extremely unlikely to receive attention from the staff. Operant conditioning would therefore predict that the probability of disordered behaviour is likely to increase the longer the child stays in a ward run along these lines.

For example, one programme used positive reinforcement to shape more desirable behaviour in a sample of 28 severely sub-normal adolescent girls whose IQs ranged from 20 to 50. The behaviours shaped included dressing for a meal, playing in a group, washing hair and working within the institution where they were in care. Reinforcements consisted of bronze tokens which could be 'spent' on such things as sweets, clothes, cosmetics, and privileges such as watching television. Reinforcements were programmed for improvements in behaviour no matter how slight. Each girl was reinforced on an individual basis with the particular response being evaluated against her baseline behaviour at the beginning of the experiment. Twenty-two weeks after the programme began, signficant gains in the more desirable behaviour were reported for the group as a whole although, as might be expected, there were considerable differences between individual improvements.

Other Applications of Positive Reinforcement. A dangerous condition of self-imposed starvation, called anorexia nervosa, has been successfully treated with behaviour modification techniques. This disorder usually affects intelligent young girls, and patients have been known to die from it. Doctors generally have assumed that anorexia nervosa is a physiological condition, and have sometimes prescribed tube feeding to prevent the death of the patient. Garfinkel, Kline, and Stancer (1973) among others, boldly assumed that the disorder is primarily psychological or behavioural, rather than physiological. Accordingly, they treated five late adolescent girls who had been hospitalised for the condition by rewarding them for weight gains. The rewards included weekend passes and the opportunity to socialise with friends. By the end of the treatment almost all of the patients' original weight had been regained.

Extinction procedures can be employed to eliminate some types of vomiting that are learned, rather than physiologically determined. Wolf, Birnbrauer, Lawler, and Williams (1970) report a case in which a nine-year-old retarded child was enrolled in a class in an institution for retarded children. The child began to vomit in class, and was sent back to her living quarters on each occasion. These investigators suggested that her vomiting was a learned behaviour that was reinforced by the opportunity to leave class. They set up an extinction procedure during which the child was required to remain in the classroom even if she vomited. As you might imagine, the vomiting behavior ended quickly.

Systematic Desensitisation

Emotional reactions may be classically conditioned. If we consistently experience pleasure in someone's company, then the mere mention of the person's name, a conditioned stimulus (CS) will set off pleasant feelings. In the same way, fear, anxiety and guilt may also be classically conditioned to stimuli and situations (e.g. the Little Albert experiment).

Some people find themselves caught in the grip of extremely strong, apparently irrational, fears. Cases have been reported in which children were terrified of such stimuli as illness, social contacts, death, cats, travel, being alone, blood, medicines and fainting, among other things. This not the mild uneasiness we may all feel in connection with some of those stimuli and situations. There are overwhelming specific fears, called phobias, that incapacitate the individual. For example, many children are so irrationally fearful of not having mother with them that they can never bring themselves to leave the protection of their homes, even to go to school or out to play. One technique used successfully to treat phobic reactions has been labelled 'systematic desensitisation' (Wolpe, 1969). This involved creating:

(1) some pleasant condition that counteracted the anxiety so that the organism came to associate the stimulus situation with pleasure;

(2) using a graduated approach to the feared situation. The basic paradigm is:–
Stage 1: Early trials link feared object into pleasurable sequence
Doing or thinking pleasant things ⟶ No anxiety
Stage 2: Later trials
Feared Object ⟶ No anxiety; pleasure and toleration of former feared object

The patient begins by making a list of all the situations that make him anxious and then arranging them in order, from those that produce the least anxiety to those that produce the most. The therapist then begins the desensitisation by asking the patient to relax as completely as possible. The therapist helps the subject learn to relax by asking him first to tighten and then to relax specific sets of muscles such as those in the hands, feet, legs and neck. By perceiving the difference between tightened and relaxed muscles, the subject learns to relax.

When the patient is relaxed, the therapist asks him to think about the situation, from those listed, that produced the least amount of anxiety. If the patient is thoroughly relaxed, he will be able to think about the situation without feeling anxiety, since the anxiety will be incompatible with the relaxed state. What usually happens is that the patient will not be able to attain sufficient relaxation on his first trials, but slowly the therapist will help him reach the point where he can contemplate the anxiety-producing idea in a state of relaxation. Once he has accomplished this, he is on the road to being able to think of and encounter the anxiety-producing situation without it producing anxiety in him.

Sometimes relaxation may be assisted by the use of drugs. It is argued that to make such presentations while the subject is in a state of profound muscular relaxation is necessary for building up the tolerance of the patient — the relaxed state being to some extent antagonistic to the presence of anxiety.

Once the weakest of the hierarchical stimuli has been desensitised and no longer elicits fear, the therapist can move up the hierarchy, presenting more and more disturbing stimuli one at a time. In each case, the patient is asked to relax in the presence of the disturbing stimulus. In this manner, a patient may overcome the fear-producing qualities of even the most frightening stimuli.

Thus, scenes which are presented to a mouse-phobic child might begin with asking the patient to imagine that he is at some distance from a small dead mouse, through those which depict a more active but small specimen, to the close proximity of a large, scuttling mouse having all the frightening characteristics specified by the patient as causing panic. It is generally found that the afflicted individual not only comes to tolerate the imagined scenes without anxiety, but that this benefit transfers to the real life situation.

There is a great deal of sound evidence that desensitisation treatment works very well indeed (and very speedily) in eliminating the fears of normal — that is not psychiatrically disturbed — individuals. Kravetz and Forness (1971) report an experiment with a six-and-a-half-year-old boy who could not speak when in the classroom. A desensitisation programme of twelve sessions (two per week) was established. The anxiety-evoking stimulus hierarchy used in this study is presented below.

(1) Reading alone to investigator

(2) Reading alone to roommate
(3) Reading to two classroom aides (repeated)
(4) Reading to teacher and classroom aides (repeated)
(5) Reading to teacher, classroom aides and small group of classroom peers (repeated)
(6) Reading to entire class
(7) Asking questions or making comments at weekly ward meeting when all patients, teachers and staff were present.

This desensitisation programme, combined with positive reinforcement, was successful in assisting the boy to overcome his fear of verbalising in the classroom.

Garvey and Hegrenes (1966) reported a similar study concerning Jimmy, a ten-year-old with school phobia. During treatment the therapist eliminated the child's fear of school by having him approach the school accompanied by the therapist and by proceeding with the following anxiety-evoking stimulus hierarchy:

(1) Sitting in the car in front of the school
(2) Getting out of the car and approaching the curb
(3) Going to the pavement
(4) Going to the bottom of the steps of the school
(5) Going to the top of the steps
(6) Going to the door
(7) Entering the school
(8) Approaching the classroom by a certain distance each day down the hall
(9) Entering the classroom
(10) Being present in the clasroom with the teacher
(11) Being present in the clasroom with the teacher and one or two classmates
(12) Being present in the clasroom with a full class.

After 20 consecutive daily treatments Jimmy resumed a normal school routine; no return of the phobia was noted during a two-year follow-up study. Before the implementation of this intervention Jimmy had participated in six months of traditional psychotherapy without apparent success.

Wainwright (1979) reports on a nine-week desensitisation programme of a 13-year-old severely mentally impaired boy who kept soiling the water in the swimming baths when he was taken for swimming lessons. The desensitisation programme was drawn up on the basis that the swimming pool had become a feared situation which produced anxiety. The full rationale behind the choice of this technique is discussed later. The aim of the programme was very gradually to reintroduce David to the pool and his swimming activities, attempting always to keep him relaxed during the sessions.

First, a desensitisation hierarchy was drawn up, as set out below, each step in the hierarchy bringing the goal of full participation in class swimming lessons nearer:

(1)   Walk to swimming pool

(2)   Walk to swimming pool
       Go inside building
       Look at water

(3)   Walk to swimming pool
       Go inside building
       Change into swimming costume
       Look at water

(4)   As for (3), plus
       Stand at top of ramp leading into water

(5)   As for (4), plus
       Walk a few steps into water
       Stand in water for a few seconds

(6)   As for (5), plus
       Walk a little further still
       Stand in water for a second time for a few seconds

(7)   As for (1)–(6), plus
       Gradually increase the number of steps down the ramp
       Gradually increase the length of time standing in the water

(8)   As for (1)–(7), plus
       Walk around shallow end of pool. Time spent doing this to be gradually increased

(9)   As for (1)–(8), plus
       Swimming in shallow end to be allowed, and extended to include a few seconds in the deep end
       Time in shallow end to be gradually decreased as time in deep end is increased

(10) As for (1)–(9), plus

Whole session to be spent in deep end, time increasing gradually up to 25 minutes.

Over a six month follow up there was no relapse.

Bed-wetting or enuresis, has been analysed in terms of classical conditioning. Normally, bladder tension is the CS that evokes a waking response (the CR). Most children probably learn this CS–CR connection in the following fashion. Bladder tension (CS) is paired with a UCS such as wet bed, which causes the child to wake up. Through repeated pairings, the bladder tension (CS) normally acquires the capacity to elicit the waking response. But some children do not learn this CS–CR connection, probably because wetting the bed does not awaken them. Therefore, these children sleep through the bladder tension and wet the bed.

As far back as 1938 (Mowrer, 1964), psychologists were attempting to control enuresis through classical conditioning. They reasoned that, since the CS (bladder tension) – CR (waking) connection has not been learned, it may be established by pairing the CS (bladder tension) with an alternative UCS that elicits the desired waking response in a more effective manner.

Mowrer devised an apparatus to help train the child to gain control. He put tiny electrical wires in a thin cloth pad that could go under the bottom sheet on the child's bed. These wires were connected to a loud bell near the child's head. Whenever the child urinated while asleep, the urine (which is a good electrical conductor) closed the circuit that rang the bell, waking the child up. Although the amount of current involved was so small that the child received no electrical shock to its body, being rudely aroused in the middle of the night was often so distressing that the unconscious parts of the child's brain often 'learned' to heed the signals coming from the bladder and woke the young person up before an 'accident' could occur. Mowrer's device has been an effective training tool for many children.

Summary

Treatment generally involves either changing the environment or 'changing' the child. The most effective forms of counselling appear to be client-centred counselling and behaviour modification. The latter is speedy, effective and capable of being operated by non-professionals under guidance.

Behaviour modification is a set of techniques, based largely on learning theory principles, which are employed to alter observable behavioural problems. Maladaptive behaviour is regarded as learned; hence it can be unlearned and new behaviour learned in its place. Positive reinforcement taken from the operant conditioning model has been used to increase the production of desired behaviour. Techniques combining extinction and positive reinforcement have also been applied effectively in the school setting to modify the behaviour of children with behaviour problems.

Systematic desensitisation has been successful with minor fears and phobias.

Activities

Behaviour Modification Activity

Operant Conditioning

1. Choose *one* child whose behaviour you wish to modify, e.g. shouting out, interfering with other children, plays alone, etc.
2. Label and describe the behaviour currently causing problems in an operational way.
3. Record baseline data over a week's period (say).
4. Carry out modification technique, i.e. positive reinforcement coupled with extinction, for a fortnight (find an appropriate reinforcer).
5. Record incidence of original problem behaviour and compare with baseline data.
6. If you have time cease reinforcing for a few days and note incidence again. Return to reinforcement and extinction procedure. Record data.
7. Graph all the data you have.

Systematic Desensitisation

1. Choose one child who appears to have a specific fear, e.g. of an animal, of reading/speaking in class, of joining in peer group activity, of school, etc.
2. Plan a sequence of exposures starting at a minimum level always associated with a context of no anxiety and relaxed conditions.
3. Keep a diary of the events for the period.

Questions

1. Do you agree with the view that behaviour modification involves imposing value judgements on children about what is acceptable/ unacceptable behaviour?
2. Describe briefly the characteristics and possible causes of
   (i) the withdrawn child and
   (ii) the school phobic.
3. Explain the use of token reinforcement.
4. Have you ever changed a child's behaviour without realising it at the time? Describe what you did and its effects. Can you explain why the behaviour changed?

Further Reading

Bandura, A. (1969) *Principles of Behavior Modification*, New York: Holt
Chazan, M. (1968) 'Children's emotional development' in H. Butcher (ed.) *Educational Research in Britain*, vol. 1, London: University of London Press
Chazan, M., Laing, A.F., Jones, J., Harper, G.C. and Bolton, J. (1983) *Helping Young Children with Behaviour Difficulties*, London: Croom Helm
Jehu, D. *et al.* (1972) *Behaviour Modification in Social Work*, London: Wiley-Interscience
Kazdin, A. (1975) *Behaviour Modification in Applied Settings*, London: Irwin Dorsey
Lazarus, A. (1971) *Behaviour Therapy and Beyond*, London: McGraw-Hill
Martin, G. and Pear, J. (1983) *Behavior Modification*, Englewood Cliffs, NJ: Prentice-Hall
Poteet, J. (1974) *Behaviour Modification*, London: University of London Press
Rutter, M., Tizard, J. and Whitmore, K. (1970) *Education, Health and Behaviour*, London: Longmans
Yule, W. and Carr, J. (eds.) (1980) *Behaviour Modification for the Mentally Handicapped*, London: Croom Helm

References

Becker, N., Madsen, C., Arnold, R. and Thomas, D. (1967) 'The contingent use of teacher attention and praise in reducing classroom behaviour problems', *J. Spec. Educ.*, *1*, 287–307
Garfinkel, P., Kline, S. and Stancer, H. (1973) 'Treatment of anorexia nervosa using operant conditioning', *J. Nerv. Ment. Disease*, *157*, 428–33
Garvey, W. and Hengrenes, J. (1966) 'Desensitisation techniques in the treatment of school phobia', *Am. J. Orthopsychiatry*, *36*, 147–52
Gelfand, D. and Hartmann, D. (1968) 'Behaviour therapy with children', *Psychol. Bull.*, *69*, 204–15
Harris, F., Johnston, M., Kelley, C. and Wolf, M. (1964) 'Effects of positive social reinforcement on regressed crawling of a nursery school child', *J. Educ. Psychol.*, *55*, 35–41

Kravetz, R. and Forness, S. (1971) 'The classroom as a desensitising setting', *Except. Child.*, *37*, 389–91

Levine, F. and Fasnacht, G. (1974) 'Token rewards may lead to token learning', *Amer. Psychol.*, *29*, 816–20

Mowrer, O.H. (1964) *The New Group Therapy*, New Jersey: Van Nostrand

Poteet, J. (1970) *Behaviour Modification*, London: University of London Press

Rogers, C.R. (1951) *Client Centred Therapy*, Boston: Houghton Mifflin

Wainwright, S. (1979) 'Behaviour therapy with the mentally handicapped', *Nursing Times*, July 19th, 1234–6

Watson, J.B. (1920) 'Conditioned emotional reactions', *J. Exp. Psychol.*, *3*, 1

Williams, C.D. (1959) 'The elimination of tantrum behaviour by extinction', *J. Abn. Soc. Psychol.*, *59*, 269

Wolf, M., Birnbrauer, J., Lawler and Williams, T. (1970) 'The operant extinction of vomiting behaviour in a retarded child' in R. Ulrich, T. Stachik and J. Mabry (eds.) *Control of Human Behaviour*, Glenview: Scotts Foreman

Wolpe, J. (1969) *The Practice of Behaviour Therapy*, Oxford: Pergamon

INDEX